# C. V. Raman

# C.V. RAMAN

*Series Editor*
**Dr. M.H. Syed**

*Editor*
**Anil Kathuria** **Bharat Singh**

Himalaya Books Pvt. Ltd.

'Ramdoot', Dr. Bhalerao Marg, Girgaon, Mumbai - 400 004
Tel : (022) 23863063. Fax : (022) 23877178
Email : himpub@vsnl.com

**Edition : 2013**

**Published by** : **H.B.P.L.**
"Pooja Apartments", 4-B, Murari Lal Street, Ansari Road,
Darya Ganj, New Delhi-110 002
Phones : 23270392, 23278631 Reliance : 30180392 to 396
Fax : 011-23256286 Email : hphdel@vsnl.com

**Sole Distributers** : **HIMALAYA PUBLISHING HOUSE PVT. LTD.**

**Branch Offices**

**Mumbai** : "Ramdoot", Dr. Bhalerao Marg, Girgaon, Mumbai-400 004.
Phones : 23860170/23863863 Fax : 022-23877178
Email : himpub@vsnl.com
Website : www.himpub.com

**Nagpur** : Kundanlal Chandak Industrial Estate, Ghat Road, **Nagpur - 440 018.**
Phone: 2738731, 3296733 Telefax : 0712-2721215

**Bengaluru** : No. 16/1 (Old 12/1), 1st Floor, Next to Hotel Highlands,
Madhava Nagar, Race Course Road, **Bengaluru - 560 001.**
Phone : 22281541, 22385461, Telefax: 080-22286611

**Hyderabad** : No. 3-4-184, Lingampally, Besides Raghavendra Swamy Matham,
Kachiguda, **Hyderabad - 500 027.** Phone: 040-27560041, 27550139,
Mobile:- 09848130433 Telefax: 040-27560041

**Chennai** : No. 85/50, Bazullah Road, T. Nagar, **Chennai - 600 017.**
Phone: 044-28344020, 32463737, 42124860

**Pune** : No. 527, "Laksha" Apartment, First Floor, Mehunpura, Shaniwarpeth,
(Near Prabhat Theatre), **Pune - 411 030.**
Phone: 020-24496323/24496333/32326733

**Lucknow** : House No. 731, Sehkhupura Colony, Near B.D. Convent School,
**Lucknow - 226 024.** Mobile : 09307501549

**Ahmedabad** : No. 114, "SHAIL", 1st Floor, Opp. Madhu Sudan House, C.G.Road,
Navrang Pura, **Ahmedabad – 380 009.**
Phone: 079-26560126, Mobiles: 09327324149,09314679413

**Ernakulam** : No. 39/104 A, Lakshmi Apartment, Karikkamuri Cross Rd.,
Ernakulam, **Cochin – 682011**, Kerala.
Phone: 0484-2378012, 2378016, Mob.: 09344199799

**Bhubaneswar** : 5 Station Square, **Bhubaneswar (Orissa) - 751 001.**
Mobile: 9861046007, E-mail:- orissa@himpub.com

**Indore** : Kesardeep Avenue Extension, 73, Narayan Bagh.Flat No. 302,
IIIrd Floor, Near Humpty Dumpty School, Narayan Bagh,
**Indore (M.P.) 452 007** Mobile: 09301386468

**Kolkata** : 108/4, Beliaghata, Main Road, Near ID Hospital, Opp. SBI Bank
**Kolkata - 700 010.**
Mobile: 09910440956, E-mail:- nkmitra@himpub.com

**Guwahati** : House No. 15, Behind Prajjyotish College, Near Sharma
Printing Press, P.O. Bharalumukh, Guwahati - 781009 (Assam)
Mobile: 07439040301; 07439040302

**Printed by** : Sri Prints & Sales, Delhi

# Preface

Biography, is now a form of literature, very much in vogue. In fact, biography is a description or account of someone's life and the times, which is usually published in the form of a book. A biography is more than a mention of personal facts (life, education, work, relationships and death), it also portrays the subject's experience of events. Technically speaking, a work is biographical, if it covers, all of a person's life. Biography writing has a long history. A biography is real. Ancient Greeks developed the biographical tradition, which we have inherited, although until the 5th century AD, when the word 'biographia' first appeared, in Damascius' "Life of Isodorus," biographical pieces were called simply "lives". It is quite likely that the Greeks were drawing on a pre-existing eastern tradition. Certainly Herodotus' "Histories" contains more detailed biographical information on Persian kings and subjects. The earliest surviving pieces, which we would identify as biographical are Isocrates' "Life of Evagoras" and Xenophon's "Life of Agesilaos," both from the fifth century BC. "Parallel Lives" by Plutarch, a Greek writing under the Roman empire, is a series of short biographies of eminent men.

The Golden Age of English biography emerged in late eighteenth century, the century in which the terms "biography" and "autobiography" entered English lexicon. The classic works of the period were Samuel Johnson's "Critical Lives of the Poets" and James Boswell's "Massive Life of Johnson". Generally American biography followed English model. By World War I, cheap hardcover reprints had become popular. The decade of the

1920s witnessed a biographical 'boom'. Later, biographical writings developed a lot and today biographies are written and compiled in the finest form of the genre. In India too, biography, as a form of literature has been evolved, cultivated and polished over the years. Here is an effort to promote this tradition further.

This series of biographies of great men, great women and celebrities in all walks of life is an adventurous academic endeavour, in its own right. A team of researchers and compilers has worked for a good period of time to accomplish the project. For this purpose, hundreds of books by eminent authors and editors have been consulted and referred to. We have benefited from various works, liberally, in order to illustrate and enrich this effort of ours. Present book is devoted to the great personality of C. V. Raman.

Sir Chandrasekhara Venkata Raman, (7 November 1888 – 21 November 1970) was a great physicist and Nobel laureate in Physics, recognised for his work on the molecular scattering of light and for the discovery of the Raman effect, which is named after him. Venkataraman was born at Thiruvanaikaval, near Trichinopoly, Madras Presidency. He gained his M.A., obtaining the highest distinctions. In 1934 Raman became the director of the Indian Institute of Science in Bangalore, where two years later he continued as a Professor of Physics. Other investigations carried out by Raman were experimental and theoretical studies on the diffraction of light by acoustic waves of ultrasonic and hypersonic frequencies and those on the effects produced by X-rays on infrared vibrations in crystals exposed to ordinary light. In 1947, he was appointed as the first National Professor by the new government of Independent India. Raman retired from the Indian Institute of Science in 1948 and established the Raman Research Institute in Bangalore, Karnataka, a year later. He served as its director and remained active there, until his death in 1970.

This is a compact and comprehensive account of the above mentioned great life, which is bound to attract the attention of scholars, researchers, students and the general readers alike. Let's hope this humble effort would receive a warm welcome and due applause.

*— Editors*

# Contents

# 1

# An Eventful Life

The great scientist of his times, Sir Chandrashekhara Venkata Raman, (November 7, 1888 - November 21, 1970) was an Indian physicist, who was awarded the 1930 Nobel Prize in Physics for his work on the scattering of light and his discovery of a unique form of scattering known as Raman scattering or the Raman effect. This effect is useful for analysing the compositions of solids, liquids, and gases. It can also be used to monitor manufacturing processes and to diagnose diseases.

## Family Background

C. V. Raman was born on November 7, 1888, in Tiruchirapalli, Tamil Nadu to a Tamil Brahmin family. Raman's ancestors were agriculturists, established near Porasakudi Village and Mangudi in the Tanjore district. His father, Chandrashekharan Iyer, studied in a school in Kumbakonam and passed the Matriculation examination in 1881. Eventually, in 1891, he got a Bachelors of Arts degree in physics at the Society of the Promotion of the Gospel College in Tiruchirapalli. Chandrashekharan became lecturer in the same college. After passing the Matriculation Exam, he got married to Parvathi Ammal, and they had eight children — five sons and three daughters. On November 7, 1888, their second child, Raman, was born in his maternal grandfather's house in Tiruvanaikkaval.

Raman's elder brother, the first child, was C. Subramanian (better known as C. S. Iyer). C. S. Iyer grew up to become world famous as an extraordinary astrophysicist, and was the Morton D. Hull Distinguished Service Professor in the University of Chicago, and was also a Nobel Laureate.

## Schooling

When Raman was four years old, his father, Chandrashekharan, moved to Vishakhapatnam to take up a post as a lecturer in the Mrs. A. V. Narasimha Rao College. There he taught physics, mathematics, and physical geography. Chandrashekharan was considered strong, both physically and mentally, as he was greatly involved in sports, physical culture, and Indian Carnatic music, among other activities.

Unlike his father, Raman was not physically strong; however, Raman had intellectually brilliant. He excelled in studies, and showed early signs of unusual talent by winning accolades from his teachers, and earning many prizes and scholarships.

Raman became interested in physics while still in school. He once built a dynamo by himself, and had deep curiosity to the workings of physical concepts and devices.

## College Education

C. V. Raman finished school at an incredibly young age of eleven, by passing the Matriculation Examination with first rank (top marks). He then joined the A. V. N. College to study for the Intermediate. He again earned accolades, and finished with top marks in the university examination. In 1903, he left for Chennai (then Madras) with a scholarship to study for the BA degree in the Presidency College, where he was the youngest. The Presidency College was the best college in Southern India at that time. Most of the professors at the time Raman went to college were Europeans. Here, Raman's interest in physics became even more focused, and he also developed a great liking for English.

## Middle Years

In 1904, Raman passed the BA examinations with first rank in the university, and won gold medals in English and Physics.

Raman's teachers advised him to go to England for further studies, but the Civil Surgeon of Madras ruled it out, claiming that the young Raman was too frail to withstand the England climate. Instead Raman did his MA in Presidency College to study Physics (he went to abroad only when he was thirty-three). With the professor of Physics at that time, R. Llewellyn Jones, Raman said he "enjoyed a measure of academic freedom which seems almost incredible. To mention only one detail, during the whole of my two years' work for the MA degree, I remember attending only one lecture..."

Pictures of Raman, his father Chandrashekharan, and Professor Jones hang at the entrance of the lecture hall of the Physics Department of Presidency College. In 1939, the Indian Academy of Sciences brought out a commemorative volume on Raman's fiftieth birthday.

## First Paper

With the great freedom Raman found with Professor Jones, he productively used the time, designing and developing experiments to answer the boundless questions he had in Physics. Only the fundamental lab instruments were found at the Physics lab at the time (only enough for class work), but Raman made use of just these. Raman's questions were often those whose answers were not found in the published literature. Thus, the essence of research came instinctively to him, and this aura was enough to push him to conduct experiments throughout his life.

While Raman was well aware of light in a wave form, and the concept of diffraction, he experimented with asymmetric diffraction of light. He compiled his findings on this experiment, and gave it to Professor Jones for comments. However, Professor Jones offered no opinion for several months. Around that time, Raman was aware of a Philosophical Magazine, perhaps those subscribed by the Connemara Public Library about five km away from Presidency College (it is not certain how Raman came to know of this magazine). Then, taking his first step towards publications, Raman sent his paper on asymmetric diffraction to the Philosophical Magazine in London, under the title "Unsymmetrical diffraction bands due to a rectangular aperture."

This paper was published in 1906 — Raman, only 18 and not yet out of college, was the sole author with no acknowledgements. Raman's achievement was even more astounding because Presidency College was not a research college, and Raman's paper was the first to come out of that institution.

Almost immediately after Raman's first publication, the famous R. W. Wood of Johns Hopkins University published another. Wood later sent a cable to Nature, exclaiming the discovery of the Raman Effect.

## Books that Influenced Raman

Chandrashekhara Venkata Raman found several books he came across in his college career very useful and often eye-opening. Of the books that influenced him, he writes, "I finished my school and college career and my university examinations at the age of eighteen. In this short span of years, had been compressed the study of four languages and of a great variety of diverse subjects, in several cases up to the highest university standards. A list of all the volumes I had to study would be of terrifying length. Did these books influence me? Yes, in the narrow sense of making me tolerably familiar with subjects so diverse as Ancient Greek and Roman History, Theory and Public Finance, the late Sanskrit writers and minor English authors, to say nothing of Physiography, Chemistry and a dozen branches of Pure and Applied Mathematics, and of Experimental and Theoretical Physics. But out of this welter of subjects and books, can I pick out anything really to mould my mental and spiritual outlook and determine my chosen path in life? Yes, I can and I shall mention three books. ... The Light of Asia. I remember being powerfully moved by the story of Siddhartha's great renunciation, of his search for truth and of his final enlightenment. This was at a time when I was young enough to be impressionable, and this reading of the book fixed firmly in my mind the idea that this capacity for renunciation in the pursuit of exalted aims is the very essence of human greatness."

About books on science, Raman says, "The next set of books that I have to mention is one of the most remarkable works of all time namely, The Elements of Euclid. ... The pages of Euclid are like the opening bars of the music of the grand opera of Nature's great drama. So to say, they lift the veil and show to our vision a glimpse of the vast world of natural knowledge awaiting study."

Raman had an innate sense of love for music and he was also influenced by the works of the great Helmholtz.

Raman said about this third of the three books of great influence on him, "It was my great good fortune, while I was still a student at college, to have possessed a copy of an English translation of his great work The Sensations of Tone... It can be said without exaggeration that it profoundly influenced my intellectual outlook. For the first time, I understood from its perusal what scientific research really meant and how it could be undertaken. I also gathered from it a variety of problems for research which were later to occupy my attention and keep me busy for many years."

## Career

Raman took and passed his Masters examination in January 1907, again, with top marks and several accolades and prizes. While he wanted to focus on science (particularly research) opportunities for research in India (specifically for Indians) were zero. His possibility of going to England was out-ruled due to his weak health at the time. Therefore, Raman's eyes looked to work in Government service, as it is known to be safe, secure, and even prestigious. Even in this case, he wanted to join the esteemed Indian Civil Service (ICS), which was the highest position in Government service, but this required studying in England and also appearing for the examination there — this choice was also ruled out for medical reasons. His next choice was the Financial Civil Service (FCS), where Raman's brother C. S. Iyer was already a member. The FCS was the forerunner of the Indian Audit and Accounts Service of today. Author G. Venkataraman states in his book Journey Into Light, "Recruitment to it was by an all-India competitive examination, but even to appear for this examination one had to first go through an interview." Raman was screened, and as usual, stood first in the written examination, though he had to study some unfamiliar subjects like history and economics. Later, Raman's other brother, Mr. Ramaswamy, confided, "After returning from the screening interview Raman said, 'I took one look at all the candidates who had assembled, and I knew I was going to stand first'." This instance shows the early formation of what was well known as the Raman Ego!

## Marriage

Raman passed the FCS examination in 1907, and before having an official position, married Lokasundari. This part of his life happened in a very untraditional manner. Usually, Indian marriages are arranged by parents — this comprised of finding a proper horoscope match for their child. This included analysing the star positions on their birth date, and other horoscopic figures. Following this is a visit by the boy and his parents to the girl's house, to check to see if they like her — during this time, the girl usually is asked to give a musical presentation. Provided these arrangements have been in agreement and the girl's family offers enough dowry, the boy is set to marry the girl on a fixed date.

Raman's marriage took a completely different course of events. As a college student, Raman was friendly with Mr. Ramaswamy Sivan, who was a freemason, theosophist, and a man with progressive views. Raman often went to visit Mr. Sivan at his house, where one day, he heard music from an Indian Classical Instrument, veenai — it was played by Lokasundari, Sivan's sister-in-law, who came for a visit from Madurai. Lokasundari was quite talented at playing the veenai, and Raman became attracted to her immediately. At that time, as Lokasundari was of marriageable age and her family was looking for a suitable groom, Sivan discussed this idea to Raman, who instantly agreed. Raman then proceeded to get his parents' approval. But it was then found that Lokasundari, though of the same cast as Raman (Brahmin), was of a different subset — this match was, in those days, strictly forbidden. Raman's father, a very liberal-minded man, accepted the idea of Raman selecting his own bride, even one from a different subset. However, the rest of the family, including Raman's mother, were displeased. Regardless of such obstacles, however, Raman followed his heart and insisted on having his own way. In fact, he even refused to accept dowry from the girl's side.

Ramaseshan said, "The story has it that on the first occasion he saw her, she was playing on the veena the Tyagaraja keertana [composition] 'Rama ni Samanam Evaro?' [Rama, is there anyone your equal?]. We shall never know whether it was by intent or by accident. Anyway, she insists that she still does not know if Raman married her for the extra allowance of Rs. 150 which the Finance Department gave to its married officers!"

Lokasundari came to be known as Lady Raman. In Bhagavantam, it was said of her, "Those who have known her ... had often said that her principal interest in life was to enable Professor Raman to carry on his scientific work with efficiency and in an uninterrupted manner ... Seldom did she permit projection in the public of her own personality as distinct from that of her husband. This aspect of hers, besides being in line with the best of Indian traditions, was so noticeable on occasions that she drew the admiration of all concerned."

Raman was given a position as Assistant Accountant-General in Calcutta in mid-1907 — he was still a teenager then. His salary was then Rs. 400, including marriage allowance. Raman and Lokasundari left for Calcutta, capital of what was then British India.

Raman made use of the diverse and scientific atmosphere of Calcutta, and was able to give full expression to his scientific creativity — Calcutta was then known as the premier city for science in the East. Apart from being posted in Calcutta, Raman was also sent to Nagpur and Rangoon; no matter the place, Raman always found ways to conduct experiments at home.

As the story goes, one evening while returning from work, he spotted the sign of the Indian Association for the Cultivation of Science. He started visiting the laboratory after office hours and did experiments, which culminated with his Nobel Prize winning work.

In 1917, Raman resigned from his government service and took up the newly created Palit Professorship in Physics at the University of Calcutta. Simultaneously, he continued doing research at the IACS, where he became the Honorary Secretary. Raman used to refer to this period as the golden era of his career. Many talented students gathered around him at the IACS and the University of Calcutta. He was president of the 16th session of the Indian Science Congress in 1929.

Raman won the 1930 Nobel Prize in Physics for his work on the scattering of light and for the discovery of the Raman effect. Raman spectroscopy is based on this phenomenon.

Raman also worked on the acoustics of musical instruments. He worked out the theory of transverse vibration of bowed strings, on the basis of superposition velocities. This does a better job in explaining bowed string vibration over Helmholtz's approach. He was also the first to investigate the harmonic nature of the sound of the Indian drums such as the *tabla* and the *mridangam*.

In 1933, Raman became the director of the newly established Indian Institute of Science (IISc) in Bangalore. The IISc was set up in 1909 with the main objective of bringing out original research and providing training in science and engineering. Up till Raman's appointment, all of IISc's directors were British and so were most of the faculty. Two years later, he continued as a Professor of Physics. In 1947, he was appointed as the first National Professor by the new government of Independent India.

He also started a company called Travancore Chemical and Manufacturing Co. Ltd. in 1943, along with Dr. Krishnamurthy. The Company during its 60 year history established four factories in Southern India.

He was knighted in 1929 and awarded the Bharat Ratna in 1954. Raman was also awarded the Lenin Peace Prize (1957).

C. V. Raman is the uncle of three world renowned Physicists Subramanyam Chandrasekhar Nobel laureate, Sivaramakrishna Chandrasekhar FRS, known for Liquid crystal research and Shivaraj Ramaseshan, former director of the Indian Institute of Science.

India celebrates National Science Day on the 28th February of every year to commemorate Raman's discovery in 1928.

## Last Days and Demise

Ramaseshan S., author of *C. V. Raman – A Pictorial Biography*, noted, "Many things happened [during the last decade of Raman's life and] time in his Institute and in the country which affected Raman greatly. The half a dozen graduate students whom he had hand-picked to work at his Institute began to leave. By 1960 all of them had gone and he chose not to take any more and (except for two assistants) he was almost all alone." It was at this time that Raman started to isolate himself from the world outside his institute — he built high walls on the compounds of his institute to discourage visitors. He underwent depression.

Much of Raman's emotional boil was caused by the way things were happening in the newly independent country. Ramaseshan said, "It seemed to him that scientific administrators, not believing that there was sufficient strength in the country for science to grow, looked outside more and more for inspiration. The policy seemed to be that expenditure (however indiscriminate), would automatically further the progress of science and technology. He felt that the universities, which till then identified and generated talent, were denuded and decertified by the exodus of scientists and teachers to better-paid positions in large, impersonal Government laboratories. Quantity appeared to be mistaken for quality. His attitude towards everyone — especially the Government — became one of suspicion and cynicism." An example of Raman's source of disappointment with the Government is the idea that purchase and use of elaborate, expensive equipment from outside the country would greatly help advance scientific and technological progress. This contradicted Raman's belief that even simple experiments can be conducted to find great scientific theories, as that is what even he had done in the Presidency College himself. Depicting such thoughts, a story from Journey Into Light goes, "... once he saw one of his students in a crest-fallen mood. Upon enquiry he learnt that (spectroscopic) experiments similar to those being performed by his student were also in progress in England at the same time and the student's worry was that whereas he had merely a 1 kW lamp his competitor abroad had a 10 kW lamp. 'Don't worry,' Raman told the student, 'put a 10 kW brain on the problem'."

He retired from the Indian Institute of Science in 1948 and a year later he established the Raman Research Institute in Bangalore Karnataka, serving as its director and remained active there until his death in 1970.

Raman gave his last Gandhi Memorial Lecture, *On the Cochlea and the Perception of Sound*, on October 2, 1970. For the first and last time in his life, he requested the audience to allow him to sit down while answering their questions. Ramaseshan said, "At the end of October he collapsed in his laboratory, the valves of his heart having given way. He was moved to hospital and the doctors gave him four hours to life. He survived and after a few days refused to stay in the hospital as he preferred to die in the gardens of his Institute surrounded by his flowers."

Two days before Raman died, he told one of his former students, "Do no allow the journals of the Academy to die, for they are the sensitive indicators of the quality of science being done in the country and whether science is taking root in it or not." Raman then gave his vision for the future of the Institute in a letter.

> "This Institute was created by me in 1948 to provide a place in which I could continue my studies in an atmosphere more conductive to pure research than that found in most scientific institutions. To me the pursuit of science has been an aesthetic and joyous experience. The Institute has been the haven where I cold carry on my highly personal research. This personal character of the Institute should obviously change after me. It must blossom into a great centre of learning embracing many branches of science. Scientists from different parts of India and all over the world must be attracted to it. With its beautiful gardens, large libraries, extensive museums, I feel that the Institute offers a perfect nucleus for the growth of a centre of higher learning. Science can only flower out when there is an internal urge. It cannot thrive under external pressures. Fundamental science cannot be driven by instructional, industrial, governmental or military pressure. This is the reason why I decided as far as possible not to accept money from Government. I have bequeathed all my property to the Institute. Unfortunately, this may not be sufficient for the growth of this centre of Learning. I shall therefore not put it as a condition that no governmental

funds should be accepted by the Institute. I would however strongly urge taking only funds that have no strings attached."

That same evening, Raman met with the Board of Management of his Institute and discussed (from his bed) with them any proceedings with regards to the Institute's management. Raman passed away from natural causes early next morning, November 21, 1970.

## Raman and his Scientific Achievements

### *Raman Scattering*

Raman scattering or the Raman effect is the inelastic scattering of a photon.

When light is scattered from an atom or molecule, most photons are elastically scattered (Rayleigh scattering). The scattered photons have the same energy (frequency) and, therefore, wavelength, as the incident photons. However, a small fraction of scattered light (approximately one in ten million photons) is scattered from excitations with optical frequencies different from, and usually lower than, the frequency of the incident photons. In a gas, Raman scattering can occur with a change in vibrational, rotational, or electronic energy of a molecule. Chemists are concerned primarily with the vibrational Raman effect.

In 1922, Raman published his work on the "Molecular Diffraction of Light," the first of a series of investigations with his collaborators which ultimately led to his discovery (on February 28, 1928) of the radiation effect which bears his name. The Raman effect was first reported by C. V. Raman and K. S. Krishnan, and independently by Grigory Landsberg and Leonid Mandelstam, in 1928. Raman received the Nobel Prize in 1930 for his work on the scattering of light. In 1998 the Raman Effect was designated an ACS National Historical Chemical Landmark in recognition of its significance as a tool for analysing the composition of liquids, gases, and solids.

The Raman Effect differs from the process of fluorescence. For the latter, the incident light is completely absorbed and the system is transferred to an energetically excited state, from which it can go to various lower states only after a certain period (resonance lifetime). The result of both processes is essentially the same: A photon with a frequency different from that of the incident photon is produced and the molecule is brought to a higher or lower energy level. But the major difference is that the Raman Effect can take place for any frequency of incident light. In contrast to the fluorescence effect, the Raman Effect is therefore not a resonant effect.

## Ideology and Philosophy

Raman was a staunch nationalist, in a sense, that whatever he had achieved in life was through sheer personal efforts and indigenously prepared equipments. He was a strong propounded of self-reliance. Raman believed that the solution to India's economic problems lay in increasing agricultural and industrial production by harnessing science and the scientists on a massive scale. While addressing the Institution of Engineers in 1948, he spiritedly declared:

> "There is only one solution for India's economic problems and that is science and more science. Let us not get away from that fact that the US is the wealthiest country in the world. What is the reason? There is no country in the world that has so consistently and steadily encouraged scientific studies and scientific research, which are the basis of all wealth. Wealth does not grow on the trees but is made by man – science, more science and science for all is the answer."

Raman strongly advocated for science and scientific temper to be created within the country without aping or importing it from abroad. He deplored following of the camps or countries, in effect meant not to depend on the others. He rather preached the doctrine of indigenous manufacture and development of technology. Expressing this view in his address delivered in 1950 at Jadhavapur Engineering College, he said:

> "In the past, India had shown her greatness in the fields of scholarship, philosophy and science but today

we are helplessly dependent on Western countries for the knowledge of science. India should not be a camp-follower but a leader in science. It is of no use getting our ideas from the West. We have to think out our problems and find the solutions to them."

He advocated self-reliance, which he practiced in his own activities and interests. To him, science was a personal endeavour, an aesthetic pursuit and above all a joyous experience.

Speaking once at St. Joseph's College, Bangalore, he forcefully said:

> "There will be no science in India if we continue to rely on imported American and German equipment for research work. I call it paying for our ignorance and incompetence. This is a terrible problem in the country. A halo of infallibility has been built around American and German-made gadgets. Do not buy such equipment but make your own at home. Science can and shall advance in very simple ways. We often pay Rs. 50,000 for something, which can be made for only Rs. 5,000. The balance in difference we pay for our ignorance. There will be no situation and no real advance at this rate."

Raman never believed in the confinement of science within the four walls of the laboratory; but felt that everyone must enjoy the fruits of science. In the first meeting of the Academy in independent India at Cuttack, Raman called the scientists to serve the common man and fight to eradicate poverty, disease and illiteracy. Thus, it will ensure true usage of science for the humanity in general.

In 1942, at the convocation address of the Madras University, he said:

> "True wealth of Nation consists not in the stored-up gold in its coffers and the banks, not in factories but in the intellectual and physical strength of its men, women and children."

In 1948, in his address to Orissa Chamber of Commerce, he said:

> "Real growth of a country was in the hearts, minds, bodies and souls of young men and women of the country."

Raman loved the youth passionately and had high hopes from them. He wished the youth to plunge daringly in the realms of science and achieve their aims in life. During a radio broadcast in 1943, he had said:

> "... the principal requisite for success in science research is not the maturity of knowledge associated with age and experience but in freshness of outlook which is the natural attribute of youth."

Thus, Raman saw bright future of India in its youth. In 1949, while speaking in Allahabad at a meeting organised by scientists to felicitate him on reaching the age of 60, he said:

> "I give myself to the younger generation. I speak to them with condor. I know that my words will not fall on barren ground because there is the quality of sincerity, feeling and understanding. I am confident they will go home to the minds of the young and take root."

Raman continuously worried about the backwardness of our universities and persistently insisted for their vitalisation. In the convocation address at Madras University in 1942, he said:

> "(Indian) Universities are not strong enough to bear the burden of free India. Let us try to make our universities best. We should not be satisfied with anything less than the best. What will be the result? Instead of a great many of our young men going out of the country, they will remain here and strive to advance our reputation and that will make us strive for more good things."

The above speaks for his foresight that is very much prevalent amongst the youth of India, who aspire to seek better opportunities leading to the phenomenon of "Brain-Drain". After acquiring necessary education in India, youth in the name of further studies, today, go abroad never to return to serve their motherland. The youth must be brought back so as to serve the country and the onerous task of doing so, rests not only on the government or politicians shoulders, but upon every Indian also.

Citing the example of the American philanthropists, he appealed to all who afforded easily to donate for the cause of education.

He once declared that:

> "Has it not been truly said that he who gives for learning will be remembered long after Kings and Emperors are forgotten. There is no greatest gift a man can make than a gift in the cause of learning."

Knowing the value of education as a force of life and culture, in 1950 at Bombay, Raman said:

> "Countryside is the best laboratory you can have. It provides far better scope than big institutions costing thousands and lacs of rupees."

In 1966, at the convocation address of IIT Madras, he said:

> "I have been on a joy ride through the campus and was thrilled to see the wonderful old Banyan trees, the wild grass, the thorns here and there and the occasional buildings.
>
> Study, lectures, books and examinations contribute a small part in a man's or woman's education. The greatest teacher of all is Nature herself — the supreme artist who creates forms of beauty, loveliness and colour that have been unsurpassed since the beginning of time. She has not been the inspiration not only of artists, painters and sculptors but to a man of science too. Life is not merely a matter of getting food, clothes and shelter. Its finer aspects are to be found in music, flowers, colours and beauty, and the aesthetic sense and satisfaction that are derived from the enjoyment of all these."

In 1941, addressing the Patna University he said about the women that:

> "I have a feeling that if the women of India take to science and interest themselves in the progress and the advance of science as well, they will achieve even what men have failed to do. Women have one quality — the quality of devotion. It is one of the most important passports to success in science. Let us therefore not imagine that intellect is the sole prerogative of males only in science."

Raman was a great humanist by heart, soul and mind. He was totally against, the wars that frequently took place between nations. At the same time he condemned the use of atom bomb too. In 1941, speaking on Science and War at Patna, he said:

> "Lust, greed and racial hatred are the three important causes of human conflict. He pleaded for the mutual understanding between nations and an effort to settle differences by peaceful means."

Such was his humanistic approach. In a way his was a belief in non-violence resembling to Gandhiji's concept of non-violence. At the same time Raman was very clear that in case of aggression, a fitting reply must be given.

Raman had great liking for Gandhiji and his operational philosophy. Once speaking to the college students in Ahmedabad, Raman said:

> "Gandhiji's teaching stressed the supreme virtue of the human spirit utterly indestructible and unconquerable. India can never hope to find a place in the sun, unless it upholds the value of human spirit."

Raman remained very active in science throughout his life. The scientific investigation was his spiritual quest. In Plato's sense spiritual quest is described as Truth, Goodness and Beauty, which our ancients referred to it as Satyam, Shivam and Sundaram.

Raman did not go after rituals and institutionalised religion. He did it all according to the Bhagwad Gita. He believed in intrinsic divinity of soul and further that Nature is the manifestation of God.

In 1950, in his convocation at Utkal University, Raman said:

> "What is science in the last analysis but the study and love of Nature displayed not in the form of abstract worship but in practical form of seeking to understand Nature? The more I pursue science, the more I am impressed with the infinite loveliness and wonders of the world. I have often gone to give an expression to this. Whenever I was asked whether I believed in God. I tell you, if there is God. He is in this world before us."

In 1955, while speaking at a Bhoodan function, Raman said:

> "God lives in us. See God in your own soul and heart. The human soul is the repository of the Divine. Never shall we lay aside that feeling of devotion, which has been India's standard through the ages."

Raman found a great resemblance between Science and Indian Philosophy. In this context, he added:

> "One aspect of Indian culture was its profound understanding of Nature. Much of India's philosophy is related itself to the understanding of the rationale and the meaning of Nature."

# 2

# Journey of Great Life

## Early Years and Education

Chandrashekhara Venkata Raman was born at Tiruchirappalli in South India on the 7 November 1888. Raman's parents, Chandrashekhara Iyyer and Parvati Ammal, lived at that time in what was then called the province of Madras, a part of India now known as the Tamil Nadu. The family, for many generations, had been pursuing the profession of agriculture and were of moderate means. Family traditions in those days were such that if anyone attempted to break off from them, it would have been regarded as a bold step. Raman's father did take such a bold step when for the first time in the family, he took to teaching in the local English High School. This bold step was followed by another when Mr. Chandrashekhara Iyyer decided to accept the post of lecturer in physics and mathematics at the Mrs. A. V. N. College, Vizagapatam; Raman was then four years old. Vizagapatam, now known as Visakhapatnam, is a seaport town on the east coast of India and situated in the State of Andhra Pradesh. Thus, the parents and with them the four-year-old son moved to Vizagapatam. The next ten years of Raman's life were spent at Vizagapatam, where he studied for eight years in the High School and two years in the College. He passed the Intermediate examination in 1902, enabling himself to join for a university degree course. In January 1903, he moved to Madras and joined the Presidency College. He passed his B.A. degree examination in 1904, winning the first place and a Gold Medal in physics. He passed the M.A. degree examination in 1907, again obtaining a first division and record marks.

It is noteworthy that while he was still a student and an undergraduate at the Presidency College, young Raman felt the urge towards scientific research and undertook original investigations in acoustics and in optics. Research in modern science in those days was quite unknown in India and it was unusual for an undergraduate to have not only evinced such interest but also to have published the results of his work in well-known international journals. Raman's first research paper was on 'Unsymmetrical diffraction-bands due to a rectangular aperture', observed when light is reflected very obliquely at the face of a prism. The paper was published in the *Philosophical Magazine* in November 1906 and it is interesting to see that it was communicated by the author himself and contains no acknowledgement for any kind of help received from anyone else. Thus, it is clear that Raman was already standing on his own legs and building up confidence in himself. This was followed by another note in *Nature* in 1907. Raman was in his eighteenth year when he contributed these publications, on all counts an early manifestation of special talent.

During his work and in all his contacts with his colleagues and teachers as an undergraduate, he displayed an enquiring and restless mind with a sharp and incisive intellect so that he was regarded as an uncommon student. It was quite clear, even at that time, to many who came into contact with him that he was cut out for a scientific career and was destined to reach great heights. However, circumstances and conditions in India, rather than his own tastes and talents, led young Raman to temporarily choose, after graduation, a career involving administrative duties in the service of the Government of India.

## Marital Bond

While still awaiting a posting in the Government, Raman married Loka Sundari Ammal, who later proved to be a worthy and life-long companion to him. Those who have known her through the decades that have since gone by, had often said that her principal interest in life was to enable Professor Raman to carry on his scientific work with efficiency and in an uninterrupted manner. Lady Loka Sundari Raman is highly talented in her own right and possesses a flair for mastery over several languages. Seldom did she permit projection in the public of her own personality as distinct from that of her husband. This aspect of hers, besides being in line with the best of Indian traditions, was so noticeable on occasions that she drew the admiration of all concerned. On several journeys she had travelled widely with Professor Raman and looked after him with great and loving care. They had two sons, Ghandrasekhar and Radhakrishnan, born in the years 1921 and 1929 respectively. Lady Raman has survived Sir Venkata Raman and she continues to live in and look after the Raman Research Institute at Bangalore.

### *Service in the Finance Department*

One of the reasons which made Raman choose in the first instance a career in the Government was that pursuit of science in India at that time offered little inducement to young and talented persons. Most college professors used to advise the bright graduates of each year to appear in one or other of the competitive examinations conducted by the government for recruitment to different types of civil service. Raman appeared for the competitive examination held in February 1907 and secured a first-class therein. Thus he joined the Indian Finance Department as an Assistant Accountant-General at Calcutta in June 1907. The next ten years of his life were spent as an officer of the Finance Department. It was fortunate that a great part of those ten years was spent in Calcutta, although immediately after joining, he was transferred for a while to Rangoon and then to Nagpur.

It is interesting to see that, though the duties of his office occupied most of his time, Raman sought and found opportunities to not only keep up his interest in science, but also to conduct experimental investigations, some-times under difficult and improvised conditions. While in Calcutta, by a chance look at its sign board while on his way to his office, he came to know of the existence in Calcutta of a privately endowed scientific institution by the name of the Indian Association for the Cultivation of Science. This Association was founded in 1876 by Mahendralal Sarkar, and at the time when it attracted the attention of Raman, Amritlal Sarkar, son of the founder, was the Association's Secretary. This Association was later to become the working place for Raman for many years and indeed it was while working in that institution that he conducted many experiments over many years which led to the discovery of the Raman effect. Even during the short spells of his stay in Rangoon and in Nagpur, he never gave up pursuit of science but continued his investigations. During this period of Government service, he contributed about 30 original papers in different branches of physics to *Nature*, to the *Philosophical Magazine* and to the *Physical Review*.

There is a story, still being recalled by a citizen of Nagpur whose collection of a few hundred-rupee notes was nearly burnt by a blazing fire. The perturbed individual went to the Accountant-General's office and presented the half-burnt bundle, but with little hope of retrieving any. Any other officer would probably have shown him the door, but Raman who was then in the office of the Accountant-General, took the trouble to scrutinise the notes under a magnifying glass, one by one, and instructed the treasurer to give him fresh notes. Raman argued that the numbers on the half-burnt notes were visible and thus it was a genuine case.

During his part-time link with the Indian Association for the Cultivation of Science, he came into contact with Sir Ashutosh Mukherjee, then judge of the Calcutta High Court and an active member of the Association. Sir Ashutosh was also the Vice-Chancellor of the Calcutta University. Raman's successes in scientific research during the period 1907-17, besides attracting the academic circles in India and abroad, also attracted the attention of Sir Ashutosh Mukherjee. That was the time when the University Science College was just being founded in Calcutta and special chairs were being established with the help of generous donations from various philanthropic persons amongst whom, Sir Taraknath Palit was one. When Sir Ashutosh wanted a Professor, capable of filling the newly-created Palit Chair of Physics, he thought of Raman and offered him the post. Although Raman knew very well that from a pecuniary point of view, he would be a great loser, with scant regard to the monetary handicap which he would bringing upon himself by accepting the professorial assignment, Raman joined the Calcutta University as Palit Professor of Physics and bid good-bye to administration and government service in 1917.

In this connection, while announcing his plans for filling the chair, Sir Ashutosh Mukherjee stated that, 'For the chair of Physics created by Sir Taraknath Palit, we have been fortunate enough to secure the services of Mr. Chandrashekhara Venkata Raman, who has greatly distinguished himself and acquired a European fame by his brilliant researches in the domain of Physical Science, assiduously carried on under the most adverse circumstances amidst the distraction of pressing official duties...'.

'I shall fail in my duty if I were to restrain myself in my expression of the genuine admiration I feel for the courage and spirit of self-sacrifice with which Mr. Raman has decided to exchange a lucrative official appointment for a University Professorship, which I regret to say, does not carry even liberal emoluments. This one instance encourages me to entertain the hope that there will be no lack of seekers after truth in the Temple of Knowledge which it is our ambition to erect.'

## The Golden Era of Calcutta (1917-32)

### *Indian Association for the Cultivation of Science*

Professor Raman left government service and joined the University of Calcutta as Palit Professor of Physics in July 1917. In 1919, following the death of Amritlal Sarkar, Raman was elected as Honorary Secretary of the Indian Association for the Cultivation of Science, then situated in a dusty old building at 210 Bow Bazar Street in Calcutta. This was one of the most crowded parts of the city and yet Raman chose to live in a house so close to the Association that he could literally walk into his work by opening a back door, any time of the day or night. Indeed, he used to do so very often, and his whole time was thus available for scientific work. He had at his disposal the facilities and the resources of both places, namely, the Department of Physics in the University College of Science of the Calcutta University and the Indian

Association for the Cultivation of Science. His position as Honorary Secretary gave him full control of the resources of the Association and proved to be of great value and help to him for the development of his scientific activities.

Professor Raman used frequently to refer to this period as the golden era in his career, Many young men gathered round him both at the University College of Science and at the Indian Association for the Cultivation of Science. The latter in particular was the scene of intense scientific activity and several of the research students used to stay inside and around the Association premises so as to be in a position to avail themselves of the meagre facilities as and when they were released by other workers. There were no fixed hours for work nor was it the tradition to observe any closed days. Raman, by his personal effort, steadily improved the resources that were available. He sought and obtained monetary help from many sources. During this period, he attracted some devoted scientists from all over India, who proved to be a succession of gifted collaborators. This enabled Raman to push forward steadily with his investigations. At that time, some of the areas that interested him were vibrations and sound; theory of musical instruments; optical studies such as diffraction, colours and interference; colloids; molecular scattering of light; X-rays; magnetism and magneto-optics, and so on.

The Raman effect, which was discovered in early-1928, stood on a different footing. That naturally became the area of his principal interest in the last four years of that era and literally the place was filled with spectrographs, mercury lamps and several young men working day and night on some aspect or other of the newly-discovered phenomenon.

## Travels Abroad

Professor Raman made his first brief visit to Europe as a delegate to the Universities Congress held in the summer of the year 1921 at Oxford. It is to be noted that by this time, he had already published numerous papers and his work was fairly well known in scientific circles. It was during this voyage, while travelling on board a steamship, that Raman's attention was first drawn to the problem of the origin of the blue colour of the Mediterranean. He conceived the idea that the colour of the deep sea is partly or even largely to be attributed to the molecular scattering of light by the waters of the sea. Observations made by him during the return voyage again confirmed this hypothesis and as we shall see later, these observations became the starting point for the detailed investigations which he undertook on the scattering of light by liquid, solid, and gaseous media. Such studies were undertaken during the seven years that followed.

His next trip abroad was in 1924, when he was invited to join the British Association for the Advancement of Science in a tour across Canada. He was a guest speaker at a Scientists' Convention in Canada and was requested to open a discussion on the scattering of light at Toronto. During that visit, Raman extensively toured Canada, USA, England and Norway. At the invitation of Professor Millikan, Raman stayed on and served as Visiting Professor for four months at the California Institute of Technology. He attended the Centenary of the Franklin Institute of Pennsylvania as the representative of India and returned to India in 1925. During the same year, he again visited Europe as a guest of the Russian Academy of Sciences to represent India at the bi-centenary celebrations of the Academy in Leningrad and Moscow. In 1929, Raman was invited by the Faraday Society to open a discussion on Molecular Spectra which was held in Bristol. During that visit, he visited and lectured in several other places in Europe. Subsequently, he again visited Europe to receive the Nobel Prize at Stockholm in 1930; to receive the Honorary Doctorate at Paris in 1932; to take part in the International Congress of Physics at Paris and Bologna in 1937; to participate in the twentieth anniversary celebrations of the discovery of the Raman effect at Bordeaux in 1948; and so on and so on. On each occasion, he lectured at other centres of research and made many personal contacts with friends and scientists of several countries.

## Awards and Honours

Raman was a highly successful teacher and investigator. His lectures were very lucid and invariably attracted large numbers of students. These qualities as well as his varied scientific achievements received world-wide recognition. The Royal Society of London elected him to its Fellowship in 1924. The British Government in India conferred a Knighthood on him in 1929. He received the Nobel Prize for Physics in 1930. He was awarded the Matteucci Medal by the 'Societa Italiana della Scienza' of Rome in 1928. The Royal Society of London gave him the Hughes Medal in 1930. In 1941, the Franklin Institute of Philadelphia awarded the Franklin Medal to Raman. The citation on that occasion, amongst other things, said that the award to Sir C. V. Raman was in recognition of his many brilliant contributions to physical science and of his leadership in the renaissance of scientific work and scientific education that has occurred in India. The Soviet Union honoured him with the International Lenin Prize in 1957.

Several Indian Universities among which are the universities of Calcutta, Bombay, Madras, Benares, Dacca (at that time in India), Allahabad, Patna, Lucknow, Osmania, Mysore, Delhi, Kanpur and Sri Venkateshwara had conferred Honorary Doctorates on him. Among the Universities outside India, mention may be made of the University of Freiburg which conferred the Hon. Ph.D. degree and the University of Glasgow which conferred the Hon. LL.D. in 1930. He also received the degree of Hon. Sc.D. of the University of Paris in 1932.

He was an Honorary Member of the Deutsche Akademie of Munich, of the Zurich Physical Society, the Royal Philosophical Society of Glasgow, the Royal Irish Academy and of the Hungarian Academy of Sciences. He was an Honorary Member of the Indian Science Congress Association as also of several other Indian Science organisations. He was General President of the Indian Science Congress in 1929, and has been President of the Indian Academy of Sciences since its foundation in 1934 until his death. He was a Foreign Associate of the Academy of Sciences of Paris and a Foreign Member of the Academy of Sciences of USSR. He was Honorary Fellow of the Optical Society of America and the Mineralogical Society of America; an Honorary Member of the Academy of the Socialist Republic of Romania and of the Catgut Acoustical Society; a Member of the Czechoslovak Academy of

Sciences. In 1961, Pope John appointed him a member of the Pontifical Academy of Sciences.

Amongst the many Indian distinctions he received, special mention may be made of the title and decoration of 'Rajasabhabhushana' conferred by the Maharaja of Mysore in 1935. This is a colourful title for, when literally translated, it would read as The Jewel of King's Court. In 1954, the Government of India awarded the title of 'Bharat Ratna' to him, the only Indian scientist to have been thus honoured.

## *Scientific Work at Calcutta*

While at Calcutta, Raman's own work as well as that of other workers in his laboratories, mostly young aspirants for the doctor's degree from different parts of India, covered diverse branches of physics. As a general observation, it appears fairly correct to say that there was a definite bias towards experimentation and that the two areas of acoustics and optics received more attention than any other.

Raman started work in acoustics by interesting himself with the physical theory of musical instruments, particularly of the violin family. This involved a study of the vibrations of stretched strings in great detail. He made fundamental contributions to the motion of the bowed point and the effect of the bridge in coupling the motion of the string to the body of the violin. Later, he worked on the Indian drums — the *mridangam* and the *tabla.* He made the remarkable observation that these drums possess harmonic over-tones — a discovery which did not fit easily with the fact that the drums have a circular membrane. It was known that the frequencies of vibration of a circular membrane are not harmonic. He quickly found that the Indian drum heads have a peculiar feature in that they are loaded by sticking at an appropriate place on the membrane, varying amounts of soft material and that this kind of loading results in a harmonic structure for the overtones.

Amongst his early publications dealing with his work in acoustics, mention may be made of Bulletin No. 15 in a series of bulletins which he used to publish on behalf of the Indian Association for the Cultivation of Science. This was an elaborate and richly illustrated memoir embodying the most important scientific contribution of those years, viz. a fully worked out physical theory of musical instruments of the violin family and an experimental verification of the results thereof. Some years later, he was asked to contribute an article on the physics of musical instruments to the *Handbuch der Physik* and he did so for the eighth volume of that serial published in 1927.

Undoubtedly, his best-known scientific work done during that period was in the field of optics generally and about the phenomenon of scattering of light in particular. Commencing with a critical observation of optical effects like the coronas, glories and haloes; studying the diffraction of light by emulsions and by colloidal solutions, passing through similar studies by molecules such as transparent media like liquids and gases and after adopting many original approaches, his work in those years had culminated in the discovery of the Raman effect. In December 1930, when awarding the Hughes Medal of the Royal Society to Sir C. V. Raman, Lord Rutherford said:

> 'Sir Venkata Raman is one of the leading authorities in optics, in particular on the phenomenon of the scattering of light. In this connection, about three years ago, he discovered that the light's colour could be changed by scattering. This had been predicted some time before, but in spite of search, the change had not been found. The 'Raman effect' must rank among the best three or four discoveries in experimental physics in the last decade; it has proved and will prove, an instrument of great power in the study of the theory of solids. In addition to important contributions in many fields of knowledge, he has developed an active school of research in physical science in the University of Calcutta.'

When Raman commenced the work around 1921, it was known that light is diffused laterally with varying degrees of intensity by matter in all states of aggregation. When a beam of white light is condensed by means of a lens into the centre of a large glass bulb containing a dust-free liquid like benzene, an observer who shields himself from the direct rays of the source and views the track in the liquid in a transverse direction, will at once see a magnificent blue scattering. This rather easily performed experiment was always explained by attributing the blue colour to a relative enhancement of what is already present in the source. It was not expected that during the process of molecular scattering, it was at all possible that in addition to what is present in the source, light of frequencies not present in the source can be generated and therefore detected in the scattered beam. Professor Raman, by using a simple device of inserting appropriate filters in the paths of incident and scattered beams in the beginning and by using monochromatic sources later, discovered that some new frequencies not present in the incident light appear in the scattered beam as a result of, so to say, inter-action between molecules of the illuminated substance and the incident radiation. Thus, in the spectrum of the light scattered by a substance, the Raman effect discloses itself by the presence of new lines adjacent to the original lines of the incident light. The effect may be briefly defined as follows: When a transparent substance is radiated with monochromatic light, a portion of the incident radiation is scattered by the substance in all directions. While a large part of the light thus scattered possesses the same frequency as that of the incident radiation (Rayleigh scattering), a small fraction thereof consists of light which undergoes a change of frequency (Raman scattering), the extent of change being characteristic of the substance.

It is best to quote here what Professor Raman himself wrote, nearly 40 years after the discovery, about how he was led to make the discovery.

'Later, I became aware of the remarkably brilliant monochromatic illumination which could be obtained by the aid of the commercially available mercury arcs sealed in quartz tubes. Towards the end of February 1928, I took the decision to make use of such lamps for all further studies in the field of light-scattering. The success which attended this forward step was immediate and highly gratifying. Experience in working with sunlight indicated the technique necessary for the observation of extremely weak phenomena, viz., the rigorous exclusion of stray light and the conditioning of the observer's vision by a prolonged stay in darkness. On setting up the apparatus and making these preparations, I found that the light of the mercury arc diffused by various materials when examined through a direct vision spectroscope showed the presence, besides the lines of mercury, also of other lines the positions of which varied with the substances under study. Amongst the numerous materials thus examined was a large block of clear ice. This showed sharp displaced lines in the spectrum of the scattered light in approximately the same positions as the rather diffuse bands observed with pure water. Within a few days of the discovery, photographic spectra were successfully recorded in which the additional lines showed up very clearly.' It is of a particular significance that the equipment which Professor Raman employed consisted of three items, a mercury lamp, a flask of benzene and a direct vision pocket spectroscope, all of which would be regarded as crude instruments, even at that time. He always took pride in the fact that his researches never involved costly equipment. On one occasion, he is said to have remarked; 'The essence of science is independent thinking, hard work and not equipment. When I got my Nobel Prize I had spent hardly Rs. 200/- on my equipment.'

## Move to Bangalore

### *Indian Institute of Science*

In April 1933 Raman left the Calcutta University and accepted a call from the Indian Institute of Science at Bangalore in South India to become its Director. Bangalore is one of the attractive cities of India and has a salubrious climate. The move came as a welcome change to Raman who, by that time had lived for the previous twenty-five years, not only in the crowded city of Calcutta but also in one of the most crowded parts of that city. It is understandable that ever since then, Raman made Bangalore his permanent home. He continued to stay in Bangalore even after retirement from the Indian Institute of Science. He built an Institute of his own in Bangalore, now known as the Raman Research Institute. He used to make frequent references to the beautiful environment which the city provided and seldom moved out of Bangalore, during his later years.

The Indian Institute of Science, a premier scientific Institution of India and founded in 1909, seemed at first as if it was going to provide afresh a venue for Raman's scientific activities. Physics was not a subject of study at the Institute and the management took the very wise step indeed of creating a Department of Physics, built around Raman soon after he moved to Bangalore. However, serious difficulties between Raman and the management quickly showed up and the former was obliged to give up administrative duties, relinquish the post of Director and accept continuing as Professor of Physics. This he did till 1949. It may be said that his association with the Indian Institute of Science was not a happy one and did not produce the results which the Institute hoped it would, when they invited Raman to become its first Indian Director. The individuals who were connected with the management of the Institute and the course of events during that period left such a nostalgic impression on Raman's mind that in later years, whenever he referred to them in retrospect, he was very bitter. However, looking back over the past, one feels that the enforced isolation did enable Raman to devote all his time to physics. During that period, he started new lines of work and attracted several young scientists to the Institute. His presence there for over 15 years was responsible for the establishment of an excellent school of physics in South India. He trained a band of first-rate physicists, several of whom are today holding important positions all over the country. While writing about Raman and the Indian Institute of Science, one cannot fail to notice that he joined the Institute almost immediately after discovering the Raman effect, after having been awarded the Nobel Prize for physics and in fact when he was at the peak of his scientific form. Thus, the conflict between individual greatness and institutional interests became a difficult one to resolve and it happened that he always turned out to be the better known when it became a matter of juxtaposition.

### *Scientific Interests*

One of the areas, in which he made significant contributions, during the early years of his work at the Indian Institute, is on the diffraction of light by high-frequency sound-waves. When a beam of light traverses a liquid cell in which sound-waves of high frequency are maintained with the help of a piezo-electric oscillator, interesting diffraction effects are noticed and several papers relating to these effects were being published at that time. It was at a chance discussion of such effects that Raman asked several questions and suggested a way by which the phenomenon should be explained. Then followed a series of papers by himself and Nagendra Nath, wherein what is now called the Raman-Nath theory of diffraction of light by ultrasonic waves was developed. This treatment not only explained fully the observed effects but led to several interesting new ideas. Those of his colleagues who saw him tackle this problem, clearly noticed in it a case in which physical intuition got the upper hand in pointing the way for mathematical logic to follow and build an exact theory. Professor Raman frequently adopted this method and quite often with resounding success.

During that period, he started work on a special type of X-ray reflections. He found that when a beam of X-rays traverses a diamond plate, the octahedral planes of the crystal exhibit well-defined reflections of the monochromatic X-radiation. These reflections appear in positions well removed from the ordinary Laue reflections of white radiation by the same planes. He concluded that in this phenomenon, we are concerned with X-ray reflections of a second kind having a dynamic origin. Diamond exhibits such reflections very conspicuously, while other crystals too have since then been found to show the phenomenon, but less conspicuously.

Many other areas, notably in optics, such as the luminescence of fluorspar, colours of stratified media as are found in iridescent crystals of potassium chlorate, optical effects caused by the twinning in felspars, etc., continued to engage his attention. Besides, problems in light scattering and Raman effect which were being studied on a continuing basis, constituted a part of the regular programme in his laboratory.

When on retirement, he left the Physics Department of the Indian Institute of Science in 1948, such good facilities for experimental work in several of the areas that interested him had been built up that he left behind him a very well-equipped laboratory.

### *Indian Academy of Sciences*

One of the significant developments, on a national scientific level, which resulted from the move of Raman to Bangalore is the establishment of the Indian Academy of Sciences. Professor Raman took steps in the year 1934 to establish an Academy, having distinguished men of science drawn from various parts of India and who were active participants in research work as its foundation fellows. He was elected founder President and continued to be elected President of the Academy until his death. In the year of its foundation, he arranged for the issue of the first numbers of the *Proceedings of the Indian Academy of Sciences* in two sections, one for physical sciences and another for biological sciences. Thereafter, they were issued as regular monthly periodicals devoted to the publication of the results of research workers in India. Bangalore was chosen as the headquarters of the Academy and there has been no parallel in the history of scientific periodicals in India to the unfailing regularity with which the *Proceedings* of the Academy were issued month after month during the 35 years of Raman's association with the Academy as its President. This naturally involved his having to devote much of his time and energy for this purpose. Nevertheless, he often referred to this effort with great satisfaction and a feeling of achievement. The Indian Academy of Sciences and the *Proceedings* issued on behalf of that Academy have been two noteworthy aspects of Indian science during the past three decades.

## Raman and the Raman Research Institute

### *Raman Research Institute*

Professor Raman, anticipating his retirement from the Indian Institute of Science and having decided to settle down in Bangalore, took steps to bring into being an independent research institute in Bangalore where he could continue his scientific work. At his instance, the Government of Mysore made a gift to the Indian Academy of Sciences of a magnificently located piece of land. He collected some private benefactions during his tours in different parts of India, sufficient for the cost of a modest building. The construction of the building was commenced in the year 1943 and was completed in the year 1948. The building was occupied in 1949. A research institute, with Raman as Director and a small number of research assistants began functioning in the same year. Thereafter a great number of additional amenities were added and other structures raised. Sir C. V. Raman himself made substantial gifts of money and securities and also gifts of valuable immovable properties for the use and benefit of the Institute to enable it to function as an independent organisation. The Institute, known today as the Raman Research Institute, by the name of its Founder-Director Sir C. V. Raman stands on an elevated site and amidst beautiful surroundings from which a panoramic view of the city of Bangalore can be obtained. The first floor of the main building in the Institute is occupied by museums, the library and a lecture theatre. The ground floor contains some research laboratories, the study room and an office for the Director. The museums consist of a very impressive collection, exclusively made by Sir C. V. Raman, of minerals, crystals, birds, butterflies, fossils and a great many other items of scientific interest. Anyone going through this museum will not fail to be impressed by the extraordinary interest which natural objects always evoked in Sir C. V. Raman. He was, indeed, a great naturalist and to him, the primary object of science was the understanding of nature. He was often called a child of nature, for he laboured unceasingly to probe into her inner workings and her hidden secrets. Those of us who were used to meeting him and talking to him in the Raman Research Institute recall vividly that wide-eyed and penetrating look of his and the infectious enthusiasm with which he used to expound the subject of his contemporary interests, to the nearly complete exclusion of all other topics during any conversation. This went on till the last day of his life. The Raman Research Institute is at present being managed by a small Board, constituted by him for that specific purpose, a little before he died.

### *Interest in Diamonds*

Raman had a great fascination for gemstones and the museum he built up at the Raman Research Institute contains some priceless specimens for study and research. In particular, his interest in the study of the diamond, of its remarkable physical properties and of its structure has been more or less a lifelong involvement with him. As long back as 1930, it was found that diamond exhibits a strong and sharp line corresponding to the frequency shift of 1332 $cm^{-1}$ in its Raman spectrum, besides a complex luminescence spectrum, the leading feature of which is a band at 415.5 nm (4155 A), its intensity varying enormously from specimen to specimen. With this as the starting point, Professor Raman built up his interest in diamonds to such an extent that at one time, every student working in his department was engaged in studying one aspect or other of the properties of diamond. Fluorescence, absorption, luminescence, birefringence, X-ray studies, specific heat, magnetic susceptibility, photo-conductivity, ultraviolet transparency, the Faraday effect and a host of other properties are amongst the several that were the subject matter of intensive studies by him and his collaborators.

He used to purchase, after a personal examination of each specimen, from auctions, shops and individual dealers, many diamonds and add them to his collection. In the museum at the Raman Research Institute today, are several hundreds of diamonds — some in their natural condition, some cut and polished, some cleavage plates, all of which altogether make up a unique collection probably unparalleled anywhere in the world as a laboratory acquisition.

His interest in the physics of the diamond was deep seated. It was both scientific and aesthetic. On many occasions, he gave expression to his views on the subject and as a specimen thereof, we may quote here from one of his writings. 'Diamond is a crystal of the cubic class and it is chemically an element. It exhibits the characteristic properties of the solid state in a superlative degree. Hence, by a study of its physical behaviour, one could hope to discover the principles which are the fundamental basis of crystal physics. It was these considerations which led me to build up a collection of some five hundred diamonds and utilise this material for investigations extending over a period of many years. Memoirs reporting the results have appeared from time to time in the *Proceedings of the Indian Academy of Sciences.*'

Amongst the many interesting conclusions he reached about diamonds are the following. Some diamonds belong to the tetrahedral class and others to the octahedral class of the cubic system. Those belonging to the tetrahedral class exhibit a visible luminescence of a blue colour when illuminated with ultra-violet light. In his collection is present a diamond of this kind which emits enough light in a dark room under ultra-violet irradiation to enable a newspaper held close to it to be read. Those belonging to the octahedral class, under the same circumstances, do not emit any visible light. He concluded that the luminescence is a property of the diamond itself and is not due to any extraneous impurity present within the crystal. His work relating to the special type of reflection of X-rays from the octahedral planes of diamond has already been mentioned.

Sir C. V. Raman was aware that India was the original home of some of the well-known diamonds which found their way to other parts of the world and helped to spread the fame of this gemstone. A couple of years before his death, he spent a great deal of time studying the geography and the geology of the Krishna valley and of the rivers that flow in and around it, because it has been known that at one time 60,000 people were engaged in diamond mining operations in that area. He concluded that the story of diamonds in the Krishna valley need not be treated as a closed chapter having only historical interest. On the other hand, he felt that it may well prove to be a subject of practical importance at the present time if pursued vigorously with the necessary circumspection.

### *Later Phase of Life*

Isolation from other scientists in India, arising partly from his disappointment with the trends that the growth of science in India was showing and partly from his desire to devote himself wholly to his chosen lines of work, was a noticeable feature of the last few years of Raman's life. He was generally critical of the post-Independence scientific efforts in India but became strongly so as time went on and bitterly complained against the growing dependence of Indian scientists on foreign institutions for their equipment and support and even for their ideas. He disapproved of young men going out of India for building up scientific careers but, during the last two decades of his life, the times were such that the so-called brain drain was gaining momentum in India as in other similar developing countries. He disapproved of organisations spending large sums of money on equipment and often said that where there is creativity of mind, the magnitude of external tools did not matter. But the expansion in Independent India was such that large sums of money came to be invested on national laboratories and other Government-controlled scientific institutions. Thus, the widening gap between Raman's intuitive ideas and India's facts of life was a phase of his association with the Raman Research Institute. It is on record that when the late Jawaharlal Nehru, then Prime Minister of India, admonished India's scientists and asked them to come out of the ivory towers in which they had confined themselves, Raman reacted in a typically sharp manner and said 'The men who matter are those who sit in ivory towers. They are the salt of the earth and it is to them that humanity owes its existence and progress.'

A few years before his death, he ventured into a new field of scientific activity, although distantly related to his original interests like colour and optics. He asked of himself two questions, namely, How do we perceive light? and What is colour and how is colour related to the physical characters of light? These questions had been asked by many a man of science in the past and answers furnished, but Raman always preferred to look at a basic problem like that in his own way. He was, as a consequence, led to make several systematic observations. More than ever before in his life, he sur-rounded himself with nature. The colours of flowers from the extensively grown garden in the Raman Research Institute fascinated him at all times and were the subject matter of intensive studies by him. The culmination of that work was the publication of a treatise entitled *Physiology of vision,* just a couple of years before his death.

While he grew into being regarded and respected as the Father of Indian Science, the Government instituted National Professorships and conferred on him the first such Professorship to enable him to do the work that he liked while functioning as the Director of the Raman Research Institute. Towards the end, he became an 'Institution' in himself and as loneliness surrounded him, work became all that mattered to him in his life. When he fell ill, and was confined to bed, the end coming nearer and nearer, he told his doctors 'do not want to survive my illness if it means anything less than a hundred per cent active and productive life'. Less than a couple of months before his death, he went up the first floor of the Raman Research Institute like a young schoolboy, delivered the Gandhi Memorial lecture on

2 October 1970 — the last lecture he gave in his life wherein he expounded his ideas about the theory of hearing. This incident is more than proof that he not only believed in work, but also practised what he believed in, and was active till the very end. After a short illness, he died in the early hours of the morning of Saturday, 21 November 1970. His mortal remains were cremated in the grounds of the Raman Research Institute. Thus, passed away Sir Chandrashekhara Venkata Raman, the legendary figure of science in modern India, into the pages of history. How much of the tradition and how many of the institutions he handed over to the present generation of Indian scientists will survive is a matter for the future and for those who have inherited the same.

### *Some General Observations*

There are some features in Raman's make-up that have been noticed and admired by those who came close to him as well as by those that knew him only from a distance. He was richly endowed with a child-like sense of wonder at the unknown and not understood facets of nature so that, throughout his life, he was pushed into exploring these aspects. Such being the motivation, he was often and appropriately referred to as the child of nature and nothing fascinated him more than nature herself. Subjects like colours, origin of minerals, birds and butterflies, the blue of the ocean, the sky and other natural phenomena were his primary concern. On the contrary, he could not reconcile himself with the fact that large human resources and material wealth are being put into programmes such as those that deal with space and so on, and do not concern themselves with things on earth and of immediate interest to mankind. He was a self-made man and had always set an example to his associates and students, of hard work, indomitable will and total dedication to science.

His intuitive abilities enabled him to jump several steps in mathematics. His capacity to expound complicated concepts in physics in a simple and appealing manner always made him a very popular speaker. Thus he attracted thousands of listeners whenever he gave public lectures. He was forthright when he criticised what he considered wrong or unscientific and by such action, he had hurt many a public man on occasions.

He was always more than generous in acknowledging the share of his co-workers, encouraged every deserving student that came to him and could never tolerate foolishness. He had a delicate sense of humour and was a great attraction when he chose to make an after-dinner speech. He loved art. He loved music. He lived, worked and died for science and in science.

Sir C. V. Raman was one of the brilliant scientists of India who won the Nobel Prize in 1930 for his discovery of the 'Raman Effect.' (The discovery that monochromatic light ray in the incident beam can be split up into a number of components with wave length smaller or greater than that of the incident ray).

In 1934, he founded the Indian Academy of Sciences and in 1948, the Raman Research Institute.

In addition to being a great scientist, C. V. Raman was a superb speaker. The following speech delivered at the convocation ceremony of the Agra University is a good example of his eloquence.

# 3

# An Illustrious Career

Raman was transferred to Nagpur for some time during his government service. Once a gentleman with partially burnt pile of currency notes came in his office to exchange them for new. The officer in charge examined the currency notes and rejected them. The officer showed the door to the aggrieved party. Raman who witnessed the event called him back. He took the pile of currency notes and examined every piece by means of a magnifying glass, which he used to keep all the time. The numbers on them were clearly legible and Raman found them to be legally tenderable. He ordered the officer in charge for the exchange. The aggrieved party was much pleased with Raman's approach. Thus, Raman proved that he was a man of humanity. He was the rarest of officers in the most orthodox times, that one could come across. The nation needed such humane officers which is the wont, even today.

## Receiving the Nobel Prize

After receiving the Nobel in 1930, when Raman returned to his seat, there were tears in his eyes. They were not tears of joy, but of sorrow. It was so because there was no flag of India next to his chair but that of colonial masters. Here again was an instance where his patriotism was at its best. He asserted that Patriotism does not flow from chorus sounding the National anthem, but through "love of the earth that bore us, feeds and sustains us".

## With Gandhiji

Once Gandhiji accompanied by Kasturba, Mahadev Desai and Sardar Vallabhbhai Patel visited the IISc in 1936. Raman interestingly and eloquently explained the scientific achievements of the Institute. When Gandhiji was about to leave the institute after the visit, Raman was eager to have their comments and the observations. Gandhiji was silent but Sardar Patel wanted to know whether anything could be done to improve the Charkha. It may be Sardar Patel's idea, in heart of this enquiry, that how science and technology be taken to the common man on the rural side. Raman was happy with this comment. He firmly believed in rural technology, and whether it could be developed indigenously. This event implied the commonality of Gandhiji and Raman views on service to humanity and use of science for society at large.

There was an international exhibition at Paris in 1937. There was no exhibit from India on display at the exhibition. But there were two beautiful items in American Pavilion. One, the bust of Mahatma Gandhiji facing that of Rockfeller and the other, a demonstration of Raman Effect besides a write-up on Raman. The positioning of these two items at the American Pavilion was indeed a matter of happiness and mystery. They (the exhibits) raised scores of questions that remained unanswered. But it is not difficult for deep thinkers to lift the veil of secrecy and interpret the meaning of the two items on display.

Could it be the same message of the materialism (through Rockefeller) and the spiritualism (through Gandhiji)? Or did it imply that ultimate happiness of man lies in the Gandhian philosophy and not Rockefellerian one? Did it mean that Raman's achievement through indigenous means held in store, a great future for India? Or did both Gandhiji and Raman, had attained the position of prophets, leading the mixed future of East and West!

## Stopped Attending Annual Sessions of Science Congress

Raman regularly attended the annual sessions of Science Congress till 1949. Then he abruptly stopped attending them. He was then asked why? Raman very boldly replied that he had nothing to do with Science Congress that were frequently inaugurated by politicians.

According to him, "They have nothing to do with the development of science. Nowhere else in the world is this done. Even after independence we are not exempted from the feudal past. It was simply a transfer of power and not a real freedom in the true sense."

Raman flatly refused to be included in any committee where he could not spare his time or where he was unable to contribute substantially. Once a feeler was sent to Raman to gauge his mind and seek his consent on whether he would take up the Vice-Presidency of India? He laughed heartily and asked, "What shall I do with it?" It is very interesting to mention the identical case of Einstein, who too was offered the Prime Ministership of Israel. He very politely rejected by saying that politics was not his business and he did not know anything of it.

## A Conscience-keeper of Science

Nehru once admonished scientists to come out of "Ivory Towers" and work for the country's progress. Raman immediately and thoughtfully reacted sharply saying, "The men who matter are those who sit in the ivory towers. They are the salt of the earth and it is to them that humanity owes its existence and progress."

Raman had a strong feeling that the administrator was the boss even in the Research Institutes. Dr. Homi Bhabha, a contemporary scientist, too had the same feelings. Not only Raman but also many others were to criticise the pattern of the establishment. Many others remained within the system while Raman did not compromise and preferred to remain outside the system. Having a high reputation and prestige, he could have easily held the highest position in the land.

History will cite Raman on record as a conscience-keeper of science as Rajaji, another astute and a respected politician turned first Governor General of independent India, who was also committed to both fields, at the same time. Both were equally unhappy with the establishment in their own ways.

## Resignation from Royal Society of London

Unscrupulous elements criticised him badly and baselessly. Under a spell of depression, born out of all such things, he resigned as member of the Royal Society of London. His resignation from the society was an uncommon event. He was perhaps second to Newton to resign from the society.

## Foundation of Raman Research Institute

Raman stayed at Bangalore to fulfil the obligation to his student. Later, the Bharat Ratna medal and the citation were routinely hand-delivered at his residence by an ordinary messenger of Mysore Government. That was the way Raman received the Nation's highest award — no one to cheer, to stand up and applaud or even to congratulate. This event (incident) speaks volumes for the founder of Raman Research Institute (RRI), a tall man and a spirited giant.

Once when the building for RRI was under construction, Padmanabham — the laboratory assistant at RRI reported to Raman that one labourer was preparing the mortar with his legs bleeding; Raman gave up all work and went to that labourer. Raman said, "Your leg is bleeding. Don't do any work today. Don't bother about the work." The labourer replied, "Bapaji, this is our life. If we do not work, what shall we eat? To work like this is common to us. We cannot afford the rest."

Raman replied, "Don't worry about your wages. You will get your wages till you are alright."

Raman returned to his office and called up the Director of a Bangalore hospital to request on behalf of the labourer. Then he requested Padmanabham to carry the patient in his car to the hospital. He further instructed to ensure that the bill was drawn in his (Raman's) favour only.

Later, Raman also called the contractor and requested him to provide such labourers with gumboots. The contractor replied, "If labourers need such boots, they should have their own. It is not our job to provide them." He went to the extent of ensuring that every labourer was provided with the necessary safety gear at work, proving once again his human nature.

In another incident, some candidates were called for the interview at RRI Candidates who did not pass written tests and interview were allowed to go with their allowances paid immediately. It so happened with one candidate that he was paid more, due to the mistake of an accountant. The candidate, who knew about over-payment, came to the accounts department to return the excess amount. Raman by chance, witnessed the incident as he approached the accountant.

He then went to his office and called candidate who had returned the excess fare. He said, "I know that you are not up to the mark in physics so I did not select you. But now I have changed my opinion and select you because of your honesty and integrity. These are innate virtues which you possess. Does not matter that you know physics less. It is my duty to teach and prepare you in physics. Efficiency can be increased by practice and training. But honesty and integrity are the qualities of culture, which are rarely found."

On the occasion of the Academy's Golden Jubilee, Dr. Homi Bhabha was to give a lecture (in 1941) on Cosmic rays at Nagpur University Convocation Hall. There was no blackboard or a chalk, nor a duster at the venue. It is known to all in science that when a lecture is to be given such tools are a must. Bhabha remarked on the absence of the board on which to draw diagrams or write the equations. Raman known to have a quick presence of mind and wit, instantly added, "It is good in a way. It stimulates the imagination."

In science, ideas, imagination and observations are prime factors for its progress. Reviewing the various activities of the Academy, Raman once said that an Academy of science is not a sheer ornament but an indispensable institution. The Academy, which Raman brought up was easily able to fulfil all the expectations.

## Honours and Awards

Raman was honoured with a large number of honorary doctorates and memberships of scientific societies. He was elected a Fellow of the Royal Society early in his career (1924) and knighted in 1929. In 1930 he won the Nobel Prize in Physics. In 1954 he was awarded the Bharat Ratna. He was also awarded the Lenin Peace Prize in 1957.

India celebrates National Science Day on 28 February of every year to commemorate the discovery of the Raman effect in 1928.

## Bharat Ratna

On August 15, 1954, Raman was announced as the recipient of the highest award of the country, the Bharat Ratna. On 19 January, 1955, Raman received a telegram from Dr. Rajendra Prashad, the then President of India which read as follows:

> "I shall be glad if you will stay in Rashtrapati Bhavan as my guest, when you come to receive your Bharat Ratna Award. Kindly let us know your mode and date of arrival for reception arrangements."

Raman sent a reply to the President on 20 January, 1955 which said:

> "I was greatly touched by your very kind telegram received last night, inviting me to be your guest at Rashtrapati Bhavan for the Investiture Ceremony on 27 January, 1955.
>
> Further, I find myself unable to come to Delhi for the function. Even ordinarily my work here is all-engrossing and prevents me from accepting assignments which call me away from Bangalore. At the present time, I am firmly tied down here to enable one of my students to complete his Doctorate thesis, which the Regulation requires him to submit to his university before the end of January 1955. Thus, my duty as a teacher has to take precedence over my own personal affairs. I feel fully confident that you will appreciate the compelling nature of the circumstances, which prevent me from accepting your kind and gracious invitation to come to Delhi.
>
> Yours Sincerely,
>
> C. V. Raman"

## Publications

*1909:*

- "The Small Motion at the Nodes of a Vibrating String", *Nature,* 1909.
- "The Maintenance of Forced Oscillations of a New Type", *Nature,* 1909.
- "The Ectara", *J. Indian Math. Club,* 1909.

*1910:*

- "The Maintenance of Forced Oscillations", *Nature,* 1910.
- "Oscillations of the Stretched Strings", *J. Indian Math. Club,* 1910.

*1911:*

- "Photographs of Vibrational Curves", *Philos. Mag.,* 1911.
- "Remarks on a Paper by J. S. Stokes on 'Some Curious Phenomena Observed in Connection with Melde's Experiment'", *Physics Rev.,* 1911.
- "The Small Motion at the Nodes of a Vibrating String", *Phys. Rev.,* 1911.

*1912:*

- "The Maintenance of Forced Oscillations of a New Type", *Philos. Mag,* 1912.
- "Some Remarkable Cases of Resonance", *Phys. Rev.* 1912.
- "Experimental Investigations on the Maintenance of Vibrations", *Bull. Indian Assoc. Cultiv. Sci.,* 1912.

*1913:*

- "Some Acoustical Observations", *Bull. Indian Assoc. Cultiv. Sci.,* 1913.

*1914:*

- "The Dynamical Theory of the Motion of Bowed Strings", *Bull. Indian Assoc. Cultiv. Sci.,* 1914.
- "The Maintenance of Vibrations", *Phys. Rev.* 1914.

- "Dynamical Theory of the Motion of Bowed Strings", *Bulletin, Indian Association for the Cultivation of Science,* 1914.
- "On Motion in a Periodic Field of Force", *Bull. Indian Assoc. Cultiv. Sci.,* 1914.

***1915:***

- "On the Maintenance of Combinational Vibrations by Two Simple Harmonic forces", *Phys. Rev.,* 1915.
- "On Motion in a Periodic Field of Force", *Philos. Mag,* 1915.

***1916:***

- "On Discontinuous Wave-Motion - Part 1", *Philos. Mag,* 1916 (with S. Appaswamair).
- "On the 'Wolf-Note' of the Violin and Cello", *Nature* (London). 1916.
- "On the 'Wolf-Note' in the Bowed Stringed Instruments", *Philos. Mag.,* 1916.

***1917:***

- "The Maintenance of Vibrations in a Periodic Field of Force", *Philos. Mag,* 1917 (with A. Dey).
- "On Discontinuous Wave-Motion - Part 2", *Philos. Mag,* 1917 (with A Dey).
- "On Discontinuous Wave-Motion - Part 3", *Philos. Mag,* 1917 (with A Dey).
- "On the Alterations of Tone Produced by a Violin 'Mute'", *Nature* (London) 1917.

***1918:***

- "On the 'Wolf-Note' in the Bowed Stringed Instruments", *Philos. Mag.,* 1918.
- "On the Wolf-Note in Pizzicato Playing", *Nature* (London), 1918.
- "On the Mechanical Theory of the Vibrations of Bowed Strings and of Musical Instruments of the Violin Family,

with Experimental Verification of Results — Part 1", *Bulletin, Indian Association for the Cultivation of Science*, 1918.

- "The Theory of the Cyclical Vibrations of a Bowed String", *Bulletin, Indian Association for the Cultivation of Science*, 1918.

***1919:***

- "An Experimental Method for the Production of Vibrations", *Phys. Rev.*, 1919.
- "A New Method for the Absolute Determination of Frequency", *Proc. R. Soc. London*, 1919.
- "On the Partial Tones of Bowed Stringed Instruments", *Philos. Mag*, 1919.
- "The Kinematics of Bowed Strings", *J. Dept of Sci., Univ. Calcutta*, 1919.

***1920:***

- "On the Sound of Splashes", *Philos. Mag*, 1920.
- "On a Mechanical Violin-Player for Acoustical Experiments, *Philos. Mag.*, 1920.
- "Experiments with Mechanically-Played Violins", *Proc. Indian Association for the Cultivation of Science*, 1920.
- "On Kaufmann's Theory of the Impact of the Pianoforte Hammer", *proc. S. Soc. London*, 1920 (with B. Banerji).
- "Musical Drums with Harmonic Overtones", *Nature* (London), 1920 (with S. Kumar).

***1921:***

- "Whispering Gallery Phenomena at St. Paul's Cathedral", *Nature* (London) 1921 (with G. A. Sutherland).
- "The Nature of Vowel Sounds", *Nature* (London) 1921.
- "On the Whispering Gallery Phenomenon", *Proc. R. Soc. London*, 1922 (with G. A. Sutherland).
- "On Some Indian Stringed Instruments", *Proc. Indian Association for the Cultivation of Science*, 1921.

**1922:**

- "On Whispering Galleries", *Indian Assoc. Cultiv. Sci.*, 1922.
- "On the Molecular Scattering of Light in Water and the Colour of the Sea", *Proceedings of the Royal Society*, 1922.
- "The Acoustical Knowledge of the Ancient Hindus", *Ashutosh Mukherjee Silver Jubilee - Vol. 2.*

**1926:**

- "The Subjective Analysis of Musical Tones", *Nature* (London), 1926.

**1927:**

- "Musical Instruments and Their Tones".

**1928:**

- "A new type of Secondary Radiation", *Nature*, 1928.
- "A new radiation", *Indian Journal of Physics*, 1928.

**1935:**

- "The Indian Musical Drums", *Proc. Indian Acad. Sci.*, 1935.
- "The Diffraction of Light by High Frequency Sound Waves: Part I", *Proc. Indian Acad. Sci.*, 1935 (with N. S. Nagendra Nath).
- "The Diffraction of Light by High Frequency Sound Waves: Part II", *Proc. Indian Acad. Sci.*, 1935 (with N. S. Nagendra Nath).
- "Nature of Thermal Agitation in Liquids", *Nature* (London), 1935 (with B. V. Raghavendra Rao).

**1936:**

- "The Diffraction of Light by High Frequency Sound Waves: Part III: Doppler Effect and Coherence Phenomena", *Proc. Indian Acad. Sci.*, 1936 (with N. S. Nagendra Nath).
- "The Diffraction of Light by High Frequency Sound Waves: Part IV: Generalised Theory", *Proc. Indian Acad. Sci.*, 1936 (with N. S. Nagendra Nath).

- "The Diffraction of Light by High Frequency Sound Waves: Part V: General Considerations — Oblique Incidence and Amplitude Changes", *Proc. Indian Acad. Sci.*, 1936 (with N. S. Nagendra Nath).
- "Diffraction of Light by Ultrasonic Waves", *Nature* (London), 1936 (with N. S. Nagendra Nath).

***1937:***

- "Acoustic Spectrum of Liquids", *Nature* (London), 1937 (with B. V. Raghavendra Rao).

***1938:***

- "Light Scattering and Fluid Viscosity", *Nature* (London), 1938 (with B. V. Raghavendra Rao).

***1948:***

- *Aspects of Science*, 1948.

***1951:***

- *The New Physics: Talks on Aspects of Science*, 1951.

***1953:***

- "The structure and optical behaviour of iridescent opal", *Proc. Indian. Acad. Sci. A38* 1953 (with A. Jayaraman).

***1959:***

- *Lectures on Physical Optics*, 1959.

# 4

# The Great Genius

The genius who won the Nobel Prize for Physics, with simple equipment barely worth Rs. 300. He was the first Asian scientist to win the Nobel Prize. He was a man of boundless curiosity and a lively sense of humour. His spirit of enquiry and devotion to science laid the foundations for scientific research in India. And he won honour as a scientist and affection as a teacher and a man.

One day in 1903, Professor Eliot of Presidency College, Madras, saw a little boy in his B.A. Class. Thinking that he might have strayed into the room, the Professor asked, "Are you a student of the B.A. class?"

"Yes Sir," the boy answered.

"Your name?"

"C. V. Raman."

This little incident made the fourteen-year-old boy well known in the college. The youngster was later to become a world famous scientist.

## A Child Genius

Tiruchirapalli is a town on the banks of the river Cauvery. Chandrashekhara Ayyar was a teacher in a school there. He was a scholar in Physics and Mathematics. He loved music. His wife was Parvathi Ammal. Their second son was born on 7th November 1888. They named the boy Venkata Raman. He was also called Chandrashekhara Venkata Raman or C. V. Raman.

Raman grew up in an atmosphere of music, Sanskrit literature and Science. He stood first in every class and was. Talked about as a child genius. He joined the B.A. class of the Presidency College. In the year 1905, he was the only boy who passed in the first class. He won a gold medal, too.

He joined the M.A. class in the same college and chose Physics (study of matter and energy) as the main subject of study. Love of science, enthusiasm for work and the curiosity to learn new things were natural to Raman. Nature had also given him the power of concentration and intelligence. He used to read more than what was taught in the class. When doubts arose he would set down questions like 'How?' 'Why?' and 'Is this true?' in the Margin in the textbooks.

The works of the German scientist Helmhotlz (1821-91) and the English scientist Lord Raleigh (1842-1919) on acoustics (the study of sound) influenced Raman. He took immense interest in the study of sound. When he was eighteen years of age, one of his research papers was published in the 'Philosophical Magazine' of England. Later another paper was published in the scientific journal 'Nature'.

## Officer - Scientist

Raman's elder brother C. S. Ayyar was in the 'Indian Audit and Accounts Service' (IAAS). Raman also wanted to enter the same department. So he sat for the competitive examination. The day before this examination, the results of the M.A. examination were published. He had passed in first class recording the highest marks in Madras University up to that time. He stood first in the IAAS examination also.

On May 6, 1907, Raman married Lokasundari Ammal.

At the age of nineteen, Raman held a high post in the government. He was appointed as the Assistant Accountant

General in the Finance Department in Calcutta. And the same year something happened to give a new turn to his life.

## 210, Bow Bazaar Street

One evening Raman was returning from his office in a tramcar. He saw the name plate of the 'Indian Association for the Cultivation of Science' at 210, Bow Bazaar Street. Immediately he got off the tram and went in. Dr. Amritlal Sircar was the Honorary Secretary of the Association. There were spacious rooms and old scientific instruments, which could be used for demonstration of experiments.

Raman asked whether he could conduct research there in his spare time. Sircar gladly agreed. Raman took up a house adjoining the Association. A door was provided between his house and the laboratory. During the daytime he would attend his office and carry out his duties.

His mornings and nights were devoted to research. This gave him full satisfaction. So he continued his ceaseless activities in Calcutta.

## From Accounts to Science

At that time Burma and India were under a single government. In 1909, Raman was transferred to Rangoon, the capital of Burma. When Chandrashekhara Ayyar passed away in 1910, Raman came to Madras on six months' leave.

After completing the last rites, Raman spent the rest of his leave period doing research in the Madras University laboratories.

The Science College of Calcutta University was started in 1915.

There a chair for Physics was established in memory of Taraknath Palit, a generous man. Raman was appointed Professor. He sacrificed the powerful post in the government, which brought a good salary.

The Indian Science Congress was started in 1913. Its aim was to bring together scientists engaged in research; they should meet and exchange ideas. Its first session was held in 1914. Ashuthosh Mukherjee was the President. Raman was the President of the

Physics section. Later he worked for many years as the Secretary of the Science Congress. He presided over its annual sessions in 1929 and 1948.

## Professor Raman

In 1917, at the age of 29, Raman became the Palit Professor. He continued research along with the new assignment.

Raman was very deeply interested in musical instruments such as the Veena, the Violin, the Mridangam and the Tabala. He began to work on them. Around 1918 he explained the complex vibrations of the strings of musical instruments. He later found out the characteristic tones emitted by the Mridangam, the Tabala, etc.

Amritlal Sircar, who was devoting all his time to the welfare of the Indian Association for the Cultivation of Science, passed away in 1919. Professor Raman became its Honorary Secretary. Two laboratories — those of the College and of the Association — were under him; and this gave a new stimulus to his researches. Both his body and his mind could do all the work that had to be done. Many students came to him from different parts of the country for post-graduate studies and research. 210, Bow Bazaar Street and the University Science College Laboratory — these became the active research centres of India. Research workers like Meghnad Saha and S. K. Mitra, who became famous later, worked at these centres.

## The Great Teacher

That was a time when Raman was completely immersed in experiments and research. According to the terms of the Palit Chair, he could have remained free from teaching work, doing research only. But Raman had great pleasure in teaching. Students were inspired by his lectures. They were eager to listen to him. He would not stick to one particular textbook. His lectures brought the fragrance of fresh research. They reflected Raman's great curiosity about the secrets of nature. Usually the lecture was of an hour's duration. Forgetting the time in the discussion of the subject, Professor Raman would sometimes lecture for two or three hours. Any doubt or question from a student would stimulate new scientific ideas.

## Not a Minute to Waste

Absorbed in experiments, it was not unusual for him to forget food and sleep. Sometimes working late at night, he would sleep in the laboratory on one of the tables.

In the mornings too, most of his time was spent in the laboratory. He worked in informal clothes. At 9.30 a.m. he would rush home. After a shave and a bath he would dress up and send for a taxi. He Would finish his breakfast in two or three minutes and get into the taxi. Racing over a distance of four miles, he would reach the class on time. He never wasted time.

## In England

The Congress of the Universities of the British Empire met in 1921 in London. Raman went to England as the representative of Calcutta University. This was his first visit abroad.

Raman lectured in the 'Physical Society' of London. People came in large numbers to listen to him. He was introduced to J. J. Thomson and Ernest Rutherford, the famous English Physicists. Raman visited St. Paul's Church in London. A whisper at one point of the church tower is heard clearly at another point. This effect, produced by the reflection of sound, aroused his curiosity.

## The Blue of the Sea

Raman's journey to England and back was by sea. In his leisure hours, he used to sit on the upper deck of the ship and enjoy the beauty of the vast sea. The deep blue colour of the Mediterranean Sea interested the scientist in him. Was the blue due to the reflection of the blue sky? If so, how could it appear in the absence of light? Even when big waves rolled over the surface, the blue remained. As he thought over the problem, it flashed to him that the blue colour might be caused by the scattering of the sun's light by water molecules. He turned over this idea in his mind again and gains. Immediately after his return to Calcutta, he plunged into experiments. Within a month, he prepared a research paper and sent it to the Royal Society of London. Next year he published a lengthy article on the molecular scattering of light.

Raman never held the wrong belief that research could be carried out only with foreign-made or very complicated equipment. No doubt, he imported some equipment. But he prepared much of the equipment he used with the help of his students.

## New Contacts

Scientists of many countries appreciated the research papers of Raman and his colleagues. The Royal Society, the oldest and the most important science society of England, honoured Raman in 1924 by electing his as its 'Fellow' (that is, a member).

The annual session of 'The British Association for the Cultivation of Science' was held in the same year in Toronto (Canada). Raman inaugurated the seminar on the scattering of light. R. A. Millikan, the famous American Physicist, who also attended, was full of admiration for Raman. They became fast friends too.

At the Mount Wilson Observatory in California (USA), a telescope of 100-inch width was in use. Those were the times when discoveries in the field of astronomy (study of stars and planets and their movements) filled people with wonder. Raman was always eager to learn new things. He spent a couple of days on Mount Wilson. During the nights he viewed the Nebula (bright or dark patch in the sky caused by distant stars or a cloud of gas or dust). Through the telescope and was thrilled.

He went to Russia in 1925 to participate in the two-hundredth anniversary of the 'Russian Academy of Sciences'.

## The Guide

Many scholars were working in the Calcutta laboratories to unlock the secrets of sound and light. To all of them Professor Raman was the 'Guru' and the leader. He had observed the blue colour of the deep glaciers (mass of ice or snow) in the Alps mountain ranges. Taking the clue from this, some of the research workers studied some scattering of light in ice and quartz crystals. They also studied the scattering of light in liquids such as pure water and alcohol, as well as in vapours and gases.

With a complete mental picture of the phenomenon, Raman would proceed to experiment systematically. After that he would write the research paper based on the results of the experiments and arrange for its early publication. Sometimes it would be late in the day by the time the final copy was prepared. Then he would rush to the General Post Office in a taxi to catch the last mail. Then he would enjoy a feast of *Rasagulla* with his students.

He started 'The Indian Journal of Physics' in 1926 to make the prompt publication of research papers possible.

Raman wanted the young men working with him to take up independent positions and to serve the nation. He felt that his laboratory was a centre of training for young talent, but not a permanent storehouse.

Raman's research on sound became famous all over the world. 'Handbuck der Physic', a German Encyclopaedia of Physics, was published in 1927. Raman was the only foreign scientist invited to contribute an article to it.

## The Raman Effect

Sometimes a rainbow appears and delights our eyes. We see in it shades of red, orange, yellow, green, blue, indigo and violet. The white ray of the sun includes all these colours. When a beam of sunlight is passed through a glass prism a patch of these colour-bands are seen. This is called the spectrum. The Spectrometer is an apparatus used to study the spectrum. Spectral lines in it are characteristic of the light passing through the prism. A beam of light that causes a single spectral line is said to be monochromatic.

When a beam of monochromatic light passes through a transparent substance (a substance which allows light to pass through it), the beam is scattered. Raman spent a long time in the study of the scattered light. On February 28, 1928, he observed two low intensity spectral line corresponding to the incident mono- chromatic light. Years of his labour had borne fruit. It was clear that though the incident light was monochromatic, the scattered light due to it, was not monochromatic. Thus Raman's experiments discovered a phenomenon which was lying hidden in nature.

The 16th of March 1928 is a memorable day in the history of science. On that day a meeting was held under the joint auspices of the South Indian Science Association and the Science Club of Central College, Bangalore; Raman was the Chief Guest. He announced the new phenomenon discovered by him to the world. He also acknowledged with affection the assistance given by K. S. Krishnan and Venkateshwaran, who were his students.

The phenomenon attracted the attention of research workers all over the world. It became famous as the 'Raman Effect'. The spectral lines in the scattered light were known as 'Raman Lines'.

Is light wave-like or particle-like? This question has been discussed from time to time by scientists. The Raman Effect confirmed that light was made up of particles known as 'photons'. It helped in the study of the molecular and crystal structures of different substances.

### *World-Wide Interest in Raman Effect*

Investigations making use of the Raman Effect began in many countries. During the first twelve years after its discovery, about 1,800 research papers were published on various aspects of it and about 2,500 chemical compounds were studied. Raman Effect was highly praised as one of the greatest discoveries of the third decade of this century.

After the 'lasers' (devices that produce intense beams of light, their name coming from the initial letters of 'Light Amplification by Stimulated Emission of Radiation) came into use in the 1960s, it became easier to get monochromatic light of very high intensity for experiments. This brought back scientific interest in Raman Effect, and the interest remains alive to this day.

## The World Honoured Raman

Raman received many honours from all over the world for his achievement. In 1928 the Science Society of Rome awarded the Matteucci Medal. In 1929 the British Government knighted him; thereafter Professor Raman came to be known as Professor Sir C. V. Raman. The Royal Society of London awarded the Hughes Medal in 1930. Honorary doctorate degrees were awarded by the Universities of Freiburg (Germany), Glasgow (England), Paris (France), Bombay, Benaras, Dacca, Patna, Mysore and several others.

## The Nobel Prize, Too

The highest award a scientist or a writer can get is the Nobel Prize. In 1930, the Swedish Academy of Sciences chose Raman to receive the Nobel Prize for Physics. No Indian and no Asian had received the Nobel Prize for Physics up to that time. At the ceremony for the award, Raman used alcohol to demonstrate the Raman Effect. Later in the evening alcoholic drinks were served at the dinner. But Raman did not touch them. He remained loyal to the Indian traditions.

## A Keen Eye

However minute the results of an experiment, they could not escape the searching eyes of Raman. And his mind retained every detail of what he observed. An incident, which took place at Walter, the seat of Andhra University, may be mentioned. After the discovery of the Raman Effect, spectra of different substances were being studied there.

On one of his visits there, Raman found the research workers puzzled at not getting the expected spectral lines. Raman examined the plate containing the spectrum and exclaimed with joy, "There it is, you see!" He immediately got a projector and made the weak spectral lines clearly visible on the white screen.

## In Bangalore

He came to Bangalore as the Director of the Tata Institute (the Indian Institute of Science) in 1933. The Tata Institute soon became famous for the study of crystals. The diffraction of light (the very slight bending of light around corners) by ultrasonic waves (high frequency sound waves which we cannot hear) in a liquid was elegantly explained by Raman and Nagendranath. This became known as the 'Raman-Nath Theory'.

## Raman's Day

Raman was an early riser and used to take morning walks regularly. The sight of tall trees against the sky at dawn delighted him. By six in the morning he would be in the chamber where he worked up to 9 a.m. he would devote his time to discussion with students who were experimenting and to the study of research papers. At 10 o'clock he would be in the Directors office. He would complete the office work and return to the laboratory. He would be immersed in research till 8.30 p.m. He used to arrange two or three seminars every week. At these seminars all the workers would come together to discuss various problems of their research.

## 'Use a 10-Kilowatt Brain'

Whenever students showed new results, Raman was delighted. He would guide them to do further work. If they appeared to be depressed he would inspire them to fresh efforts.

A student was once experimenting with an X-ray tube of one-kilowatt power. He learnt that a scientist in England was experimenting on the same problem with a five-kilowatt X-ray tube, and grew depressed. When Raman, who was on his rounds, came to know of this, he said with a smile, "There is a very simple solution; use a 10-kilowatt brain on the problem."

Raman possessed supreme self-confidence and he generated it in his students also.

Raman used to enquire about his students even after they left his Institute. If they had any difficulty he would help them as best he could.

## Judging Talent

Raman had his own method of judging the merit of a student. Once he set a question concerning the vibrations of the Mridangam at the Post-graduate Examination of the Allahabad University. This was different from the other questions based on textbooks. Only one student answered it and he had spent all the allotted time on this one answer. Raman was pleased with his talent and personally congratulated him.

Once a candidate attended an interview for a research post in the Tata Institute. He had passed in the first class. He was asked, "Are there any scientific problems you would like to work on?" There was no satisfactory answer. Physically also the candidate was weak. Raman advised him, "Research is strange work. Success in it brings limit less joy whereas failure pushes one to deep despair. Joy and despair — both require bodily strength. You should first improve your bodily strength through sports and exercises."

## The Indian Academy of Sciences

In order to encourage scientific research in India, Raman established the Indian Academy of Sciences in 1934. From that year the science journal 'The Proceedings of the Academy' is being published every month.

The Government of Mysore granted 24 acres of land to promote the activities of the Academy. It was his earnest desire 'to bring into existence a centre of scientific research worthy of our ancient country, where the keenest intellectuals of our land can probe into the mysteries of the Universe'. He fulfilled his wish by establishing a Research Institute at Hebbal, Bangalore. He did not seek help from the Government but have away all his property to the Institute. The Executive Committee of the Academy named the centre 'Raman Research Institute'.

## The Raman Research Institute

In 1948 this great scientist entered on one more active phase of life when he became the Director of the Raman Research Institute. The Institute became the centre of all his activities. A garden and tall eucalyptus trees surrounded it. He used to say, "A Hindu is required to go to the forest in old age, but instead of going to the forest, I made the forest come to me." At the Institute he could concentrate on things that interested him. He was alone with his work and was happy. At the entrance to the Institute was a board bearing the words, "The Institute is not open to visitors. Please do not disturb US."

He did research on sound, light, rocks, gems, birds, insects, butterflies, sea shells, trees, flowers, atmosphere, weather and physiology of vision and hearing. His study covered such different fields of science as Physics, Geology, Biology and Physiology. Among them sound and colours particularly attracted him. Once he even went round shops to select sarees of different colour designs.

## Delight in Colour and Light

Raman collected rocks and precious stones. His invaluable collection included hundreds of objects such as sand that melted due to lightning, rock indicating the lava flow during a volcano and diamonds, rubies and sapphires. Many fluorescent minerals (that is, minerals having the property of receiving short invisible rays and sending out long visible rays) were kept in a dark room. There he could create a small twinkling world by switching on the ultra-violet light. Thin layers of some crystals were prepared for study. No colour was seen when they were viewed perpendicularly. But the viewer had only to change the angle — and blue, green and yellow colours delighted the eye. After a deep study of diamonds Raman explained many of their characteristics.

Once in Paris he went shopping for diamonds and crystals. There two beautiful butterflies with blue wings in a shop window attracted him. He bought them and later collected thousands of specimens.

Raman loved flowers for their colours. He grew many flower plants. He used to visit flower exhibitions to examine flowers.

Raman used to announce his new scientific discoveries at the annual sessions of the Academy. At the Madras session (1967) he discussed the influence of the earth's rotation on its gaseous envelope. Next year he put forward his theory of the physiology of vision.

Many countries and institutions continued to honour him. The membership of the American Optical Society (1941), the National Professorship of India (1948), the Franklin Medal of the Franklin Institute (1951), the International Lenin Prize (1957), the Membership of the Pontifical Academy of Science (1961) — these were some of the honours conferred on him.

The greatest honour the Government of India confers on an Indian is the award of 'Bharat Ratna'. Raman became a 'Bharat Ratna' in 1954.

## 'A General Practitioner in Science'

When Raman stepped into the field of research, Modern Physics was in its infancy. It developed numerous branches by the time he began working in his own Institute. Then research workers had access to modern equipment and methods, which were not available six decades earlier. They tended to study a small field and to specialise in it. But Raman never limited his activities and interests to a narrow field.

Raman once inaugurated the 'General Practitioners Conference' in Bangalore. A general practitioner is a doctor who treats common illnesses. Raman humorously commented on that occasion that he was a general practitioner in science. He liked all scientific problems whether they were small or big. His interest and satisfaction lay in finding a solution to the problem.

In 1969, the daughter of Nagendranath (who had been a research student under him thirty years earlier) was married; Raman and his wife attended the reception. Raman drew Nagendranath aside and explained his new problem; he was trying to find a theory of earthquakes taking into account the actual shape of the earth and the wave-like nature of the quakes. Raman was not a person to be satisfied with his past achievements. He was always seeking new and vaster fields of study.

Raman was a delightful speaker. Sprinkled with good humour, his talk was usually focused on realities. Raman used to say that the colour of the sea interested him more than the fish, which lived in it. He thought that we should have our own ships for oceanographic research (the study of the sea). He often said that India lost her freedom because she took no interest in the seas.

## The True Research Student

Raman was studious. He kept in touch with the latest developments in science in the world around him. He had personal contact with many scientists. He used to read new books and research papers from different centres. On one occasion he was addressing the students of Presidency College, Madras. Like an elder brother he told them, "How much can you learn in an hour's lecture? Spend more time in the library." Studying and experimenting, he remained a student throughout his life.

"The equipment which brought me the Nobel Prize did not cost more than three hundred rupees. A table drawer can hold all my research equipments," he used to say with pride. It was his conviction that if the research worker is not inspired from within an amount of money can bring success in research.

He hoped that scientists of free India would win worldwide fame by their discoveries. "If there are no facilities here, what is wrong with their going abroad and spreading the fame of India? Did not the workers of the East India Company come and rule India?" he used to say.

Raman was not conservative in his outlook. He used to spell out his opinions boldly. When he was called 'India's illustrious scientist' he would correct the description with humility: "I am just a man of science." When scientists were criticised he would retort with confidence that they were the salt of the earth.

## A Lion's Heart

Friends and admirers organised a special function at the Annual Session of the Academy at Ahmedabad to honour him on his eightieth birthday. Many people expressed warm sentiments. Raman never took much interest in birthday celebrations. Still, at the end. He thanked the organisers; and with a twinkle in his eyes, he said, "I wish some one had said that I had a lion's heart!" All who had spoken forgot to make mention of his great asset, namely courage.

## Interest in Music

Raman was a great lover of music. He used to say, "I should live long, because I have not heard all the music I want to hear." He was a frequent visitor to a shop selling musical instruments in Balepet, in Bangalore. He collected a variety of musical instruments like the Mridangam, the Tabla, the Veena, the Violin and the Nagaswaram.

'The Catgut Acoustical Society' of America is devoted exclusively to the study of violins. It elected Raman as its honorary member.

5

# The Great Indian Scientist

Many people know Chandrashekhara Venkata Raman (more popularly known as C. V. Raman) because he was the first Indian Nobel Laureate in science. Till date Raman remains the only Indian to receive a Nobel Prize in science. The other two Indian-born scientists, viz., Har Gobind Khorana and Subramanyan Chandrasekhar (who became US citizens) got Nobel Prizes in science.

Raman was also the first Asian to get Nobel Prize in science. Raman's celebrated discovery, the Raman Effect, experimentally demonstrated that the light-quanta and molecules do exchange energy which manifests itself as a change in the colour of the scattered light.

However, this phenomenon was earlier predicted theoretically by Hendrik Anthony Kramers (1894-1952) and Werner Heisenberg (1901-76). It was the most convincing proof of quantum theory of light. This does not diminishes the importance of Raman's discovery. As Albert Einstein (1879-1955) wrote : "C. V. Raman was the first to recognise and demonstrate that the energy of photon can undergo partial transformation within matter. I still recall vividly the deep impression that this discovery made on all of us...."

Raman's interests in science were wide, from astronomy and meteorology to physiology. 'Raman published 475 research papers and wrote five remarkable monographs on topics so varied that one's mind boggles'.

Raman made many major scientific discoveries in acoustics, ultrasonic, optics, magnetism and crystal physics. Raman's works on the musical drums of India was epoch-making and it revealed the acoustical knowledge of the ancient Hindus. It may be noted here that it was Pythagoras who first formulated what makes a sound musical to the human ear.

On the occasion of awarding the Hughes Medal of the Royal Society of London, Lord Rutherford (1871-1937) commented on Raman's scientific achievements as follows: "Sir Venkata Raman is one of the leading authorities in optics, in particular on the phenomenon of the scattering of light. In this connection, about three years ago, he discovered that the light's colour could be changed by scattering. This had been predicted some time before, but in spite of search the change had not been found. The `Raman effect' must rank among the best three or four discoveries in experimental physics in the last decade; it has proved and will prove (to be) an instrument of great power in the study of the theory of solids. In addition to important contributions in many fields of knowledge, he (Raman) has developed an active school of research in physical sciences in the University of Calcutta".

Raman developed a vibrant and excellent school of physics. He established the Indian Academy of Sciences Bangalore (1934) and the Raman Research Institute (1948).

## A Great Populariser of Science

Raman deserves to be remembered not only for his towering scientific accomplishment but also for his indomitable will. Raman was a staunch patriot and he had great faith in India's potential for progress. He excelled under the most adverse circumstances. Raman was a great populariser of science. "He was perhaps the greatest salesman science has ever had in this country", says S. Ramaseshan, a pioneer of X-ray crystallography in India and a nephew of Raman. During his popular science lectures (or 'performances' as Raman called them) Raman held his audience spellbound. His lectures were always accompanied by lively demonstrations. Raman had a deep sense of humour. According to Ramaseshan, the popular science lectures of Raman were so gripping because, "He talked only of those things about which he felt intensely or those things which he understood well or wanted to understand better. He brought out things in their simplest and their most basic elements. He made his audiences feel that they had seen it all too." Raman was a lecturer par excellence. Even his critics had to agree on this point. Throughout his life Raman lectured. He lectured to diverse audiences. However, he was at his best when he delivered popular science lectures. Raman also gave radio talks. The texts of his nineteen radio talks were brought out in a book form. The book was titled The New Physics: Talks on Aspects of Sciences and it was published by the Philosophical Library of New York. The topics covered by Raman ranged from the microscopic world of atoms to the universe itself. The quality of Raman's lectures can be guessed from what Francis Low, a distinguished theoretical physicist then working at the Institute for Advanced Studies, Princeton, wrote in the introduction to this book: "Physics by its very nature requires extreme specialisation on the part of its students. Its conclusions, which must eventually predict numbers for the results of actual measurements, are best expressed in mathematical formulae. This has the disadvantage of making the subject well-nigh unintelligible to the layman. There are unfortunately few teachers who are able to surmount this handicap. Professor Raman has written a book which avoids this pitfall and thus should give the lay reader an opportunity of penetrating at least part of the way into the mysteries of this interesting and important science".

Raman believed in excellence *per se*. He never compromised on quality and he firmly believed that if India was to make any economic advance it could only be based on such excellence. He had a great fascination for art and music. He was not confined to a particular narrow speciality. He believed that 'real fundamental progress is always due to those who had ignored the boundaries of science and who treated science as a whole.'

Raman was a very simple man. He was also a supreme egotist. But then in private conversation he often showed utmost humility. He was a man of emotion. He never bothered to suppress his feelings. He could get violently angry. He hurt many. He feared no authority. On some occasions he publicly wept like a child. Raman had "all-too-human" drawbacks in abundance. But then he was an excellent physicist and totally devoted to the pursuit of science.

## His Solid Foundation

C. V. Raman was born on 7 November 1888 in his maternal grandfather's house, in a small village of Thiruvanaikaval near Tiruchirapalli, on the bank's of Kaveri in Tamil Nadu. Raman's maternal grandfather Saptarshi Shastri was a great Sanskrit scholar, who in his younger days travelled on foot to distant Bengal (over 2,000 km away) to learn navya nyaya (modern logic).

Raman's parents were R. Chandrashekhara Iyyer and Parvathi Ammal. Raman's father, who initially taught in a local school for many years and later became a lecturer in mathematics and physics in Mrs. A. V. Narasimha Rao College, Vishakapatnam (then Vizagapatnam) in Andhra Pradesh. Raman passed his matriculation examination at the age of 11 and he passed his F.A. examination (equivalent to today's Intermediate) with a scholarship at 13. In 1903 Raman joined the Presidency College in Chennai (then Madras) from where he passed the B.A. (1904) and M.A. (1907) examinations. He stood first both in B.A. and M.A. examinations and won all the prizes available. To get some idea we quote here Raman himself.

Raman wrote:

> "I finished my school and college career and my university examination at the age of eighteen. In this short span of years had been compressed the study of four languages and of a great variety of diverse subjects, in several cases up to the highest university standards. A list of all the volumes I had to study would be terrifying length. Did these books influence

me? Yes, in the narrow sense of making me tolerably familiar with subjects of so diverse as Ancient Greek and Roman History, Modern Indian and European History, Formal Logic, Economics, Monetary Theory and Public Finance, the late Sanskrit writers and minor English authors, to say nothing of physiography, chemistry and dozen branches of Pure and Applied Mathematics, and of Experimental and Theoretical Physics. But out of this welter of subjects and books, can I pick out anything really to mould my mental and spiritual outlook and determine my chosen path in life? Yes I can and I shall mention three books.

A purposeful life needs an axis or hinge to which it is firmly fixed and yet around which it can freely revolve. As I see it, this axis or hinge has been, in my own case, strongly enough, not the love of science, not even the love of Nature but a certain abstract idealism or belief in the value of the human spirit and the virtue of human endeavour and achievement. The nearest point to which I can trace this source of idealism in my recollection of reading Edwin Arnold's great book, The Light of Asia. I remember being powerfully moved by the story of Siddharta's great renunciation, of his search for truth and of his final enlightenment.

The next set of books that I have to mention is one of the most remarkable works of all time, namely, The Elements of Euclid. Familiarity with some parts of Euclid and a certain dislike of its formalism have dethroned this great work from the apparently unassailable position which it occupied in the esteem of the learned world for an almost incredibly long period of time. Indeed, my own early reactions to the compulsory study of Euclid were anything but favourable... Not until many years later however, did I fully appreciate the central position of Geometry in relation to all natural knowledge. I can illustrate this relationship by a thousand examples but will content myself with remarking that every mineral found in Nature, every crystal made by man, every leaf, flower or fruit that we see growing, every living thing from the smallest to the largest that walks on earth, flies in the air or swims in the water or lives deep down on the ocean floor, speaks aloud of the fundamental role of geometry in Nature.

The pages of Euclid are like the opening bars of the music of the Grand Opera of Nature's great drama. So to say, they lift the veil and show to our vision a glimpse of a vast world of natural knowledge awaiting study.

Of all the great names in the world of learning that have come down to us from the remote past, that of Archimedes, by common consent, occupies the foremost place. Speaking of the modern world, the supremost figure in my judgement is that of Hermann von Helmholtz. In the range and depth of his knowledge, in the clearness and profundity of his scientific vision, he easily transcended all other names I could mention, even including Isaac Newton. Rightly he has been described as the intellectual colossus of the nineteenth century. It was my great good fortune, while I was still a student at College, to have possessed a copy of an English translation of his great work The Sensations of Tone. As is well-known, this was one of Helmholtz's masterpieces. It treats the subjects of music and musical instruments not only with profound knowledge and insight, but also with extreme clarity of language and expression."

While Raman was a student, he independently undertook original investigations in acoustics and optics. Raman was the first student of the Madras Presidency College to get a research paper published, that too in a prestigious international journal. His first paper on 'unsymmetrical diffraction bands due to a rectangular aperture' was published in the Philosophical Magazine (London) in November 1906. This was the result of Raman's measuring the angles of a prism using an ordinary spectrometer in his college. This was followed by a note in the same journal on a new experimental method of measuring surface tension. Lord Rayleigh (1842-1919) took note of the papers published by Raman as a student. Rayleigh was an outstanding mathematical physicist and a good experimenter, who was awarded the Nobel Prize for the discovery of argon. Raman and Rayleigh exchanged some correspondence. It is interesting to note that Lord Rayleigh addressed Raman as Professor.

## Into the Pursuits of Science

Though Raman proved his brilliance in scientific investigations but as were the norms of those days he was not encouraged to take up science as a career. At the instance of his father Raman took the Financial Civil Service (FCS) examination. He stood first in the examination and in the middle of 1907 Raman proceeded to Kolkata (then Calcutta) to join the Indian Finance Department as Assistant Accountant General. He was then 18½ years old. His starting salary was Rs. 400 per month, a fabulous sum in those days. At that point of time perhaps nobody would have even dreamt that Raman would again venture into the pursuits of science. Raman's prospects in the Government service were too lucrative. And during those days opportunities for doing research were rare. But then one day while going to office Raman saw a signboard with the words "Indian Association for the Cultivation of Science" written on it. The address was 210, Bowbazar Street. On his way back he came to the Association where he first met an individual named Ashutosh Dey (Ashu Babu) who was to be Raman's assistant for 25 years. Ashu Babu took Raman to the Honorary Secretary of the Association, Amrit Lal Sircar, who was overjoyed when he came to know about Raman's intention — to do research at the Association's laboratory. Amrit Lal had reason to be overjoyed because it was his father Mahendra Lal Sircar (1833-1904), a man of vision, who established the Association in 1876. This Association happened to be the first institute to be established in India solely for carrying out scientific investigations.

## In Contact with Mahendra Lal Sircar

Mahendra Lal Sircar, who took the MD degree in 1863, was appointed a Fellow of the Calcutta University in 1870 and Sheriff of Calcutta in 1887. He was also a member of the Bengal Legislative Council from 1887 to 1893 and was associated with many learned societies of Kolkata. Mahendra Lal was a staunch patriot and his interest ranged beyond medicine. Being a visionary he had visualised that many problems faced by the country could only be solved by the application of modern science. Mahendra Lal had shown a great foresight by realising that 'science would never strike a deep root in this country through the process of its introduction in the educational curriculum alone.' To realise his dreams Mahendra Lal founded the Association. Mahendra Lal stated the objective of the Association as follows: "The object of the Association is to enable the Natives of India to Cultivate Science in all its departments with a view to its advancement by original research and (as it will necessarily follow) with a view to its varied applications to arts and comforts of life." At the beginning the major activity of the Association was to organise popular science lectures by well-known scholars and scientists. The Association had built a Laboratory in 1891 with the generous donation by the Maharaja of Vizianagram. However, during Mahendra Lal's lifetime nobody came forward to do research under the aegis of the Association. Mahendra Lal was dismayed by the apathy of Indians towards the cultivation of science. A few weeks before his death Mahendra Lal had stated his wish in the following words: "Younger men must come and step into my place and make this into a great institution." So when Amrit Lal Sircar saw Raman, perhaps he felt that he (Raman) would realise his father's dream. And as we know today Raman indeed realised Mahendra Lal Sircar's dream.

It was not an easy task. Till 1917 Raman continued his research at the Association in his spare time. Doing research in his spare time and that too with very limited facilities Raman could publish his research findings in leading international journals like Nature, The Philosophical Magazine and Physics Review. During this period he published 30 original research papers. His research carried during this period mainly centred on areas of vibrations and acoustics. He studied a number of musical instruments, viz., ectara, violin, tambura, veena, mridangam, tabla, etc. He published a monograph on his extensive studies on the violin. The monograph was titled 'On the Mechanical Theory of Vibrations of Musical

Instruments of the Violin Family with Experimental Verifications of the Results Part- I'. During this period Ashu Babu, who never entered the portals of a university, was his only collaborator. This did not prevent Ashu Babu from becoming a joint author in many papers that Raman published. Even Ashu Babu was the sole author of a paper published in the Proceedings of the Royal Society of London. It was in 1919 Raman took research students for the first time.

There was an interruption to Raman's work at the Association. He was transferred to Rangoon (1909) and Nagpur (1910). However, Raman's research work was not completely stopped. At both places he converted his home into a laboratory and continued his work. He came back to Calcutta in 1911.

## Rigorous Involvement in Science Work

In 1917, Raman was invited by Ashutosh Mukherjee (1864-1924), to be a professor in the newly established Science College. Mukherjee, who was a judge of the Calcutta High Court for twenty years, was a great educationist and jurist of his time. On being appointed as the Vice-Chancellor of the Calcutta University he not only started a post-graduate department for various disciplines of science but he also persuaded people to create endowment Professorships. Raman was offered the Palit Professorship in Physics. The salary for the professorship was about half the amount that Raman was getting in the Finance Department. Moreover, Raman was successful as a Finance Officer. In fact the Finance Department was reluctant to let him go. Thus the Member (Finance) of the Viceroy's Council wrote: "We find Vankataraman is most useful in the Finance Department being, in fact, one of our best men". However, Raman happily accepted the offer. He joined the Calcutta University as Palit Professor in July 1917. That Ashutosh Mukherjee was touched by Raman's total devotion to science is obvious from his following remarks: "For the Chair of Physics created by Sir Taraknath Palit, we have been fortunate enough to secure the services of Mr. Chandrashekhara Venkata Raman, who has greatly distinguished himself and acquired a European fame by his brilliant research in the domain of Physical Science, assiduously carried on under the most adverse circumstances amidst the distraction of pressing official duties. I rejoice to think that many of these valuable researches have been carried on in the laboratory of the Indian Association for the Cultivation of Science, founded by our late illustrious colleague, Dr. Mahaṇdra Lal Sircar, who devoted a lifetime to the foundation of an institution for the cultivation and advancement of science in this country. I should fail in my duty if I were to restrain myself in my expression of genuine admiration I feel for the courage and spirit of self-sacrifice with which Mr. Raman had decided to exchange a lucrative official appointment with attractive prospects, for a University Professorship, which, I regret to say, does not carry even liberal emoluments. This one instance encourages me to entertain the hope that there will be no lack of seeker after truth in the Temple of Knowledge which it is our ambition to erect."

Ashutosh Mukherjee had to change the provision of the endowment before appointing Raman. Because one of the requirements, for appointment to the Palit Chair was to have been trained abroad. But Raman refused to go abroad to be 'trained'. The terms of Raman's appointment as the Palit Professor did not entail any teaching responsibilities. His duties were :

- to devote himself to original research in his subject to extend the bounds of knowledge;
- to stimulate and guide research by students; and
- to supervise the laboratory in the College of Science.

Though he was free from teaching responsibility but Raman, being a born-teacher, could not be away from the class room. He took a prominent part in M.Sc. teaching. Here we quote L. A. Ramdas, one of his students : "Prof. Raman took 'Electricity and Magnetism' in the year 1920-21 and 'Physical optics' in 1921-22. Both sets of M.Sc. students felt that they were indeed listening to a type of inspired teaching to which was brought all the original flavours and excitement of the past.... We shared with him much of excitement and superb thrill that Banjamin Franklin, Oersted, Arago, Gauss, Faraday, Maxwell, Hertz, Lord Kelvin and many others must have felt while they were making their actual discoveries... Often he used to take the entire forenoon, for 2 and sometimes even 3 hours — such was his tremendous love of teaching....And after each lecture we used spontaneously to look up original papers and treatises like Maxwell's Electricity and Magnetism, J. J. Thomson's Conduction of Electricity, Faraday's Experimental Researches, Lord Raylegh's and Kelvin's Collected Papers, and so farther".

## In Indian Institute of Science

Even after joining the Calcutta University Raman was allowed to continue his work at the Association's Laboratories. In fact the Association became the research arm of the University. Following the death of Amrit Lal Sircar in 1919 Raman was elected as Honorary Secretary of the Association, the post he held till 1933, when he left Kolkata. It was not that Raman was very willing to leave Kolkata. His exit was the result of the clash between him and Meghnad Saha, another great personality of Indian Science. Raman was voted out of the Honorary Secretaryship of the Association. It was certainly a moment of bitter humiliation for Raman and it was more so because he had Himalayan ego. And so he decided to take up the pending invitation from the Indian Institute of Science (IISc), Bangalore, to become its Director. He was the first Indian to become its Director. Raman succeeded Sir Martin Forster, FRS. He served IISc both as its Director (1933-37) and head of the Physics Department (1933-48).

When Raman joined IISc its academic accomplishments were not very high. Its funding position was much better than Calcutta University where Raman was working. Raman brought out the following changes:

- A new physics department came into existence.
- Some of the existing departments were reorganised.
- Steps were initiated to establish a central workshop for fabricating precision instruments.
- The surroundings were improved by planting beautiful flowering gardens.

For achieving academic excellence he himself gathered a team of talented students and started doing high quality research in many fields of physics. Raman also wanted to initiate basic research in fields like quantum mechanics, crystal chemistry and vitamins and enzyme chemistry by recruiting outstanding faculty. At that point of time many reputed scientists were forced to leave Germany because of Hitler's racist policy. Raman wanted to bring some of these scientists to IISc. Raman had many names on his list, both foreign and Indian'. However, he was only successful in bringing Max Born, that too for a short time.

Some of the Raman's moves were opposed by the existing staff. In fact Raman's moves to reorganise some of the existing departments and the Institute's workshops led to the resignation of two professors — the Professor of Chemistry (Prof. Watson) and the Professor of Electrical Engineering (Prof. Modawalla). Raman's act of reapportioning the Institute's budget to aid the newly established physics department invited charges of embezzlement. He was accused of patronising the physics department at the cost of other departments. His attempt to keep Max Born in the institute was also not liked by many. As time passed Raman found himself increasingly in isolation. Seeing the growing turmoil in the campus, the Council, the body charged with overseeing the management of the Institute, recommended to the Visitor (then Viceroy of British India) in July 1935 to appoint a Review Committee to review the Institute's affairs. The Committee, the appointment of which was formarlly announced on January 19, 1936, consisted of Sir James Irvin, Principal and Vice-Chancellor of St. Endrews University, Dr. A. H. Mackenzie, Pro Vice-Chancellor, Osmania University and Dr. S. S. Bhatnagar, then Professor of Chemistry at the Punjab University at Lahore. Irvin was to head the Committee. The Committee in its Report to the Viceroy submitted in May 1936 more or less reaffirmed the accusations made against Raman. The Report stated : "Making full allowance for possible exaggeration, we greatly fear that there is much truth in these allegations. The resignations of Professor Watson and Professor Modawalla can now be readily understood". According to the Irvin Committee Report, Raman was guilty not only of administrative irregularities, but of financial lapses as well. The Committee branded Raman inimical to applied science. Besides castigating Raman, the Committee also proposed measures to curtail the powers of the Director. For example the Committee suggested that the budget be processed "through no fewer than four bodies in succession before it is finally sanctioned." Raman's warning that "it would place insuperable obstacles in the path of progressive administration such as is essential for success of a scientific institution" went unheeded. The Council endorsed the Report of Irvin Committee and the friction between the management of the Institute and Raman continued to grow. Finally the situation became such that there was no alternative for Raman other than to resign the Directorship of the Institute. In fact he was asked to resign or face action. However, he remained in IISc as Professor of Physics. Raman retired as Professor from the Institute in 1948.

After retirement from the Institute he concentrated his attention in building an institute of his own — the Raman Research Institute (RRI). Even before his retirement Raman had started to build an institute where he could retire and enjoy science. To quote Raman: "You know, I was to retire at 60. So two years before my retirement I started building this institute so that on the day I retired I took my bag and walked right into this institute. I can not remain idle for a single day". Raman had to gather money for building the Institute. Raman had lost most of his life's savings including his Nobel Prize money in an investment. The Institute was built on a ten acre plot of land gifted by the Maharajah of Mysore way back in 1934 the land of given to the Indian Academy of Sciences, and for its related activities. Raman travelled extensively for raising donation for constructing the building for housing the institute. When Raman moved to the institute the facilities were far from complete. Raman was opposed to the idea of taking grants from the government for running the institute. To earn money for the institute he started a few chemical industries (in association with one of his former students). The dividends from these industries were sufficient to support the institute to start with. He gifted away most of his personal properties to the Academy for the benefit of the institute, as also the Lenin Peace Prize money. A museum was built to house Raman's collection of crystals, gems, minerals, rock specimens, shells, stuffed birds, butterflies and so on. Raman had fascination for colours and so he collected everything that had colours.

## The Foundation of Indian Academy of Sciences

The Indian Academy of Sciences Bangalore, which now publishes some of the best science journals in the country, was established by Raman. The Academy was formed on April 27, 1934. It was registered in Bangalore under the Societies Registration Act. Besides Raman, there were 160 Foundation Fellows. The inaugural meeting of the Academy was held in the campus of Indian Institute of Science in August 1934. The best scientists from all over India were elected to the Raman's Academy. Commenting on the composition of the Academy Raman, in his address at the first annual meeting, observed: "Our list of Fellows is also representative of all parts of India. Bombay heads the list with 38 Fellows closely followed by Madras Presidency with 35, and Mysore State with 33. Other provinces are also well represented. We have 21 Fellows in the United Provinces, 13 from Punjab, 11 from Bengal, 8 from Central Provinces; Bihar, Orissa, Hyderabad, Travancore and Burma are also represented in our list."

The objectives of the Academy were:

- to hold meetings for discussing the results of research;
- to hold symposia on special subjects; and
- to publish the proceedings.

Unlike in other countries India has three Science Academies. Raman formed the Academy on his own. The need for an Academy was first highlighted by Raman in his editorial in Current Science published in May 1933. Raman wrote: "The conviction that research is civilization and determines the economic, social and political development of a nation has not yet been unreservedly accepted as part of the administrative policy of India, and we are disposed to ascribe the tardy and perhaps unwilling recognition of this fundamental fact to the absence of an all-India scientific organisation whose function would be to concentrate enlightened public opinion on the doctrine that science is material and spiritual wealth..... It seems to us that early establishment of a National Academy of Science would secure closer and better organised cooperation of activities among all research institutes in India and exercise through its official journal a wider influence for the consolidation and promotion of the best interests of science." Raman further wrote: "While the foundation of the scientific reputation of a country is established by the quality of work produced in its institutions the superstructure is reared by the national journals which proclaim their best achievements to the rest of the world". After writing the editorial Raman circulated a questionnaire among the Indian scientists to ascertain their views. The idea of an Academy proposed by Raman was discussed in the 1934 Session of Indian Science Congress presided over by M. N. Saha, who supported the idea and proposed Royal Society of London as a model. After discussing the matter in a General Committee, it was referred to an Academic Committee consisting of 25 members including Raman. However, when the Academic Committee could not take a quick decision Raman resigned from the Committee and formed an Academy on his own.

The National Institute of Sciences came into existence on January 3, 1935. Its inaugural meeting was held in Calcutta on January 7, 1935. It functioned in Calcutta till 1946 when it moved to New Delhi. Its name was changed to Indian National Science Academy in 1970. The idea behind establishing the National Institute of Sciences was not just to form just another Academy but to form a co-coordinating body. Thus in its inaugural meeting, Lewis L. Fermor, the first President of the National Institute of Sciences said:

> "During the past year the word Academy has been much before us... It seems desirable, therefore, that we should first enquire what the word Academy means. It will surprise most of you to learn that the first Academy was a pleasure garden in Athens which is supposed to have belonged to an ancient Attic hero named Academus ....In this garden the Greek philosopher Plato taught for nearly 50 years; and the Academy thus started lasted from the days of Plato to those of Cicero, that is, for over 300 years.... While Academies, if we go to the original meaning, must, therefore, function locally or regionally in the most important portion of their activities, they can also

> legitimately make a wider appeal... When in 1933 the proposal was mooted to found an Indian Academy of Sciences, some of us overlooked the fact that there were already two such academies in existence — one called the Asiatic Society of Bengal and the other of the United Provinces Academy of Sciences. The proposal, therefore, to found a third Indian Academy...logically meant either the creation of a fresh garden in another part of India, or of a body to coordinate the already existing gardens. Our friends in Bangalore knew all the time that they needed a Society of Academy status with its headquarters in Bangalore. Had they boldly said so at the beginning, the confusion that has arisen in scientific circles during the past year would have been avoided, because it is obviously correct that southern India should have its own philosopher's garden. However, Bangalore did not do this ...Object as we may to the manner in which our Bangalore friends cut adrift...we... welcome the Indian Academy of Sciences found at Bangalore....But we still need a coordination body and that is why it is necessary to found the National Institute".

The National Institute of Sciences had 125 Foundation Fellows including Raman.

The United Provinces Academy of Sciences was founded at Allahabad in 1930. It has now been renamed National Academy of Sciences Allahabad.

The journal Current Science, the most visible journal of the Indian Academy of Science Banglore was launched even before the formation of the Academy. It was founded as a result of resolution passed at a special meeting held during the Session of the Indian Science Congress in Bangalore in 1931. The Proceedings of the Indian Academy of Sciences also started in 1934. Its objective was to provide all scientific men with an opportunity of obtaining at least a general idea of what is being done in India in fields of knowledge other than their own speciality. However, as the amount of published matter grew rapidly the Proceedings was separated into a number of theme journals —, viz. Proceedings — Chemical Sciences, Earth and Planetary Sciences, Mathematical Sciences, Animal Sciences, Plant Sciences and Engineering Sciences (later renamed as Sadhana). The other journals published by the Academy are : Pramanan-Journal of Physics, Bulletin of Materials Science, Journal of Biosciences, Journal of Astronomy and Astrophysics, Journal of Genetics and Resonance: Journal of Science Education. It may be noted here that the Journal of Genetics was founded by William Bateson in 1910 in England. Subsequently the journal was brought to India by J. B. S. Haldane. However, the journal ceased its publication in 1977. Later it was revived by the Academy.

The Academy has instituted a prestigious Raman Professorship. It has started a scheme of Young Associateship to provide opportunity for outstanding young scientists to be associated with the Fellows of the Academy. Since the days of Raman, the Academy continues to sponsor symposia and discussions. Raman was of the view that science alone could solve India's problems. He said: "There is only one solution for India's economic problems and that is science and more science." But then Raman insisted that India should not be dependent on others for ideas. India is capable of tackling her own problems. He said: "In the past, India had shown her greatness in the fields of scholarship, philosophy and science but today, we are helplessly dependent on Western countries for knowledge of science. India should not be a camp-follower but a leader in science. It is no use getting our ideas from the west. We have to think out our problems and find the solutions to them."

## The Future of Indian Science

However, Indians need to be convinced of their strength. While once addressing young people Raman said: "I would like to tell the young men and women before me not to lose hope and courage. Success can only come to you by courageous devotion to the task lying in front of you and there is nothing worth in this world that can come without the sweat of our brow. I can assert without fear of contradiction that the quality of the Indian mind is equal to the quality of any Teutonic, Nordic or Anglo-Saxon mind. What we lack is perhaps courage, what we lack is perhaps driving force which takes one anywhere. We have, I think, developed an inferiority complex. I think what is needed in India today is the destruction of that defeatist spirit. We need a spirit of victory, a spirit that would carry us to our rightful place under the sun, a spirit which will recognise that we, as inheritors of a proud civilization, are entitled to a rightful place on this planet. If that indomitable spirit were to arise, nothing can hold us from achieving our rightful destiny."

He believed that the future of any country rests with its accumulated knowledge and younger generation. He observed: "If you ask me what is the greatest industry of a Nation — the key industry — I have no hesitation in saying that it is the production and diffusion of knowledge...There is no nobler work for a man or an institution than to bring up a young generation in health and strength and in the vigour of intellectual and physical activity."

Raman had a holistic view of science. He thought nature is the best teacher. He said: "What is science in the last analysis but the study and the love of nature, displayed not in the form of abstract worship but in the practical form of seeking to understand nature?" Further he said: "One aspect of Indian culture was its profound understanding of Nature. Much of India's philosophy related itself to the understanding of the rationale and the meaning of the phenomena of Nature." Raman had displayed great faith in Mahatma Gandhi's ideas. He remarked: "Each textbook must contain as frontispiece a portrait of Gandhiji and there must be lessons containing the sermons of Gandhiji from Sabarmati to Birla House. This would be the best and the most potent way of offering homage to the memory of the world's greatest man and the Father of the Indian Nation, and is better than building memorials and erecting statues." Further he said: "His (Gandhiji's) teachings stressed the supreme virtue of the human spirit, utterly indestructible and unconquerable. India can never hope to find a place in the sun, unless it upholds the value of the human spirit." In the honour of Gandhiji he instituted the Gandhi Memorial

Lecture in the Raman Research Institute. Till his death Raman never failed to deliver this lecture. Raman's wife Lokasundari was well-known to Kasturba Gandhi.

Raman strongly espoused the cause of women. He once said: "I have a feeling that if the women of India take to science and interest themselves in the progress and advance of science as well, they will achieve what even men have failed to do. Women have one quality — the quality of devotion. It is one of the most important passports to success in science. Let us therefore not imagine that intellect is a sole prerogative of males only in science."

Raman had displayed his great leadership in institution building and training students. Raman made both the Indian Association for the Cultivation of Science and the Physics Department of the Calcutta University vibrant and excellent centres of learning. His reputation attracted students from all corners of the country. Raman was among the founders of the Indian Science Congress, which was established in 1914 and served as its Secretary for several years and also became its President. He established the Indian Journal of Physics. During his stay for over fifteen years in the Indian Institute of Science, Bangalore, he established an excellent school of Physics and trained a band of first-rate physicists. As mentioned earlier in 1934 Raman established the Indian Academy of Science. Raman was elected Founder President of the Academy and remained so till his death.

He wanted that the scientists should not be concerned with their own research alone, they should also try to develop the scientific institutions, the edifice on which the superstructure of science can be built. He remarked: "While the foundation of the scientific reputation of a country is established by the quality of work produced in its institutions, the superstructure is reared by the national journals which proclaim their best achievements to the rest of the world. Manifestly the edifice of science in India is incomplete...It is true that the spirit of science and its service are international, but is it not also true that every nation has its own Academies, learned societies, magazines and journals? India will have to organise and develop her national scientific institutions before she can enter into the comity of international scientists."

He emphasised the importance of strengthening our universities. He said: "Let us try to make our universities the best — we should not be satisfied with anything less than the best. What will be the result? Instead of a great many of our young men going out of the country, they will remain here and strive to advance our reputation and that will make us strive for more and more good things."

Raman was elected as a Fellow of the Royal Society of London in 1924 in recognition of his outstanding researches in physical optics, molecular diffraction of light, X-ray scattering by liquids and a molecular anisotropy. It may be noted that Raman had resigned the Fellowship of the Royal Society. He was conferred a Knighthood by the British Government in 1929.

He received the Nobel Prize for Physics in 1930. The Government of India awarded him the title of "Bharat Ratna" in 1954. The erstwhile Soviet Union honoured him with the International Lenin Prize in 1957. Some of the other awards/ honours, received by Raman were: Mattencci Medal of the Societe Italiana della Scienzia of Rome (1928); Hughes Medal of the Royal Society of London (1930) and Franklin Model of the Franklin Institute of Philadelphia (1941).

Raman loved children and he derived immense pleasure in showing them his museum and the laboratories of the Raman Research Institute. He believed that "The true wealth of a Nation consists not in the stored-up gold in its coffers and banks, not in the factories, but in the intellectual and physical strength of its men, women and children."

Towards the end of his life Raman chose to make himself a recluse. He not only built high walls around the Raman Research Institute but also put up a prominent signboard announcing that visitors were not welcome. He was not at all happy the way the Government was trying to build up science and technology in the country. "To Raman, scientific activity was the fulfilment of an inner need. His approach to science was one of passion, curiosity and simplicity. It was an attempt to understand. To him science was based on independent thought. Combined with hard work, science was a personal endeavour, an aesthetic pursuit and above all a joyous experience." Raman believed that science can be promoted only by doing it. He did not see any role for professional organisers of science. "For such people" Raman thought "The So-called organisation of science becomes more important than science itself or its values".

Raman died on November 21, 1970. As per his desire he was cremated in the gardens of his institute.

6

# The Great Physicist

## Passion for Physics

The most obvious characteristic was his great passion for physics coupled with an intense enthusiasm and volcanic energy. Even the most casual observer could not fail to miss the fire in his sparkling eyes which seemed to radiate this energy, and to be animated by the dynamic force of an active brain. He lived for his work as few men do, and by his exceptional tenacity of purpose, and of hard work in the pursuit of research he had set a shining example to others.

He had a deep insight into physical processes, and an intuitive sense of physical reality. He had often shown the ability to illuminate a whole subject with a few crucial ideas. His highest work showed the inevitable simplicity of all great work, and had been achieved by spontaneously taking the significant step at the right moment. He possessed in a remarkable degree the gift of seizing the vital point from apparently trivial observations. This genius for picking out the true significance of what to others was to be an unimportant detail, and transforming it into a clue to the understanding of fundamental problems was brought out strikingly in his work leading to the discovery of the Raman effect itself.

## Born Experimental Physicist

Raman was a born experimental physicist, and had been guided by the conviction that real progress in physics could be achieved by the application of considerations based on experience and reason to experimental observations of properly chosen phenomena. He had advanced directly and successfully along this straight path without often branching into mathematical physics. Yet whenever occasion arose he had shown that he possessed the mathematical equipment essential to the interpretation of his work. He had also recognised and acknowledged the fundamental importance of ideas of a mathematical or deductive nature. Thus, in the realm of his researches in crystal physics, he had realised the importance of group theory, and the theory of group representations, and encouraged investigations based on such theoretical considerations. He had also shown facility in choosing the right type of mathematical technique needed in his work, and an uncanny faculty for seeing clearly through a mass of complicated mathematical calculations. His theory of the diffraction of light by high frequency sound waves was a striking example of this. Like all great physicists, however, he had placed facts first, and hypothesis always second.

Though the work of Raman and his school had lain in apparently diverse fields it was easy to discern a coherence and unity in them. The central and guiding theme of all his physical research had been optics in all its aspects. His special love has been for crystal physics, and in particular, physics of the diamond, in which subject he was a recognised authority. He later struck new paths in crystal physics, and introduced new concepts regarding crystal structure.

## Sturdy Individualism

Another noticeable characteristic of Raman's scientific work was its sturdy individualism which was a consequence of the fact that when he started his career he belonged to no particular school of physics, but had to build one himself. He was thus a true pioneer who had had the vision and courage successfully to explore unknown lands in physics. This circumstance had made him attach great importance to an independent approach to problems, and his valuable example of striking out new and independent paths of research infected other scientific workers in our country, and assured of a bright scientific future indeed. Further, the fact that he had to start work as an independent investigator without the facilities of an already well-equipped laboratory had brought out to the full his skill as an experimenter. Most of his experiments had required neither costly machinery nor any type of special techniques, but had been so simply devised as to be easily understood even by a layman. In fact, the apparatus with which he demonstrated the Raman effect was a model of simplicity and by no means a costly one, but nevertheless that simple experiment was one of the important milestones in the world's knowledge of nature.

It is perhaps not very well known that Raman had shown a fine aesthetic outlook in his research work. His choice of topics for investigation, and his way of handling them brought out clearly his innate artistic nature. His love of music, colour, light, vibration, symmetry, harmony, pattern, structure, and architecture was but the result of a deep appreciation of the beautiful in nature. His researches on musical instruments, numerous beautiful phenomena of wave optics, the colour of the sea, colour in the plumage of birds, iridiscent shells and mother-of-pearl, vibration in crystals, and above all his studies on the form, symmetry and structure of diamond based on fluorescence, phosphorescence and birefringence patterns were a few examples of his aesthetic tastes in research. He had one of the finest private scientific collections of diamonds and other beautiful crystals, and loved them as only a true artist could.

## Interest in other Branches of Science

None who had come in contact with Raman could have failed to notice his very wide and catholic interest in many branches of science besides physics. He did perhaps as much for chemistry as for physics. His interest in geology based on deep knowledge, specially in the fields of mineralogy and crystallography, had been a stimulant for the geological research of many workers in India. Some aspects of plant life, and animal life, specially birds, had always had a deep fascination for him. He had shown keen interest in and appreciation of astronomical and astrophysical research, both observational and theoretical. Indicative of his wide interests were his plans to build an astronomical observatory, a biological research unit, and a mineralogical laboratory in the new Raman Research Institute. In spite of criticism from some quarters, it can be confidently said that by his collaboration and encouragement he had given the necessary incentive to studies in mathematics even of the purest type. It is safe to say that there is no branch of science in which he had not encouraged creative and original work, and this augurs well for the development of fundamental research in the country in its new set-up.

## Popular among Students

Raman was not only a great investigator but also a great teacher in the true sense of the word. His ideas and personality had attracted many young research students, and he had held their loyalty and affection by extending a never-failing friendship to them. He had not only taught methods of physical research to his students, but by his own shining example made them realise the necessity of endurance, steadiness and hard work in the pursuit of knowledge. While giving help and encouragement in plenty, he always expected and sometimes demanded from his students the best that they could give.

The feelings of respect and admiration which his students had towards him could be ascribed to his fairness and even generosity in acknowledging a pupil's ideas or originality. He was very liberal minded and gave away whole lines of research which lesser men would be tempted to keep for themselves. Whenever he discovered any originality in a pupil he would do all he can to develop it. His simplicity and informality are best seen in his discussions with students. Some penetrating remark made by him at such discussions were the starting point, as some of his pupils had confessed, of a complete line of investigation undertaken by them later. This has been true not merely in his own special field of research, but in other subjects as well.

Raman rendered signal service to scientific advance in India as much by his contributions to knowledge as by his training of students in methods of research. He had exerted a profound influence on the work and outlook of not only his students but most of his contemporaries.

Unlike many scientific investigators who are giants in their own laboratories but dwarfs outside unable to take a due share in the national life of their country, Raman fully participated in several walks of national activity, and was eager to serve the cause of scientific and technological advance in India. Possessing in a rare measure the extraordinary gift of making the most difficult problems in physics appeared simple, and with a keen and irresistible sense of humour, he admirably filled the role of an eminent popular lecturer on scientific subjects. Popularisation of science in the country owes not a little to his gifts of eloquence and exposition.

7

# Nobel Laureate Raman

In 1930, C. V. Raman was the first 'non-white', Asian and Indian to receive the Nobel Prize in physics for his work on scattering of light and discovery of the Raman effect. The documents were obtained from the Nobel Committee connected with the proposal and selection of C. V. Raman for the Nobel Prize and the results of the studies are reported in this text.

The Nobel Prize is one of the prizes known to a great part of the non-scientific public and is considered as the highest honour to be awarded to scientists. A short life sketch of the founder and the foundation of the Nobel Prize is included in this text. The Statutes of the Nobel Foundation (SNF) which were approved by the Crown on 29 June 1900 had been decreed by the Swedish Government on 27 April 1995. The rules and regulations quoted here are taken from these statutes.

Raman received the Nobel Prize in a record time of two years after his prize-winning discovery. Several questions have been raised about not sharing of the prize by Raman either with his colleagues or the Russian scientists. It will be shown here that it was not in Raman's hand to take this decision. The reasons for these are elaborated in this text.

India's only Nobel Laureate and the first Asian to be awarded the Nobel Prize for physics, C. V. Raman was born on 8 November

1888 in Madras. Later, the family moved to Visakhapatnam, where his father was appointed a lecturer. Raman was a brilliant student. In 1907, he joined the Financial Civil Services, as an Assistant Accountant-General in Calcutta.

In his spare time, Raman started working on some problems in the field of acoustics at the Indian Association for the Cultivation of Science, founded by Maherdra Lal Sarcar (1833-1904) based on the model of the Royal Institution in London. For nearly ten years, he worked independently and established his reputation as a scientist in India as well as in Europe. In 1917, he was appointed professor at the University of Calcutta. His first trip outside India was to Oxford in 1921 to represent the University of Calcutta.

During his voyage, he conducted some experiments and published a note in Nature entitled 'The Colour of the Sea'. It was a generally held belief that the blue colour of the sea is due to the reflected sky-light as well as due to absorption of the light by the suspended matter in the water. Raman showed that the blue colour of sea is independent of sky reflection as well as absorption, but rathter it is due to the molecular diffraction. These initial experiments opened up a new field of research in Calcutta. Further work on the scattering of light led to the discovery of the Raman effect in 1928. The effect deals with the change in the frequency of the monochromatic light after scattering. The spectrum of the scattered light gives clues about the molecular structure of the material under study, thereby helping to understand its properties.

The list of honours bestowed on Raman for his scientific findings is long. However, in this text we have restricted ourselves to a discussion of the reasons for his being awarded the Nobel Prize, as well as some of the questions that have been raised on his receiving of this award. A short biography of the founder of the Nobel Prize has also been included.

Alfred Nobel was born on 21 October 1833 in Stockholm, Sweden. His father Emmanuel Nobel was an engineer who built bridges and buildings. In connection with this, he experimented with different techniques for blasting rocks. In 1837, he had to declare himself bankrupt. He left Stockholm and moved to Russia. In 1842, the rest of family joined him in St. Petersburg, where Alfred and his brothers were tutored privately till 1850. After the

Crimean War (1853-1856), once again, Emmanuel Nobel had to declare himself bankrupt and he returned to Sweden in 1859.

In Paris, Alfred Nobel worked in the private laboratory of a famous chemist T. J. Pelouze, and came in contact with an Italian scientist, A. Sobrero, an inventor of highly explosive nitroglycerine. This idea was extended further by Alfred Nobel to conduct explosions under controlled conditions. After a long period of experimentation he was able to turn liquid nitro-glycerine into a ductile explosive and patented this material as dynamite in the year 1867. He also invented a detonator which could be ignited with a fuse. These inventions helped to reduce the costs for drilling tunnels, building canals and other construction works.

At the end of his life, he had as many as 355 patents. Some of his industrial enterprises still exist, e.g. Imperial Chemical Industries, UK; Dyno Industries, Norway; and AB Bofors, Sweden.

Through his skill as industrialist, and his number of patents he became one of the wealthiest men in the world. Alfred Bernhard Nobel died in Italy on 10 December 1896. This day is taken as the Nobel Prize ceremony day to honour the testator.

The Nobel Foundation is established under the terms of the Will of Alfred Bernhard Nobel, drawn up on the 27 November 1895, which in its relevant parts runs as follows: 'the whole of my remaining realisable estate shall be dealt with in the following way: the capital, invested in safe securities by my executors, shall constitute a fund, the interest on which shall be annually distributed in the form of prizes to those who, during the preceding year, shall have conferred the greatest benefit to mankind. The said interest shall be divided into five equal parts, which shall be apportioned as follows: one part to the person who shall have made the most important discovery or invention within the field of physics; one part to the person who shall have made the most important chemical discovery or improvement; one part to the person who shall have made the most important discovery within the domain of physiology or medicine; one part to the person who shall have produced in the field of literature the most outstanding work of an idealistic tendency; and one part to the person who shall have done the most or the best work for fraternity between nations, for the abolition or reduction of standing armies and for the holding and promotion of peace congresses. The prize for physics and chemistry shall be awarded by the (Royal) Swedish Academy of Sciences; that for physiological or medical works by the Karolinska Institute in Stockholm; that for literature by the (Swedish) Academy in Stockholm; and that for champions of peace by a committee of the persons to be elected by the Norwegian Storting (Parliament). It is my express wish that in awarding the prizes no consideration whatever shall be given to the nationality of the candidates, but that the most worthy shall receive the prize, whether he be a Scandinavian or not'.

Most probably, it was due to the influence of his secretary-cum-house-keeper that the Nobel Prize for peace is one of the five Prizes that have been instituted, whereas the sixth Nobel Prize for economic sciences has been established by the Swedish Riksbank since 1968.

The other version about the Nobel Prize for peace is that 'Evidence suggests that the award for peace may well have been the fruition of the inventor's long standing aversion to violence. Early in 1886, for example, he told a British acquaintance that he had a more and more earnest wish to see a rose red peace sprout in this explosive world'.

As stated above, the Nobel Prize for physics and chemistry is awarded by the Swedish Academy of Sciences. Here, the discussion has been limited to the field of physics only. In general, the Nobel Committee consisting of 3-5 members is elected for a period of three years for each Swedish Prize section by the Academy. (In later years, the number of members for the physics and chemistry groups has been fixed to 5 for each group). The Nobel Committee sends out invitations during September to the competent persons to put forward proposals together with evidences. The persons who are eligible to submit proposals are:

- Swedish and foreign members of the Academy of Sciences.
- Members of the Nobel Committees for physics and chemistry.
- Scientists who have been awarded the Prize by the Academy of Sciences.

- Permanent and assistant professors in the sciences of physics and chemistry at the universities and institutes of technology of Sweden, Denmark, Finland, Iceland and Norway, and the Karolinska Institute.
- Holders of corresponding chairs in at least six universities or university colleges selected by the Academy of Sciences with a view to ensuring the appropriate distribution of the commission over the different countries and their seats of learning.
- Other scientists from whom the Academy may see fit to invite proposals. Decisions as to the selection of the teachers and scientists referred to in paragraphs 5 (Expert's scrutiny) and 6 (Opinion of 3-5 members of the Nobel Committee) above shall be taken each year before the end of the month September.

According to Nobel's will, the prize should have international character. Between the years 1901 and 1929; 28.6%, 20%, 20%, 8.6% and 8.6% Nobel Laureates belonged to Germany, France, England, USA and Scandinavian countries respectively; whereas the nominators who made proposals from the above countries were 25.9%, 13.9%, 7.6%, 11.0% and 13.4%, respectively. As most of the nominators and proposed candidates belonged to these countries, the chances for others such as Russians were limited. On the other hand, these circumstances make the case study of Raman more interesting. It is in itself a proof of his pioneer work and his reputation among the scientists of these countries.

## Nobel Prize Proposals

In 1929, C. Fabry from Paris recommended J. Cabannes (Montpellier) and C. V. Raman (Calcutta), whereas N. Bohr proposed that either R. W. Wood or R. W. Wood and Raman should be considered for receiving the Nobel Prize for physics. In that year 48 nominators sent 97 proposals and proposed in all 29 persons. Out of these 29 persons, L. de Broglie, Cabannes, Raman and Wood were declared by the Committee as the persons who fundamentally deserved the prize; but it was L. de Broglie who finally received the Prize for that year.

For the year 1930, 39 competent persons were asked to submit proposals. Out of them, 37 persons sent proposals. There were 21 valid recommendations for a full or shared Prize. Most of the recommendations were concerned with atomic theory and atomic physics. The atomic theory proposals had been worked out by Oseen.

Out of the 21 nominations, Raman was the most suitable person; he was proposed 10 times, either as a single candidate for the Prize, or to share it with other physicists (Table 1).

In that year some of the other scientists proposed included, M. Born, A. Sommerfeld, E. Schrdinger, W. Heisenberg, H. F. Osborn, and M. N. Saha (an Indian astrophysicist).

## Nobel Prize in Record Time

According to the Will of Nobel: '. . . the annual award of prizes shall be intended for works "during the preceding year" shall be understood in the sense that awards shall be made for the most recent achievements in the fields of culture referred to in the Will and for older works only if their significance has not become apparent until recently'.

The application and significance of the Raman effect becomes clear from the number of papers published within a period of one-and-half years after its discovery. 'By August 1929, Ganesan was able to compile a bibliography of 150 papers!'.

The last date of sending the proposal was the first of February (in our case February 1930); and the list of original literature on the Raman effect, compiled by Kohlrausch13, contained 225 entries till 31 January 1930, starting from the first publication of Raman and Krishnan in Nature on the discovery.

The relevance of this discovery in the area of quantum mechanics can be judged from the statement of R. W. Wood, 'It appears to me that this very beautiful discovery which resulted from Raman's long and patient study of the phenomenon of light scattering is one of the best convincing proofs of the quantum theory' (emphasis added).

***Table: Names of the persons who recommended Raman alone or Raman with others for the Nobel Prize for the year 1930 (ref. 10)***

| *Nominator* | *Candidadels* |
|---|---|
| E. Bloch (Paris) | W. R. Wood* and C. V. Raman |
| N. Bohr (Copenhagen) | Wood or Wood and Raman |
| O. Chwolson (Leningrad) | Half for Raman and the rest for Lansberg and Mandelstam |
| J. Perrin (Paris) | Raman or Raman and Heisezerg |
| F. I., de Broglie (Paris) | Raman |
| H. M. de Breglie (Paris) | Raman |
| R. Pfeiffer (Breslau) | Raman |
| J. Stark (Grosshessclohe) | Raman |
| E. Rutherford (Cambridge) | Raman |
| C. T. R. Wilson (Cambridge) | Raman |

*W. R. Wood (1868-1955) was famous for his work on fluorescence and resonance radiation.

As shown above, because his discovery found immediate applications in the field of experimental and theoretical physics; Raman was found to qualify for receivihg the Prize in such a short period of time. The opinion of experts in the scientific community about Raman's scientific work, further substantiates his candidature for the prize.

## Western Connections

Raman's work on musical instruments was well known outside India even before he joined the University of Calcutta as a professor. He began his work on light scattering in 1921 and soon established his reputation in this field. In 1924 he was invited by the British Association for the Advancement of Science in Toronto to open a discussion meeting on the scattering of light. As a scientist, he established several contacts with the scientists in the West.

The report prepared by the Nobel Committee was signed by H. Pleijel, Manne Siegbahn, V. Carlheim-Gyllenskld, Erik Hulthen and C. W. Oseen. Some amongst these were known personally to Raman. For example, M. Siegbahn (1886-1978), who received the Nobel Prize in 1924 for his discovery and researches in the area of X-rays, had contacts with Raman. C. W. Oseen (1879-1944) who held the chair of theoretical physics at the University of Uppsala and later was appointed the director of the Nobel Institute for Theoretical Physics, was also known to Raman. In one of his letters to Raman, he wrote: '. . . Several months ago, you had the great kindness to send me a copy of your German pamphlet Forschritte der Chemie, etc. on anisotropic fluids.

***Table: Nobel laureates from German-speaking area who received the Nobel prize before C. V. Raman***

| *Scientist/s* | *Achievements* | *Year of invention* | *Year of Nobel Prize* |
|---|---|---|---|
| W. C. Roentgen | The discovery of the X-rays | 1895 | 1901 |
| P.E.A. von Lenard | For his work on cathode rays | 1893/1902 | 1905 |
| K.F. Braun* | Contribution to the development of wireless telegraphy | 1897 | 1909 |
| W. Wien | The laws governing the radiation of heat | 1893 | 1911 |
| M. von Laue | The discovery of the diffraction of X-rays by crystals | 1912 | 1914 |
| M. Planck | For the services he rendered to the advancement of physics by his discovery of energy quanta | 1900 | 1918 |
| J. Stark | For his discovery of the Doppler effect in canal rays and the splitting of spectral lines in electric fields | 1905/1913 | 1919 |

*Contd...*

| *Scientist/s* | *Achievements* | *Year of invention* | *Year of Nobel Prize* |
|---|---|---|---|
| A. Einstein | For his services to theoretical physics, and specially for his discovery of the laws of the photoelectric effect | 1905 | 1921 |
| J. Franck and G.L. Hartz | For their discovery of the laws governing the impact of an electron upon an atom | 1913 | 1925 |

*Braun shared the prize with the Italian scientist G. Marconi.

During the sea-voyage now nearing its termination, I have spent my time very pleasantly and profitably studying your exposition of this subject. I had not written to you earlier acknowledging your presentation, so I am taking this opportunity of expressing my gratitude to you for sending me this publication. It has deeply interested me, and the explanations you have given are so clear and masterly that their perusal has made a deep impression on my mind. I hope this will bear fruit before long' (dated 16 December 1929).

Niels Bohr (1885-1962), who received the Nobel Prize in 1922 for investigation on the structure of atoms and the radiation emanating from them, had contacts with Raman. In a letter dated 21 March 1923 he wrote: 'I hope you will pardon the liberty I am taking in writing to you concerning Bidhubhusan Ray, who is on the staff of this college and is one of the promising young physicists of the Calcutta School. . . I have suggested to Ray that he might follow a different course (not to go to England and Germany like most Indians were doing) and that he cannot do better than spend a greater part of his period of deputation at Copenhagen working under your direction.' Raman visited Copenhagen, about which Bohr states, 'We often think of your visit here some years ago, and I hope very much that I shall have the pleasure of meeting you again before too long' (dated 18 September 1929). In the same letter he wrote, 'I take this opportunity to express my most cordial congratulations to you to your great discovery of the new radiation phenomenon which has added so immensely to our knowledge of optics and atomic physics'.

Raman wrote back to him, 'The great kindness you have shown me in the past encourages me to make a request of a personal character. As you know, my work on the new radiation effect has been received with enthusiasm in scientific circles, and I feel sure that if you give your influential support, the Nobel Committee for physics may recommend that the award for 1930 may go to India for the first time. The proposal for the award has to reach the Nobel Committee before 31 January 1930. I have greatly hesitated in writing to you about this, and it is only because I felt sure that you sympathise with the scientific aspirations of India that I have ventured to do so. With many apologies. I am, yours sincerely' (letter dated 6 December 1929). Raman was not aware that he had been already nominated by Bohr for the year 1929. He repeated this decision for the year 1930.

However, the following paragraphs clearly bring out that it was not the contacts alone, but rather it was his scientific contributions which fetched Raman the Prize.

## Opinions of the Nominators

The comments of some of the scientists who nominated Raman are:

> C. T. R. Wilson (1869-1959), who received the Nobel Prize in the year 1927, and E. Rutherford (1871-1937) wrote, '... There seems to be no doubt that a study of the change of frequency in liquid and solid media provides valuable information on the natural frequencies associated with the molecules-information which is difficult to obtain by other methods-and will prove of great service in increasing our knowledge... We are both of (the) opinion that Raman is a physicist of exceptional ability, who in the difficult conditions in his own country has built up a successful school

> of research which has already produced work of high quality. He is a man strong both on the theoretical and experimental side and this is well illustrated by many of his papers. We are of the opinion that his work is of the outstanding quality required for this great honour.' (Rutherford and Wilson to the Chairman, Nobel Committee, 25 January 1930).

J. Stark (1874-1957), who also got the Nobel Prize in 1919 for his discovery of the Doppler effect in canal rays and the splitting of the spectral lines in an electric field, pointed out the practical side of the discovery by Raman. He observed, 'Answering your invitation I present to you a proposal for the Nobel Prize in physics for the year 1930, and to be precise I propose: Professor C. V. Raman in Calcutta for the discovery of the effect of the change in the frequency of light when scattered which was named after him. This discovery means-independent of the transience of theories-a permanent progress in the knowledge of physical reality.' (J. Stark to the Nobel Committee, dated 7 January 1930. Translated from German).

R. Pfeiffer from Breslau praised not only the discovery of the effect but also the earlier research works of Raman. He stated, 'I propose the professor of physics at the University of Calcutta Venkata Raman (Fellow of the Royal Society) for this year's Nobel Prize for physics. Professor Raman has developed a fruitful research work since several decades from which I want to mention only his extensive investigations about the acoustics of Indian musical instruments and those about the diffraction of light in molecules (Tyndall phenomenon). These latter investigations led him to his great discovery namely the establishment of the effect which was named after him (Raman effect); as a result, Raman moved up to the very front of those physicists studying the problems of modern atomic physics. The Raman effect provides inner eigenfrequencies of the molecules that means a property of them due to their inner Constitution, that means it (the effect) provides a powerful method for the exploration of molecules. It is of particular interest that the eigenfrequencies determined by this method which are situated in the spectral range of ultra-red frequently cannot be found by the help of spectroscopic methods. Therefore ultra-red research and Raman effect have a stimulating influence upon one another so that everyday surprises us with fresh evidence. In summary, I have to express my conviction that the Raman effect is one of the most important and most fruitful discoveries of the last years.' (R. Pfeiffer to the Nobel Committee, 22 January 1930. Translated from German).

Niels Bohr (1885-1962) stated, 'This phenomenon (Raman effect), the explanation of which agrees so well with the quantum theoretical ideas, will undoubtedly become a most important source in increasing our knowledge of the states of the atoms or molecules of matter in transitions, between which their characteristic spectra are emitted.' (N. Bohr to the Nobel Committee for physics, 29 January 1929. Translated from Danish).

The above evidences amply show that experts in the field recognised his work, which qualified him for the Nobel Prize.

### *Why did not Raman Share the Nobel Prize with His Co-workers?*

In his book Raman and His Effect Keswani wrote, 'Raman was a great teacher and beloved of his pupils but he could have given more credit to K. S. Krishnan who contributed no less to the discovery of the effect now known as the Raman effect'; and further, 'Many have felt that K. S. Krishnan should have been acknowledged as the co-discoverer of the effect now bearing Raman's name exclusively'. As far as the coining of the term Raman effect (in English and German-speaking areas) or Smekal-Raman effect is concerned. The term was coined by scientists other than Raman. In the same book Keswani has raised some interesting questions, such as 'Why did the Nobel Committee for physics not vote for the sharing of the prize by the Indian(s) and Russians?'.

The names of the collaborators were known to the Committee as well as to the expert who prepared the report. The name of candidates given in the report of the Nobel Committee shows that not a single collaborator of Raman was nominated. Also, according to the SNF 7 '. . . Personal applications for an award shall not be considered' (emphasis added). Thus it was not possible for Raman to put his name or any of his co-workers for the nomination. The prize was awarded not only for the discovery but for 'his work on light scattering and the discovery of the Raman effect'. The committee had to base their decision on the proposals and the opinions of the experts. If there was a controversy among the members of the Committee regarding awarding the prize to the co-workers as well, it will never come to light because under the rules of SNF 10, 'Proposals received for the award of a prize, and investigations and opinions concerning the award of a prize may not be divulged. Should divergent opinions have been expressed in connection with the decision of a prize-awarding body concerning the award of prize, these may not be included in the record or otherwise divulged'.

### *Why did not Raman Share the Nobel Prize with Russian Scientists?*

There existed a controversy between Raman and his Russian colleagues on the priority of the discovery. Raman wrote in Nature, 'The Russian physicists, to whose observation on the effect in quartz Darwin refers, made their first communication on the subject after the publication of the notes in Nature of 31 May and 27 April. Their papers appeared in print after sixteen other printed on the effect, by various authors, had appeared in recognised scientific periodicals.' Most probably, there was more one-sided correspondence between Raman and the Mandelstam school, as I. L. Fabelinskii's who was a co-worker of Mandelstam states, '. . . due to its impudent and domineering nature it has been left without reply and no correspondence has been kept' (I. L. Fabelinskii, private commun).

Since the controversy was a public knowledge, the Committee had to pay special attention to this issue despite the fact that the Russian scientists were recommended only twice Papalexis of Leningrad (now St. Petersburg) proposed that the prize should be awarded to Mandelstam (1879-1944) alone, whereas Chwolson stated that Raman should get half of it and the rest of it should go to Landsberg (1890-1957) and Mandelstam.

## Opinion of the Nobel Committee

The arguments put forward by Chwolson from Leningrad in his proposal follows: 'that Raman shares the honour of his discovery with Landsberg and Mandelstam; because undoubtedly, they discovered the named phenomenon in quartz crystals at the same time and independently from Raman. Only due to the external circumstances and the negligence of the Russian researchers in publishing their discovery, is according to Chwolson, the cause that the effect has been named as the "Raman effect". Raman's discovery was made on February 16 and Landsberg and Mandelstam's on 21 February 1928. Letters by Raman and Krishnan to Nature were published on 31 March 1928, whereas Landsberg and Mandelstam's first publication in Naturwissenschaften on 13 July. By giving Raman alone the prize the Russian scientists would be severely punished due to this negligence, said Chwolson. Also he gives the reference of M. Born from Goettingen, who was said to know the exact situation and to have given his opinion publicly. Chwolson obviously refers to Born's article in Naturwissenschaften (1928, 16, 741) on the Fourth Russian Physicists Conference, where Born was a guest. Born mentions in his lecture that the phenomenon was discovered in Moscow and Calcutta at the same time and the Russian physicists should share the honour with Raman' (translated from Swedish).

About the proposal of Papalexis from Leningrad the Committee observed, 'An even stronger impression of this opinion we find in the proposal of Papalexi, Leningrad in which he writes that Mandelstam alone should get the prize. He supports his proposal as follows: Mandelstam has been working since 1907 on the theoretical and experimental aspects of the diffusion light. Since 1918 through his theoretical interpretations he came to the idea of the existence of the scattering light, which corresponds to the Raman effect. Papalexi refers to an article of Mandelstam in Journal of Russian Physical Society (Journal d. russ. phys. Gesellschaft) 1926, 58, 831, (in Russian language)' (translated from Swedish). The Committee was of the opinion that Smekal in 1923 and Kramers and Heisenberg in 1925 had already given this explanation.

In order to make the position of the Committee on this matter clear, it will not be out of place to quote the comments of it, which stated, 'If we see Mandelstam's and Landsberg's first publication in Naturwissenschaften (1928, 16, 557), we get a different picture. The short note had been dated 6 May and explains the discovery of combination lines of the diffuse light in crystalline quartz. The existence of these lines has been shown experimentally, but about the interpretation of the lines the authors say, "We consider it to be premature at this moment to give a definite interpretation of the phenomenon in question. One of the theoretical interpretations which are possible consists of the following" . . . (translated from German), in which the authors gave the same statement as Raman. And further they said, "Whether and in what way the phenomenon observed by us is connected with the one which was recently described by Raman cannot be judged at the moment because of its rather summary description" (translated from German). However, Raman's and Krishnan's letters of 31 March as well as that of 21 April gave a very clear explanation of the nature of the phenomenon, (both cited by Mandelstam and Landsberg). Under these conditions, Mandelstam and Landsberg cannot argue to have obtained their experimental results independently' (translated from Swedish).

## Opinion of an Expert

'A work may not be awarded a prize, unless it by experience or expert scrutiny has been found to be of such outstanding importance as is manifestly intended by the Will'. The expert who gave this report was Erik Hulthen, professor and the director of the Physical Institute and the member of the Nobel Committee from 1929 to 1962. He prepared the report on the Raman effect under the title 'The complete explanation of the Raman-Effect'. The report was in favour of Raman and cited work done by different scientists on the topic in the past years. The conclusion of the report (translated from Swedish) follows:

1. The proposal by Chwolson that the Nobel Prize should be divided between Raman and Landesberg- Mandelstam had been rejected because they did not come to an independent interpretation of their discovery.
2. For the same reasons, the proposal of Papalexis in favour of Mandelstam had not been taken into account.
3. The uncertainties concerning the explanation of the intensity of Raman and infrared lines in the spectrum, could be explained during the last year.

4. The Raman method has been applied with great success in different fields of molecular physics.
5. The Raman effect has effectively helped to check the actual problems of the symmetry properties of molecules, thus the problems concerning the nuclear-spin in the atomic physics'.

The Nobel Committee said, 'the Raman effect is useful for the study of atomic physics and the constituents of compound. It also gives valuable information to prove modern theories in atomic physics. The Committee finds Raman's discovery on diffusion light is worth the Nobel Prize for physics' (translated from Swedish).

We have seen that the expert as well as the Nobel Committee had given their award-adjudication in favour of Raman. Thus he cannot be held responsible for not sharing the prize.

## The Nobel Dream

According to the regulations, the Nobel Committee submitted its report with proposal and opinion to the Swedish Academy of Sciences on 20 September 1930 (the regulation says-by the end of September) with the conclusion, 'The Committee has decided to ask the Academy to award the Nobel Prize for physics for the year 1930 to Chandrasekhra Venkata Raman, Calcutta, for his work on the diffusion of light and for the effect named after him' (translated from Swedish).

According to the regulations, 'the Committee shall take up the matter for a final decision before the middle of the following November'. Another committee, 'Physic-class' comprising about 25 members is responsible for controlling all the proposals, recommendations and other documents concerning the Nobel Prize for physics. It gives its opinion and final decision to the Academy about the selection of the Nobel Laureate. According to the Special rules of SNF 7, '. . . The Academy shall take the matter for a final decision before the middle of the following November'. 'The laureate is immediately notified of the decisions, which are then announced internationally at a press conference held in Stockholm and attended by representatives of the international news media. The messages contain the names of the laureates and a short statement describing the reason for award'. Raman would not have been in time to attend the Nobel Prize giving ceremony on 10 December 1930, if he had been informed by proper channels. '. . . Two months before Raman knew that he was awarded the Nobel Prize. He had the supreme audacity of booking his steamer passage to be in time for the ceremony at Stockholm. That not only did he take such a step but went further and declared publicly that he did so are both interesting facts of his life'. Whatever might be the source of his information, on 10 December 1930 he and Lady Raman were in Stockholm to receive the prize.

According to SNF rules under 9, '. . . It shall be incumbent on a prize-winner, whenever this is possible, to give a lecture on a subject relevant to the work for which the prize has been awarded. Such lecture should be given within six months of the Festival Day in Stockholm, or, in the case of the Peace Prize, in Oslo.' Raman delivered his Nobel lecture on 11 December 1930, entitled 'The Molecular Scattering of Light', in which he gave the point of motivation of his research, i.e. the blue colour of the sea and further extension of this work on the scattering of light which led to the discovery of the effect.

After receiving the prize Raman stayed on for further five days. On 17 December 1930 he was in the Grand Hotel Olso from there he wrote a letter to Bohr which dictates, '. . . We next proceed to Goeteborg and then to Copenhagen which we reach on the night of the 19 December or perhaps the 20 December. . . . It is my hope to (be) able to meet you and your group of investigators and to spend three or four days in Copenhagen much to the advantage of my knowledge of physics' (dated 17 December 1930). The telegram which he sent from Goeteborg shows that in Copenhagen he delivered a lecture on 'Scattering of light in crystals'. Raman met A. Sommerfeld in Munich. After this tour through Europe he returned to India.

## C. V. Raman, M. N. Saha and the Nobel Prize

In 1930, Sir C. V. Raman and Meghnad Saha were both nominated for the Nobel Prize for physics. The documents from the Nobel Committee connected with the proposal and selection of the Nobel Laureates were obtained. The investigation based on the report of the Nobel Committee will show that the 'Raman effect' was evaluated as an important discovery with its applications in the field of physics and chemistry. The effect was hailed as a proof of modern theories in atomic physics. Although Sana's scientific achievements were appreciated, they were not regarded worth of the Nobel Prize. Saha's main discovery, that is, his 'thermal ionisation equation' was seen as an application on the astrophysical data. The committee considered his work on 'selective radiation pressure' not a new discovery but a logical consequence of his ionisation equation.

The Nobel Prize is considered to be the highest honour for scientists. The Statutes of the Nobel Foundation (abbreviated as SNF) which were approved by the Swedish Crown on June 29, 1900 had been decreed by the Swedish government on April 27, 1995. Also the Statutes of the June 29,1973 containing special regulations (abbreviated as SNF-Special Rules) concerning the award by the Royal Academy of Sciences had been decreed on April 7, 1994. The rules and regulations quoted are taken from these Statutes.

A very short view is given about the education and scientific interests of C. V. Raman and M.N. Saha until 1930. The opinion of the Nobel Committee about the achievements and discoveries of the two scientists are given in detail, to show the facts which convinced the Committee to make its decision in favour of Raman, although the work of Saha was also evaluated an important achievement.

According to the Statutes of the Nobel Foundation of April 27, 1995,

> "The Nobel Foundation is established under the terms of the will of Dr. Alfred Bernhard Nobel, drawn up on the 27th of November, 1895, which in its relevant parts runs as follows : § 1 the whole of my remaining realisable estate shall be dealt with in the following way: the capital, invested in safe securities by my executors, shall constitute a fund, the interest on which shall be annually distributed in the form of prizes to those who, during the preceding year, shall have

conferred the greatest benefit to mankind. The said interest shall be divided into five equal parts, which shall be apportioned as follows: one part to the person who shall have made most important discovery or invention within the field of physics; one part to the person who shall have made the most important chemical discovery or improvement; one part to the person who shall have made the most important discovery within the domain of physiology or medicine; one part to the person who shall have produced in the field of literature the most outstanding work of an idealistic tendency; and one part to the person who shall have done the most or the best work for fraternity between nations, for the abolition or reduction of standing armies and for the holding and promotion of peace congresses. The prize for physics and chemistry shall be awarded by the (Royal) Swedish Academy of Sciences; that for physiological or medical works by the Karolinska Institute in Stockholm; that for literature by the (Swedish) Academy in Stockholm; and that for champions of peace by a committee of the persons to be elected by the Norwegian Storting (Parliament). It is my express wish that in awarding the prizes no consideration whatever shall be given to the nationality of the candidates, but that the most worthy shall receive the prize, whether he be a Scandinavian or not."

### *The Nobel Prize and the Western Monopoly*

According to Nobel's will, the prize should have international character. It has been observed that between the years 1901-29, the nominators from the great scientific countries Germany, France, England, and America nominated in both disciplines (Physics and Chemistry) nearly 70 per cent of the proposed candidates from their own countries (translated from German). As most of the nominators came from these countries, the chances for others were rare.Under such circumstances, the scientists from other countries have to seek for 'help' from their influential western colleagues as the next two examples of Bohr-Raman and Bohr-Saha show.

***Bohr and Raman:*** Niels Bohr (1885-1962) received the Nobel Prize in 1922 for the investigation of the structure of atoms and the radiation emanating from them. Raman had known him since 1923. In one of his letters he wrote:

> "I hope you will pardon the liberty I am taking in writing to you concerning Dr. Bidhubhusan Ray, who is on the staff of this college and is one of the promising young physicists of the Calcutta School....I have suggested to Dr. Ray that he cannot do better than spend a greater part of his period of deputation at Copenhagen working under your direction"
> (Raman to Bohr, letter dated March 21, 1923).

On December 6,1929 Raman wrote to Bohr to support his nomination for the Nobel Prize as:

> "The great kindness you have shown me in the past encourages me to make a request of a personal character. As you know, my work on the new radiation effect has been received with enthusiasm in scientific circles, and I feel sure that if you give your influential support, the Nobel Committee for Physics may recommend that the award for 1930 may go to India for the first time.... I have greatly hesitated in writing to you about this, and it is only because I felt sure that you sympathise with the scientific aspirations of India that I have ventured to do so. With many apologies."

Raman was not aware that he had already been nominated by Bohr for the year 1929.

***Bohr and Saha:*** Saha's contact goes back to 1926. At this stage, he did not mention the Nobel Prize. On November 13, 1926 he wrote to Bohr:

> "I am visiting Europe next year, and I shall be there from June to September. I wish to spend a month in your laboratory from June 15 to about July 15.1 shall be obliged if you kindly let me know whether you and other physicists of your school (Kramers, Pauli, Heisenberg, and others) will be there during these times."

On the advice from his American colleagues he took the step to mention a nomination and on September 30, 1929 he wrote to Bohr:

> "I wish to write to you on another matter of some delicacy. Recently I have been travelling in America, and met many astronomers, and physicists. They were kind enough to tell me that I have not been given proper recognition for my work on Astrophysics which was a pioneering work, and opened up a great field in Astrophysics. There have been much mathematical elaboration to my work, but no new physical thought has yet been introduced."

He wrote further:

> "Prof. A. H. Compton has been kind enough to discuss the matter with me, and subsequently he has written to me that he is going to send up my name for the award of the Nobel Prize and he has secured the assent of Dr. I. Langmuir. Probably he will also get more support from the Britishers and others. Our relations with the Britishers are a bit delicate and I do not know whether I shall be wise in writing to them. Moreover I am sailing for India on Oct. 3, hence I shall have very little opportunity of meeting any of them and I do not wish to commit myself in writing. I shall be glad if you can see your way in supporting Prof. Cornpton's proposal. I shall be glad to give any further information, if you are kind enough to take up the matter."

These two examples show the interaction between the nominators and the candidates. As far as the contacts between the members of the Committee or the Swedish scientists and the Indian candidates are concerned, there does not seem to be such an interaction. For example, there was close contact between Saha and S. A. Arrhenius (1859-1927), who was a famous chemist and got the Nobel Prize for Chemistry in 1903 . He was one of those persons who wrote reports on the work of the candidates. Although there was contact between Raman and some of the members of the Nobel Committee, the letters of the Indian Scientists show that they have never asked their Swedish colleagues to support their nomination.

***C. V. Raman (1888-1970):*** Raman began his work on light scattering in 1921 and soon established his reputation in this field. In 1924 he was invited by the British Association for the Advancement of Science in Toronto to open a discussion meeting on the scattering of light.

The initial experiments on the scattering of light opened a new field of research in Calcutta. Further work in this direction led to the discovery of the Raman effect in 1928. The effect deals with the change in the frequency of the monochromatic light after scattering. The spectrum of the scattered light gives clues about the molecular structure and thus helps to understand the properties of materials.

His fields of research were mainly acoustics, optics and scattering of light. For his work on the diffusion of light and the Raman effect, he was awarded the Nobel Prize in 1930. Till this time he had published about 157 papers and a monograph.

***M. N. Saha (1893-1956):*** A scholarship permitted Saha to visit Europe when he was a lecturer in the Calcutta University. In England, he met the astrophysicist A. Fowler (1868-1940) at the Imperial College of Science and Technology, London. In Berlin, he worked in the laboratory of the famous physical chemist H. W. Nernst (1864-1941). In Germany Saha came in contact with M. Planck, A. Einstein, M. von Laue and A. Sommerfeld, who were the renowned scientists at that time.

After his return to India, he accepted a professorship at the University of Calcutta, but left it in 1923, as the University could not afford enough funds to support his research. He moved to Allahabad, where he taught till 1938.

In the beginning of this century, a theory of the radiative equilibrium in the outer atmosphere of the stars had been proposed. A.S. Eddington (1882-1944) had shown that the theory of equilibrium in stars must take account of gravitation, gas pressure and radiation pressure. The high temperature of the photosphere and gravitational acceleration, both are expected to influence the density variation of the chromosphere as the height varies. It was predicted that under such conditions, there should be hardly any heavy element like calcium if the height is about 3,500 kilometres. But the observations in the flash spectra had shown the existence of calcium. To explain this phenomenon, Saha treated light made of quanta as suggested by Einstein. He showed that the radiation pressure acting on a particular type of atom depends on two factors, i.e. the type of absorption frequencies which are available in the atom, and the intensity of the blackbody spectrum at those frequencies. Under such conditions, only particular atoms will absorb the quanta of the photosphere, thus experiencing the radiation pressure and under this effect, they are thrown out of the photosphere.

His main achievement was an equation named after him as 'Saha ionisation equation," which is a relationship between temperature, pressure, ionisation potential and the fraction of atoms in an ionisation process. This equation explained the sequence of stellar and solar spectra and various physical conditions which they embody.

Saha published his first paper in 1917, "On Maxwell's Stresses" in the Philosophical Magazine. Till 1930 he had 52 publications in highly reputed scientific Journals. Most of his papers belong to astrophysics. Also he was the co-author of the book on The Principles of Relativity.

### *C. V. Raman, M. N. Saha and the Nobel Prize Proposals*

The Nobel Prize for physics and chemistry is awarded by the Swedish Academy of Science. In general, the Nobel Committe consisting of three, four of five members was elected for a period of three years for each Swedish Prize section by the Academy. Later in SFN, Special Rule 1994 § 2, the number of members for the Physics and Chemistry groups had been fixed to 5 for each group. The Nobel Committee sends invitations during the month of September to the competent persons to put forward proposals, which had to be submitted with evidences before the first of February of the following year. According to SFN special Rules § 1, the folllowing persons are competent to submit proposals:

1. Swedish and foreign members of the Academy of Sciences;
2. Members of the Nobel Committees for Physics and Chemistry;

3. Scientists who have been awarded the Prize by the Academy of Sciences;
4. Permanent and assistant professors in the sciences of Physics and Chemistry at the universities and institutes of technology of Sweden, Denmark, Finland, Iceland and Norway, and the Karolinska Institute;
5. Holders of corresponding chairs in at least six universities or university colleges selected by the Academy of Sciences with a view to ensuring the appropriate distribution of the commission over the different countries and their seats of learning; and
6. Other scientists whom the Academy may see fit to invite proposals. Decisions as to the selection of the teachers and scientists referred to in paragraphs 5 (Expert's scrutiny) and 6 (Opinion of 3-5 members of the Nobel Committee) above shall be taken each year before the end of the month of September.

Now for the year 1930, 39 competent persons were asked to make proposals. Out of them 37 persons sent proposals. There were 21 valid recommendations for a full or shared Prize. Most of the recommendations were concerned with atomic theory and atomic physics. (translated from Swedish).

Out of these 21 nominations for the Nobel Prize, Raman and Saha were two Indian candidates. Raman was proposed 10 times and Saha twice.

> Sovereign Louis de Broglie and duke Maurice de Broglie, Paris, the Professors R. Pfeiffer, Breslau, J. Stark, Grosshesselohe, and E. Rutherford and C.T.R. Wilson, Cambridge, the two latter ones in a joint letter, proposed Raman on the basis of the effect named after him for an unshared Nobel Prize in Physics. Professor E. Bloch,Paris, suggests that the prize should be shared between Wood and Raman, while Prof. Niels Bohr, Copenhagen, repeats his proposal from the previous year that the Prize should be given to Wood or that it should be divided between Wood and

> Raman. Prof. O. Chwolson, Leningrad, proposed that half of the Prize should go to Raman and the other half to Profesor G.S. Landesberg and L.J. Mandelstam, Moscow. Professor J. Perrin, Paris suggests that either Raman should get the Prize alone or it should be shared between Raman and Heisenberg. (translated from Swedish).

The renowned person like N. Bohr (1885-1962) appreciated Saha's work, as a letter of one of his colleagues (O. Klein) shows which he wrote to Saha on February 13,1927. It states, *He (Bohr) would be very glad indeed to meet you when you come to Europe, since he has taken the greatest interest in your work* (emphasis added). The following example clearly indicates that he was one of the most famous physicists in 1920s.

In 1927, the "Volta Centenary Celebration" was held at Como, Italy; where the reputed scientists of that time such as M. Planck, E. Rutherford, M. von Laue, W. L. Bragg, M. Born, A. Smekal and N. Bohr were invited. M. N. Saha had the honour to be invited in this conference by the Italian society of Physics. This clearly shows that his scientific work was considered to be a landmark in the field of modern astrophysics. But strangely enough, he was not nominated by any western scientist for the Nobel Prize. Only *"D. M. Bose and S.K. Mitra, both from Calcutta nominated him"* (translated from Swedish). On the other hand, the selection of the candidate by the Committee and the Academy is not based on the system that the candidate with most proposals gets the prize. For example, in 1910, Poincare had 49.3 per cent of the proposals in his favour, but the prize was awarded to Van de Waals In 1929, de Broglie had only 12.4 per cent of the proposals, but he got the Nobel Prize.

### *Opinion of Experts and the Report of the Nobel Committee*

According to the SNF, *A work may not be awarded a prize, unless it by experience or expert scrutiny has been found to be of such outstanding importance as is manifestly intended by the will.* The Nobel Committee prepares a list of the candidates which are proposed. The next step is to opt the opinion of the experts about the work of the candidates. In order to get detailed information on the work of the candidates and to give complete reports to the Academy, the experts are asked to give their opinion about all the candidates; but not all the candidates are dealt with in detail. Generally, first, the opinion of the experts is given only for those candidates whose files are to be sent to the Academy for recommendation. It is determined at this stage whether all the scientific works of the candidate, or only the works recommended by the nominators should be taken into consideration while preparing the opinion. If the candidate has been nominated in the previous years, his works are added to the old report and new opinions are prepared.

For the year 1930, the general report about the candidates was prepared by C. W. Oseen (1879-1944), who was a member of the Nobel Committee and professor of theoretical physics at the University of Uppsala, Sweden. The work of three scientists namely R.W. Wood, M. N. Saha and C. V. Raman came under special consideration, because the Committee opted the opinion of experts only about their achievements. Since 1914, R. W. Woods has been nominated 24 times. The opinion about his work was completed. The report on Sana's work is titled, "Short report on Saha's achieve-ments", which are mentioned for the Nobel Prize. In length it is little more than four pages. The report was prepared by Carlheim-Gyllenskoeld (1859-1934) who was a geophysicist.The summary of the opinion given in the next paragraphs is taken from the report of the Committee.

### *Opinion of the Committee about Saha's Achievements*

It has been stated in the SNF that *the Nominations should be explained and accompanied by evidence in support of them* D.M.Bose and S.K. Mitra, in their nomination letter which they wrote to the Nobel Committeee on Janury 25, 1930, mention the scientific achievements of Saha under the title, *References to original publications. It* contains 7 publications on the treatment of the theory of *Thermal Ionisation* and 3 publications on *Selective Radiation Pressure*. In the letter they wrote:

> The first is the most outstanding and fruitful contribution to the subject of astrophysics since Kirchhoff made his discovery of spectrum analysis in

> 1859, and opened a way for studying the physical conditions of the stars and the sun. Saha's theory provides for a physical explanation of the data on Stellar spectra accumulated for over half a century by the labours of Sir Norman Lockyer in England, and of Prof. Pickering and Miss Canon in the Harvard College Observatory, USA. The theory has stimulated further work all over the world amongst physicists and astrophysicists. Further extensions have been made by H. N. Russel, R. H. Fowler, EA. Milne, and W. Wolther. Prof. Saha also has improved the theory in a further series of papers published in the Philosophical Magazine, and has secured experimental verification of the theory. (Bose DM. and Mitra S. K. to the Nobel Committee, letter dated January 25, 1930).

The report prepared by Carlheim-Gyllenskoeld discusses the detail of the papers given by the nominee and its summary in the report of the Nobel Committee starts on the basis of Saha's ionisation equation. It follows:

> Saha has started with some definite, already for long time well-known facts about the appearance of the spectral lines of different characteristics at different heights within the chromosphere of the sun. As the (spectral) lines of the arc are caused by the neutral atom, and the flash spectral lines are caused only by ionised atoms, the relative intensity of the two types of lines should indicate the relative number of neutral and ionised atoms. Under the supposition, that one finds a relation between the relative number, the temperature and pressure, on the basis of the conducted spectroscopic observations, one can find the explanation on the temperature and pressure existing in the stellar atmosphere, shortly before Saha's first publication, Eggert had applied Nernst formula for the isobar reaction on the problem of the gas equilibrium, inside a star and had shown that many supposition about the inner Constitution of the stars

> can be found Saha applied Eggert's method on the problem of state of the gases on the outer surface of the stars. With the help of the Formula which Saha obtained in this way, the ionisation grade of an element under any pressure and temperature can be calculated, under the condition that the ionisation potential of the element is known. The value of ionisation potential for different elements has been determined by Franck and Hertz, Mclennan and others (translated from Swedish).

In the next paragraph Saha's two important papers are mentioned which he wrote during his stay in England and Germany in which he gave the final shape to his theory and summarised his results from the previous papers. The discussion of these papers follows:

> In 1921 Saha has published a paper, in which he himself gave a summary of the fundamentals of the theory. Also, he named further applicatons of these fundamentals for the solar spectrum and the different classes of stellar spectrum. In his next paper, Saha gives more information about the application of the theory on the spectrum of celestial bodies. He concludes that the continued variation in the stellar spectrum only depends on the changing temperature of the stellar atmosphere. On this basis, the classification in different types B, A, F, G, K, M, which the Harvard astronomers set up as a result of several year long studies, seems to get a deeper physical meaning. However, several minor differences can be realised. Saha mentions several, but here, only one of these is mentioned. Adam and Kohlschuetter have recently shown that there exist considerable difference in the spectra of the giant and the dwarf stars of the same spectral class, when the intensity of certain groups of lines are compared..... But as Saha remarks, the spectrum isnotonlytemperature dependent, but also the concentration of atoms in the stellar

> atmospher, and this may give the explanation for shown deficiency in the conformity (translated from Swedish).

About the other scientific achievements the nominators wrote:

> The theory of selective radiation pressure was pronounced by Saha in a letter to Nature and in a paper published in the Journal of Science of the Calcutta University. This provides a basis for the explanation of abnormal heights of elements in the solar chromosphere. The theory has been further extended by Prof. E. A. Milne in a series of papers to the Month. Not. R. Astronomical Society of England. (Bose D. M. and Mitra S. K. to the Nobel Committee, letter dated January 25, 1930).

This achievement of Saha was not considered important. The Committee observed:

> The other important investigations by Saha which were mentioned partially seem to be considered to be logical consequences of the above mentioned research work and by no means, have the same importance. (translated from Swedish).

It seems that the nominators could not convince the Committee that Saha's work was revolutionary. Raman's work was evaluated as a proof of quantum mechanics. His nominators like N. Bohr hailed his discovery as:

> This phenomenon (Raman effect), the explanation of which agrees so well with the quantum theoretical ideas, will undoubtedly become a most important source in increasing our knowledge of the states of the atoms or molecules of matter in transitions, between which their characteristic spectra are emitted (N. Bohr to the Nobel Committee for Physics, January 29, 1929. (translated from Danish).

Another nominator wrote:

> .... I have to express my conviction that the Raman effect is one of the most important and most fruitful

> discoveries of the last years, (R. Pfeiffer to the Nobel Committee, January 22,1930, translated from German).

The Committee Concluded:

> Saha's work is proved to be very important for modern astrophysics, but this can hardly be seen as a new physical discovery, more as an application to known physical accumulated astrophysical data. With all recognition for the value of Saha's achievements, jhe Committee find itself not in the position, to recommend him for the reception of the Nobel Prize for physics (translated from Swedish).

### *Opinion of the Committee about Raman's Work*

E. V. Hulthen, a professor for experimental physics and the member of Nobel Committee for physics from 1929 to 1962, wrote a report about Raman's work which has been entitled as "Complete Report on Raman Effect" and is signed on May 26, 1930. It contains eight pages. The detailed report of the Nobel Committee as well as the expert on Raman's work are given by Singh R. *et al.* in a separate article. Here only a short review is given.

The report starts with the work of French scientist Cabannes on the light-scattering and gives the work of Raman and his colleagues before and after the discovery of the Raman effect. The report also includes the experimental technique, its advantages and the applications of the Raman effect. The work done by different scientists on this topic is also given. The Committee says one disadvantage of Raman's method is that the exposition time to take spectra of diffusion light in some cases takes hundreds of hours, but it wrote:

> This disadvantage can be compensated because the apparatus needs not at all or very little maintenance. (translated from Swedish).

The Committee said:

> Since the short time of its discovery the Raman effect proved to be a very important and applicable tool for the study of atomic physics and the chemical

> composition of the compounds. Also, it supplies us with important material for the proof of the modern atomic theory in atomic physics. The Committee finds that the Raman effect is useful for the study of atomic physics and the constituents of compound. It also gives valuable information to prove modern theories in atomic physics. The Committee finds Raman's discovery'on diffusion light is worth the Nobel Prize for physics (translated from Swedish).

The Nobel Committee and the Academy gave their award-adjudication in favour of Raman.

### *Other Factors*

***Significance of the Discovery:*** According to the will of Nobel, dictated under the SNF, §2 the annual award of prizes shall be intended for work during the 'preceding year' shall be understood in the sense that awards shall be made for the most recent achievements in the fields of culture referred to in the will and for older work only if their significance has not become apparent until recently.

The application and significance of the Raman effect becomes clear from the number of papers published on this topic. The last date of sending the proposal is the first of February (in our case Feb. 1930); and the list of original literature on the Raman effect compiled by Kohlrausch contains 225 entries till January 31,1930, starting from the first publication of Raman and Krishnan on the discovery in *Nature.* This was not the case with regard to Sana's discovery. The explanation is given in the next paragraph.

***Apparatus***: The number of publications depends upon the experimental technique and its availability in the laboratories. Raman was independent to perform his experimental work, as the only apparatus needed to do experimental work on the Raman effect were a Mercury lamp, spectroscopes and probe, available in almost every laboratory. Different people in India, USA, Russia, England and France were working on the scattering of light and spectroscopy. The discovery has its applications in physics as well as chemistry. The simplicity of apparatus and the experimental technique was one of the reasons for such a high number of publications.

Whereas in the case of Sana's work, the people needed complicated instruments. To perform the experimental work instruments were needed which could work under high temperature. To collect data about stellar spectra good telescopes were needed. Only the scientists in the United States had the facility to collect these data. Even in England these facilities were not available. Unfortunately, Saha did not get any help from the scientists in the USA.

In order to perform his experiments Saha was dependent on others. During his stay in Europe, he experienced that for research work a well equipped laboratory is required. One of his letters which he wrote to A. Einstein on August 26, 1921 states:

> ...and in my institute, there is a lack of needed apparatus and also of money to buy them. I have spoken to a representative of a very rich firm in India, which has founded a charitable endowment for scientfic work. As I am still young and an unknown person in the country, he said to me, if I can bring a recommendation letter from a renowned physicist that my work is good and useful, he can help me with the money
> If you can do me a favour and give your recommendation for my work, it will be very easy for me, to get money out of this foundation, and to buy the necessary apparatus (translated from German).

As Saha could not afford to have necessary instruments for his work, a part of his theory was verified in the USA by Russell who had access to the famous Mount Wilson observatory, where data about stellar and the sun had been collected.

## The Declaration of the Nobel Laureate

According to the regulations, the Nobel Committee submitted its report with proposal and opinion to the Swedish Academy of Science of September 20, 1930 (the regulation says — by the end of September) with the conclusion:

> The Committee has decided to ask the Academy to award the Nobel Prize for physics for the year 1930

> to Sir Chandrashekhara Venkata Raman, Calcutta for his work on the diffusion of light and for the effect named after him (translated from Swedish).

Although in general, the decision given by the Nobel Committee is accepted by the Academy, the Academy is independent of this recommendation. For example, in 1908 the Committee recommended M. Plank for the Nobel Prize in Physics, but the Academy decided for Lippmann The next decision-making Committee in the case of the Nobel Prize for physics is named "Physic-class" consisting of about 25 members. Once again, it checks all the proposals, recommendations, and other documents concerning the Nobel Prize. It gives its opinion and decision to the Academy about the selection of the Nobel Laureate. According to the Special rules of SNF § 7:

> ...The Academy shall take the matter for a final decision before the middle of the following November. The laureate is immediately notified of the decisions, which are then announced internationally at a press conference held in Stockholm and attended by representatives of the international news media. The messages contain the names of the laureates and a short statement describing the reason for award.

For the year 1930, it was stated that the Nobel Prize goes to Sir C. V. Raman, for his work on the diffusion of light and for the effect named after him. On December 10, 1930 Raman received the Nobel Prize and became the first Asian who got the prize for physics.

It has been concluded here that Raman received the Nobel Prize because the Nobel Committee and the Academy found his work worth a Nobel Prize. The Raman effect was seen as a tool which gives valuable information to prove modern theories in atomic physics and has its applications in the field of chemistry. Whereas Saha's achievements in the field of astrophysics were appreciated,but were not seen as a new discovery, more as an application to known accumulated astrophysical data. Similarly his work in the case of selective radiation pressure was an application of quantum mechanics. On the other hand the Raman effect was a proof of quantum mechanics. Sana's nominators were not influential persons, whereas Raman was nominated by renowned scientists like Bohr, Stark and Rutherford, who themselves were Nobel Laureates.

### *Summary*

Thus, Raman received the Nobel Prize 'for his work on diffusion of light and for the effect named after him'. The objections raised by some historians that Raman did not share the Nobel Prize with others or that the Committee ignored Raman's collaborators as well as Russian colleagues is not correct; as he was awarded the Prize not only for the Raman effect, but for other work in this field as well. The Nobel Committee had to take the decision according to certain rules and regulations imposed on it by the Nobel Foundation. Raman was nominated 10 times and the nominators wrote convincing recommendations in favour of him; thus the Committee decided for Raman. He received the Nobel Prize in record time due the practical significance of the discovery, as well as the good opinion of the famous contemporary scientists about his work.

8

# Raman's Global Status

## Contacts with European Scientists

In 1928 C. V. Raman (1888-1970) and K. S. Krishnan (1898-1961) observed that if monochromatic light is passed through a transparent medium, thereafter the scattering light is accompanied by other colours. This phenomenon was later named as Raman effect. The effect helps to find out the molecular structure of substances. In 1930 Raman was award the Physics Nobel Prize for his work on light scattering and the discovery of the effect named after him. He was the first Asian to receive this honour. This made him extremely popular.

C. V. Raman interacted with the wide scientific community for about half a century and visited many countries. Some of the important physicists who corresponded with Raman were Wladyslaw Natanson, Niels Bohr, Max Born, Erwin Schrodinger, Arnold Sommerfeld and Ernest Rutherford.

First, we scantly discuss Raman's interaction with some of the these physicists. Our second point deals with the visit of one of the secretaries of the Royal Society of London, AV Hill to India in 1943. He came to organise the scientists for war efforts. We show that this visit preshaped the role Raman had to play after India's independence in 1947.

## Contacts with Other Western Scientists

Lord Rayleigh's reply to Raman of date July 15th, 1906 indicates that the latter started communication abroad while he was a student. Unfortunately, little is know about Raman's correspondence until 1921. We know definitely that he started writing letters after his first visit to England in the beginning of 1920s. In this decade he established contacts, in particular either with the Nobel Laureates or those closer to the Nobel Committee. After winning the Nobel Prize in 1930, he became much more influential and famous. In the beginning of 1930s he was at the peak. It was also during this period, that the Nazi came in power. It is a well-known fact that many were forced to leave Germany. However, less know part of the story is that some of the scientists tried to get positions at Indian Universities. Raman was one of the persons to support them.

***Raman's Activities for the Displaced Scientists:*** In 1933 Raman was elected as the first Indian Director of the Indian Institute of Sciences, Bangalore. At the same time he was the Head of the Department of Physics, which was yet to be founded. He was well aware that theoretical physics (in particular quantum mechanics) was missing in India. Not surprisingly, he wrote a letter to Max Born — one of the founders of quantum mechanics and asked to suggest a few names of theoretical physicists.

In the end he decide to come himself for a period of 6 months. He was hoping to stay longer, but due to various reasons he had to return back after finishing his term of 6 months. Like Born, the father of Wave Mechanics, Erwin Schrodinger also got invitation for working at Indian universities. Born-Schrodinger correspondence shows that the latter declined the offer, as the salary was too low. Another scientist from German speaking area was Hungarian chemist Georg de Hevesy, who was working in Freiburg. He declined Raman's invitation, as he was afraid that his knowledge might stagnate in India.

Some of the fleeing scientists, who managed to come to India, had to face problems. One such example is that of R. Samuel, one of Born's students from Gottingen. He was working at the Muslim University Aligarh. On April 22, 1936 Raman wrote a letter to the

Rector of the Hebrew University, Jerusalem. In the letter he explained the difficult situation Samuel had to face in Aligarh and recommend him for the chair in Jerusalem.

Another example of Raman's activities is his proposal for the Nobel Prize in favour of Otto Stern. In his letter of October 25th, 1933 Raman stated as follows:

> I understand, however, that Professor Stern has been displaced from his chair by the present Government in Germany. The award of the Nobel Prize to him will have at least this great merit that it would relieve him from distress and enable him to continue his most important investigations.

The forgoing discussion clearly shows that Raman was a political active scientist, and was well aware of the political situation in Europe. However, his sense of politics was different, namely, the politicians should listen scientists and not others way round.

## Historical Meeting of the Royal Society in India

Raman got his entire education in India. Due to historical reasons, British men of science were the first, who influenced his educational and scientific carriers. Before he made his first journey to Europe in the beginning of 1920s, he was well known due his researches in the field of acoustics. The available documents suggest little about Raman's political views before the Second World War. It was during the war that he gave a statement, which appeared in a local newspaper on July 23rd, 1940. It follows:

> When Indian cities are bombed by Nazis — we will become war-minded — force can be vanquished only by greater force. Raman pooh-poohed Mahatma Gandhi's theory of non-violence. Indian should support British victory.

Hill's letter to Born of Oct. 13th, 1941 indicates that during this year, there was a discussion among British scientists that Indian men of science should be supported for their work and ought to be involved in war efforts. However, the representatives of the Government of India did not show any interest. It was only in

1943 that the Royal Society was asked by the Secretary of State for India to send a representative who should advice on the organisation of scientific research. In this connection A. V. Hill, a secretary of the Royal Society was informed about the possible fields for extra-mural work in connection with the armed forces in India like signals and electrical equipment, wireless communication, airborne forces. On November 16th, 1943 Hill arrived India. Three days later he wrote a letter and asked for information about the Heads of Enquiries on Scientific Research Resources in India in the field of Engineering, Chemistry, Biology and Health Researches. On November 18th, 1943 A. V. Hill wrote to Sahni that the former had been empowered as a Vice-President of the Royal Society by the President Henry H. Dale — and had been asked to forward latter's letters to Birbal Sahni (Biologist), Raman, Homi J. Bhabha (Physicist) and Shanti S. Bhatnagar (Chemist). In the same communication Hill wrote to Sahni as follows:

> ... The Council of the Royal Society asked me to do a thing which will be unique in the history of the Society, and to act on behalf of the President in admitting four Fellows (Bhatnagar, Bhabha, Krishnan and Sahni) of the Society who have never yet been able to present themselves at a meeting of the Society in London for their admissions.

In Dale's letter of Oct. 29th, 1943 to Sahni it was written that the ceremony of signing the parchment (by Bhabha, Bhatnagar, Krishnan and Sahni) at the occasion of the Indian Science Congress session would be preferred. Another letter of Dale written on October 29, 1943 was directed to the President of the National Academy of Sciences, Allahabad. It reads:

> I am asking Professor Hill to transmit, through you, the cordial greetings and friendly sentiments of the Fellows of the Royal Society of London to the Members of the National Academy of Sciences. We have the confident hope that one of the results of Professor Hill's visit will be to strengthen the bonds of understanding and true comradeship between our Indian colleagues and the men of science of this country.

At that time India had three science academies (which still exist), namely, the National Academy of Sciences (Allahabad), the National Institute of Sciences of India (today known as the Indian National Science Academy) and the Indian Academy of Sciences (Bangalore). Each considered herself representing Indian scientific community.

Regarding attending the meeting in Delhi, Raman (the founder of the Indian Academy of Sciences) consulted the matter with Bhabha and Krishnan, and they formulated a letter, in which they appreciated Dale's offer of cooperation between British and Indian scientists. They were suspicious of losing the opportunity to sign the Charter Book in the historic room of the Society in Burlington, and also their objection was:

> We ... feel that if a function of the kind proposed, which clearly affects only the Fellows of the Royal Society, is held for the purpose of obtaining our signatures in India, then it should be entirely unconnected with the meeting of any other society or organisation in India.

Raman who was not at all affected supported his candidates in the letter by writing an extra sentence: I entirely agree with and support the views expressed above. In a separate letter of December 3, 1943 he asked Sahni that if he agreed to the content of the accompanying letter he should sign it on the first place being the senior. He was also informed that including him (Raman), Bhabha and Krishnan were not going to attend the Indian Science Congress (ISC). In a letter of Dec. 10th, 1943 Sahni informed Hill about the joint letter and their decision not to attend the ISC. From Hill's response of December 14th, 1943, it is evident that he was not happy with it and was of the opinion that the ceremony of signing the parchment should take place before the inauguration of the meeting. It seems that the reason for preferring this occasion was that the Indian Science Congress was a general body of Indian scientists opened to Universities and Colleges teachers as well as research institutions; thus a better platform to attract the attention of participants to show the recognition by the Royal Society, and motivate the scientists for war efforts and post-war programmes.

In the history of 281 years of the Royal Society it was the first meeting that took place outside England. According to *The Hindustan Times* of January 4th, 1944, Hill inaugurated the historical meeting in Delhi. Hill's lecture shows that only Bhabha and Bhatnagar were present to sign the parchment. On December 21st, 1943, Bhabha had written a letter to Sahni and indicated about his decision. He also suggested that he and Krishnan should attend the special meeting. If Raman will not attend, it will not be seen as unfriendly.

On April 6th, 1944 Hill left India. He ensured the cooperation between two countries. To put it into practice, the Government of India decided to send a delegation of the Indian scientists. *The Hindustan Times*, of April 6th, 1944, shows that some the Indian scientists accepted the invitation, but Raman declined. Raman's omission was a matter of concern in India, and was interpreted as a nationalistic action, which fitted to the political situation of those days. A local periodical *The Blitz* on October 28th, 1944 reported:

> An Indian Scientists Mission without C. V.? A Hamlet without the Prince of Denmark! No, the clue perhaps lay elsewhere; C. V. Raman is not merely a scientist, dead to all life around. He is also a patriot. Under Prof. Hill's auspices, in a mission sponsored by the Government of India, will they be touring at own will? Will they be touring at their free discretion? Is there a free Government behind them? C. V. Raman is a great scientist, but not a good salesman for British wares.

After his return to England, Hill had prepared a report entitled, *Scientific Research in India*. It deals with various fields of research and possible cooperation between the scientists from the two countries. It was meant not only for war period, but also thereafter. It was a preparation for the so called the *Empire Scientific Conference*, which followed later. In the report, on pages 49 to 52 he wrote about different science academies. according to his opinion,

> Of the three, the body best suited by Constitution and membership to assume the role of a national academy

> of science, such as, The Royal Society (London), .... etc., is the National Institute of Sciences of India. It is oddly named for such a body, but that was due to a compromise which was necessary at the time it was founded.

Hill — a schrewed political-scientist — a representative of the Royal Society gave leading role to the NIS. It had far reaching consequences. It was evident that Raman and most of the south Indian scientists will not accept it.

For preparations for the *Empire Scientific Conference*, on March 1st 1945 a preliminary meeting was held in Delhi. The committee examined the subjects which were proposed by the Royal Society for discussion at the conference. Eight subjects for the evening sessions were proposed. Saha was suppose to prepare on *Nuclear Research, Scientific aspects of radio communication and Meteorological research and climate*. Bhabha had to communicate *Cosmic Rays*. In his absence, it was decided that Raman should prepare a paper on:

> Discussion of measures for improving the dissemination of scientific information within the Empire including the dissemination of scientific news to the public generally and of scientific and technical information to industry, as well as abstracting the library service.

If he did not wish to represent a paper, MN Saha was requested to do so. Sahni attended the meeting. His name did not appear in the list of those whose were to present a paper. However, in the list of *Subject for evening session* he was the last person.

On March 4th, 1946 Bhatnagar as the Director of Council of Scientific and Industrial Research (CSIR) wrote a letter to Edward Appelton — Secretary, Department of Scientific and Industrial Research, London and sent the names of candidates for the Empire Scientific Conference. Raman, Saha and Sahni appeared as the first three candidates, but they were listed as unofficial delegates, while Bhatnagar and 7 more as official candidates, with Bhatnagar as the leader of official delegation. The list was forwarded to OF Brown — Department of Scientific and Industrial Research, London on March 5th, 1946. Next day, that is, on March 6th, 1946 Bhatnagar sent a list to Alfred Egerton — Secretary of the Royal Society. Though the list contains the same candidates, the order in the list is not so as that of date March 4th, 1946.

It seems the Royal Society was not happy with the list, which was sent by the Government of India. A letter from the Office of the High Commissioner for India, London reached to the Secretary of the India. In part it reads: The Royal Society have now enquired which one of the Indian Deligates would be its leader, adding, in this connection, that amongst those named in the list Sir C. V. Raman is the senior Indian Fellow. I am to request that the information now asked for may kindly be sent as early as possible and preferably by cable. The Government of India took a diplomatic step. Its representative H. V. R. Iengar on March 13th, 1946 sent the following reply:

> In view of certain delicate personal problems of which Prof. Hill will be aware, we have decided not to appoint anyone as leader of the Delegation. Bhatnagar will be leader only of the official group and we propose that he should be treated as convener of the Delegation for purposes of general conference.

In January 1946, the Economic and Overseas Department sent a copy to Bhatnagar, in which a Programme for the British Commonwealth Scientific Conference was chalked out. The conference was to take place in July 1946. Though the Presidents or the Nominee of the three Academies were invited, Raman refused to join. As we have seen above, the NIS was declared by Hill as the real Academy. Raman wrote to Akbar Hydari — Member-in-charge of the Department of Planning and Development (Delhi). In the same letter he pointed out that his action should not be understood as disrespect to the Government and further:

> I am most anxious that my action should not be misunderstood by that society which had treated me with great consideration during the past years.

He requested Hydari to forward a copy of this letter and also about his withdrawal from the delegation to the Royal Society.

From the forgoing discussion, one gets the impression, as if Raman was an egoist and self-centered, considering his own interest, trying to bring his Academy in the centre. It is only a minor part of the story. The fact is that he had different understanding of science and politics as we shall see below. To argue the case I give three examples from different periods.

Already in the 1930s, a local newspaper *The Leader*, (December 2nd, 1931) give some glimpses on this issue. While addressing convocations at the alumni of the Agra and Allahabad Universities he mentioned that the universities should be freed from the baneful effects of political intrusion.

> The day when universities are run not by your teachers but by your politicians will be the day when Indian will slip down on the road and become a fifth class power like Rumania and Bulgaria. She will not then be able to rise the height of Great Britain and Germany.

The second case is directly related to the Royal Society. After Hill's visit and the role played by the Royal Society in the following years, Raman judged the political situation correctly. In the late-1940s he felt the political elements are dominating in the Royal Society, as is evident from the following statement:

> We need not to look at the Royal Society for guidance. The Royal Society today, in spite of its distinguished past, was unfortunately tending to become more a political than a purely scientific body. Some of the official of the Royal Society seemed to be more interested in maintaining British connections with India than to any purely scientific research. The mixture of politics and science ... was not likely to prove a success and it was not well that Indian had taken a step, which would enable her to take an independent line in the international scientific field.

Even in independent India Raman reflected his way of thinking again. For instance, after 1948 he hardly ever attended the Indian Science Congress..., on the ground that they are inaugurated by politicians. ... The politician who invariably inaugurated the yearly Congress from 1949 until his death in 1964 was Jawaharlal Nehru.

Raman who did not agree with the existing development in India, distanced himself from the state policies, but continued his scientific activities in the IAS and the Raman Research Institute.

To conclude we see that Raman was a politically active scientist, but his understanding of the relation between scientists and the state was different. He was of the opinion that politicians should take the advise of scientists, and not others way round.

Raman's invitations to Western men of science was a partial success. One of the reasons being a lack of support from the colonial government. Obviously, the success of a project depends on financial support. Interpreting the above story in European context, it can be suggested that bodies like the Royal Society (London) will play active roles to push the benefits their own countries.

So far the migration of individual scientist with European Community is concerned, it will be influenced by monetary and scientific factors.

## Sir C. V. Raman and His Contacts with Hungarian Scientists

### *Raman's Nominators*

***Karoly Tangl (1869-1940):*** Tangl was assistant to Baron Lorand [Roland] Eotvos (1848-1919) — who was known as the 'Grand Old Man' of Hungarian Physics. Tangl later became a Professor of Experimental Physics at the University of Budapest. Due to his efforts cosmic radiation and crystal physics in Budapest were initiated. However, his still greater contribution to Hungarian physics was to select and promote talented students. For instance, in the end of the first decade of the twentieth century he took Rudolf Ortvay (1885-1945) as his assistant. Later Tangl sent him to the University of Gottingen (Germany), which was a centre of learning in Europe in those days. Again it was due to Tangl that Ortvay had the chance to work under Arnold Sommerfeld (1868-1951) — one of the founders of modern atomic physics and known as a great authority. In the Hungarian science community (which was dominated by theoretical physicists), Tangl's pupils Zoltan Gyulai and Sandor Szalay established experimental researches in the field of crystal and nuclear physics at the University of Debrecen.

***Rudolf Ortvay (1885-1945):*** Unfortunately, due to the political situation the Hungarian science suffered much during the first half of the twentieth century. Some of its scientists like Todor [Theodore] von Karman (1881-1963), Gyorgy [George] de Hevesy (1885-1966) and Leo Szilard (1898-1964) were forced to emigrate for fear of right-extremists, where as Jeno [Eugene] P. Wigner (1902-95), Ede [Edward] Teller (1908-...), Janos [John] von Neumann (1903-57) went abroad due to the spreading anti-Semitism in their home land. They returned to their native land for short periods under favourable conditions. However, the case of Rudolf Ortvay is different.

Ortvay is supposed to be the man who 'kept physics alive in Hungary by his famous colloquia', which he initiated in 1929. He is considered as 'Pioneer of Modern Physics'. Ortvay who early was interested in medical and biology later spend some time under scientists Peter Debye (1884-1966) and Arnold Sommerfeld in Zurich and Munchen respectively. After finishing his education he taught at Kolozsvar (today Cluj-Napoca, Rumania), Budapest and Szeged Universities. His fields of interest were the theory of relativity, corpuscular theory of matter, and quantum mechanics. Already in 1930s, when quantum mechanics was in its infancy Ortvay organised teacher training on quantum mechanics.

Ortvay was one of the main linking persons between Hungarian and foreign physicists. He nominated renowned scientists like Arnold Sommerfeld, Arthur Eddington (1882-1944), Niels Bohr (1885-1962), P. Debye, Max Planck (1858-1947) and C. V. Raman for the Fellowship of the HAS.

### *Raman's Hungarian Connections*

Ortvay who visited India delivered two lectures at the Indian Institute of Sciences, Bangalore. The lectures published in the journal, *Current Science*, Bangalore are valuable documents to give some background of Hungarian-Indian connections. In one of the lectures entitled *Physics in Hungary - Past and Present - 1*, the author informed that the Hungarian Sandor [Alexander] Korosi-Csoma, whose tomb was in Darjeeling, was the first person to compile a vocabulary of the Tibetan language. In the same communication after praising Baron Eotvos' work in the field of gravity and capillarity he stated that these methods were used in the field of oil/petroleum production. Three expeditions related to this topic were made between 1923 and 1926 in different parts of India under the leadership of Pekar Dezso, who directed these researches as Head of the Eotvos Geophysical Institute.

In 1927, nearly 10 years before Ortvay's visit, Von Karman, known for his work on lattice- and aerodynamics visited Calcutta. However, his interest was to meet the great Indian politician Mohan Das Gandhi. In his memoir *The Wind and Beyond,* Von Karman wrote about a scientist from Delhi who made possible this contact and arranged a talk with Mahatma Gandhi. As a technician Von Karman found Gandhi's ideas anti-scientific and classical primitive. Whether he met Raman or any other physicist in Calcutta is uncertain. After many years, that is, in 1961 he (Von Karman) was elected Foreign Fellow of the Indian Academy of Sciences. Other Hungarian scientists to become Fellows of the IAS were Pal [Paul] Erdos (1913-1996) — a genius mathematician, and G. Hevesy (elected in 1950). The latter who is known for the discovery of the element Hafnium and the reception of the Nobel Prize in 1943 had closer contacts with Raman.

Hevesy, who due to political reasons, had voluntarily resigned his position on October 16, 1919 and on April 12, 1920 his lecturing right was revoked, later moved to Denmark to work with the eminent Danish physicist N. Bohr in his newly founded Institute in Copenhagen. There he stayed between 1920 and 1926. Raman came in contact with Hevesy during one of his visits to Denmark. For example on February 25, 1925. Hevesy wrote to the Director of Radium Institute in Vienna, Stefan Meyer (1872-1949) about Raman's visit.

It is well known that in Germany after Adolf Hitler came in power a law was passed that allowed the state to send a person in pre-mature retirement or devoid of his position under different pretexts. Scientists of Jewish origin or belonging to the political opposition were affected by it. Many left the country. Ernest Rutherford (1871-1937) — the famous British physicist known for his atomic model — on September 12,1933 in a letter expressed his grievances for Hevesy if he had to leave his laboratory at the Institute for Physical Chemistry at the University of Freiburg,

Germany. In July 1934 Hevesy himself asked for his dismissal and the request was met on August 25, 1934. Before this incident a special Readership in Chemistry created by Raman with tine consent of the Council was offered to Hevesy. According to the Minutes of the Council of the IIS, dated July 16-17,1934:

> "The Director laid before the Council the unanimous recommendation of the Senate that Professor George Hevesy and Dr. Max Born be appointed as Reader in Chemistry ... for a period of six months during the year. This recommendation had been circulated to the Council together with a proposal that the honorarium for the period of 6 months ... be fixed at Rs. [Rupees] 15,000 inclusive of all expenses".

And further it was stated that 'A reply had been received from Professor Hevesy expressed his willingness to spend a period of six months at Bangalore from I$^{s}$ October, 1934, to 31$^{st}$ March, 1935'. Under Resolution III this appointment was approved by the Council.

In August 1934 Hevesy wrote a letter to Rutherford and informed him about his resignation in Germany and his wish to move to Copenhagen in the middle of September. In the same communication he stated,

> "Raman invited me to spend the winter in Bangalore and take over temporarily the Chemical Institute. To spend a winter in India where I have not yet been is very tempting especially as the conditions offered are very liberal, however it is very doubtful if it will be possible to me to postpone the beginning of my activities in Copenhagen".

Just a month ago, i.e. in July 1934, Hevesy wrote a letter to the physicist James Franck (1882-1964) who had been immigrated to the United States; and informed about Raman's offer and asked for advice. He mentioned that the financial conditions were very good (total 1100 British Pounds). But from scientific and intellectual points of view he was sceptical and was of the opinion that he had hardly a chance to broaden up his knowledge in India. Also he was worried that he had to leave his children in Freiburg.

Apart from that in the middle of September (1935) he had to be in Copenhagen. On August 18, 1934 in the next letter Hevesy thanked Franck for the prompt reply. In the end he was happy to give up his Indian plan. It seems that he did not inform Raman immediately as the Minutes of the Council from November 19-20, 1934, page 12 suggest. Here it was reported that Hevesy accepted the invitation from October 1, 1935 onward for a period of six months under the early stated conditions. At which stage Hevesy gave his final decision is unknown.

Before we proceed further, in the above context, it will be worthwhile to see the case of German theoretical physicist Max Born, who accepted Raman's offer and came to India. Different authors have written about this stay. I have explored the details of Born-Raman issue in a separate article *'Max Born's role in the lattice dynamic controversy'*. There I have shown that from Born's private correspondences it is clear that his contract of three years in Cambridge was going to end. At the right time he got Raman's offer. Born's correspondence gives no clue about his expectations from this stay. According to his autobiography, his stay in India was scientifically uninteresting. Other authors also interpret Born's stay in India as not particularly productive scientifically. According to my own opinion, they ignore Born's five publications in the *Proceedings of the Indian Academy of Sciences,* and his activities for the cause of displaced Jews within India. Born initially came for six months. After Raman gave him a hope for permanent chair, Born wished to stay longer as the salary was good, Born's wife also felt happy, and moreover, Born was not feeling well with his refugee status in England and wanted to settle down definitely. That is what Max Born wrote to Paul Dirac on October 28, 1935.

***Ortvay in India:*** So far as Ortvay is concerned, it was Von Neumann who tried to help as is evident from Max Born's letter to the British physicist Paul Adrien Maurice Dirac (1902-84). It reads: 'Ortvay is not an outstanding personality. May be that Raman has never heard of him. But I leave it to you to decide whether you will respond to Von Neumann's wish' However, Born suggested Dirac to contact Raman who might arrange some lectures. But for a long time there was no reply, as Raman was in a critical position due to disputes in the IIS. In order to avoid further delay Born wrote to Raman's assistant P. Krishnamurty and asked to contact Raman's pupils in Calcutta or Waltair (Andhra Pradesh). Most probably due to the Born-Dirac plea, Raman decided to help Ortvay.

On October 17, 1936, Ortvay informed Dirac that he had an invitation to deliver a lecture in Benares [Hindu University]. He was also expecting to get similar invitations from other universities and colleges in India. His plan was to sail with a German steamer 'Potsdam' on December 22" from Genoa and arrive in Colombo (Sri Lanka) the 2 of January (1937). He wished to stay in India for two months and visit Bangalore, Benares, Calcutta and Rangoon.

On December 22, 1936 Raman wrote to Ortvay that 'I shall be extremely delighted to welcome you to this Institute.... We shall be extremely pleased if you could give us one or two lectures on the subjects of your choice'.

For this work Ortvay was offered 350 Rupees. Dirac was informed about the invitations and friendly letters from Raman and the founder of Bose-Einstein statistics — [Satyandra Nath] Bose. Ortvay stayed in Ceylon and India nearly three months and delivered lectures in Bangalore, Benares, Calcutta and Waltair. 'Unfortunately I had spent only two weeks in Bangalore, which had the biggest scientific institute', wrote Ortvay.

There is no doubt that Ortvay was impressed by the hospitality of Indian physicists. After his return from India, he along with his teacher Tangl nominated Raman for the Honorary Foreign Membership of the HAS, as is obvious from Raman's letter that he wrote on June 24, 1937. It reads:

> "I am sorry for the delay in replying to your kind letter of the 24th March (1937) from Kandy (The Hotel Suisse-Kandy Limited, Manager's Office, Ceylon). Since receiving it, I have also read your letter of 14th May and Archduke Joseph's letter informing me of my election to the honorary foreign membership of the Hungarian Academy of Sciences. I appreciate this honour very much indeed, and I am grateful to you for having proposed me for it".

Raman who was always conscious to make the work of Indian scientists known abroad lost no opportunity and in the same letter wrote: 'I am ... arranging that the Hungarian Academy will get the Proceedings of the Indian Academy of Sciences regularly'.

It seems in the following years there was no deep contact as the nominators expired in the 1940s. Apart from that the political factors also played an important role. Hungary adopted the political and economic system shaped on the pattern of the Soviet Union. The HAS was reorganised, and got the status of a supreme scientific body. However, the negative effects were that the humanity and arts group scientists as well as persons 'unfit for a political system' were no more members of the Academy. In 1989 all those members which were unjustly excluded in 1949 from the Academy were rehabilitated.

### *Raman's Visit to Hungary*

Under these political changes, the membership of the Foreign Fellows was also affected. The Hungarian scientific community found Raman as a worthy Fellow and in 1958 he was re-elected. Istvan Rusznyak — President of the Hungarian Academy of Sciences confirmed his early election of November 21, 1937 and on June 17, 1958 wrote to Raman as follows: 'I have the pleasure to invite you and your wife to participate at the meeting taking place in honour of your visit to Hungary'. Raman gladly accepted this invitation, to visit this country second time.

In Hungary, Raman and his wife were entertained by the Hungarian scientific community. Under the auspices of the Hungarian Physical Society, Raman delivered three lectures on *"The physics of crystals"*. Raman not only visited Budapest, the capital of Hungary but also the University of Szeged. Raman gave an informal talk on *"The discovery of the Raman-effect"* at the Physical Institute of the Szeged University. The participants of the talk were the Hungarian scientists Agoston Budo, Istvan Kecskemety, Laszlo Szalay, Jozsef Dombi, R. Horvai, Jozsef Gyulai, Ferenc Pinter, Laszlo Gombai.

***Raman's Talk at the University of Szeged:*** As in his unpublished lecture (its copy was supplied to the present author by Professor Laszlo Kovacs) there are some less known aspects, it is worthwhile to reproduce its details. Raman told that he enjoyed to see the blue colour of the sea. He asked himself why it was blue and stated:

> "During sunshine, I investigated the scattering of light at the surface of the sea. In the meantime I held lectures in Bombay on X-ray spectra. I discussed the phenomenon on the basis of the wave theory of light. The audience of the lectures were very pleased with the lectures and they (promised me to) publish them and offered 500 Rupees, if I would write down the text. I wanted to get 500 Rs., and I wanted to write the lectures for publication, but I was busy, I had no time. In the meantime I read a book on X-rays, discussed on the basis of the particle model of light. I saw that I have to rethink the text of my lectures. I have a keen interest to know which discussion is true. I worked a lot, calculated all things on the basis of the wave theory. All were O. K, except the Compton-effect. It could not explain the larger wavelengths of the scattered X-rays" (Tr. from Hungarian).

Raman, who in between derived 'A classical derivation of the Compton effect' informed in the talk that 'I thought there must exist an analogy in visible light as well. I made scattering experiments'.

He went on,

> "The sunlight was passed through a dark blue filter to the water and the scattered light was observed with the help of a mica grating. I used simply a paper tube. It was closed with a slit on one end, and the grating on the other end. In this very simple spectroscope, I have seen in the scattered light in addition to the blue region a pale (faint) green stripe; this light was very weak. I used a green filter and I observed in the scattered light a yellow stripe. It seemed I found the analogy of the Compton effect because of the appearance of the larger wavelengths. I have also to know if the larger wavelengths of the

light were coming really from the scattered light. They could come as a luminescence in the water as well. I saw two ways to find the real answer. First I investigated the polarisation of the scattered light. I found that the degree of the polarisation was greater. We know from the investigations of Vavilov, that the polarisation of the emitted luminescence is greater in the viscous solution, in the water practically zero. Second I visually investigated the scattered light of a mercury lamp [presumably light scattered by probe] using a simple spectrometer. I found in the spectra in addition to the strong mercury lines (which were thick in my spectroscope) new lines (not a diffuse strip) in the region of the larger wavelengths. If the primary light was more monochromatic the strip in the larger wavelengths region was narrower. This situation does not exist in luminescence. I was sure that I had discovered the optical analogy of the Compton effect. Later this effect was named Raman-effect. Naturally I investigated the phenomena with a better spectroscope as well. I began these investigation in 1924 and finished in 1928.1 was nominated for the Nobel Prize in 1929, and the prize was going to me next year" (Tr. from Hungarian).

So far as the first part of Raman's lecture is concerned there is nothing to comment. However, the section related to the experimental work needs careful reading, as it differs from the narration given in the two publications from the year 1928. For instance, in their first paper "A new type of secondary radiation", Raman and his co-worker K. S. Krishnan used sun as source of light and, they write:

> "A blue-violet filter, when coupled with a yellow-green filter and placed in the incident light, completely extinguished the track of the light through the liquid or the vapour. The reappearance of the track when the yellow filter is transferred to a place between it and the observer's eye is proof of the existence of a modified scattered radiation".

In the above referred paper they stated that the intensity and the polarisation being different than in the case of fluorescence (which is an effect also with change of wave length). Thus they were sure that a new effect has been discovered.

In the second publication related to the discovery, Raman stated:

> "A greater surprise was provided by the spectroscopic observations. Using sunlight with a blue filter as the illuminant, the modified scattered radiation was readily detected by the appearance in the spectrum of the scattered light of radiation absent from the incident light. With a suitably chosen filter in the incident light, the classical and modified scatterings appeared as separate regions in the spectrum separated by a dark region. This encouraged us to use a mercury arc the source of light..".

The comparison of published paper and unpublished lecture shows that: Firstly in the lecture Raman did not mention the complementary filter method, which was the real step towards discovery.

Secondly, in the publications there is no mention of mica grating and a provisional spectroscope (made out of paper tube, slit and grating). Also, Raman's other publications show that he started intensively his work on scattering in 1921-1922 and not in 1924. The difference between the two statements seems to be due to the fact that Raman recalled an event after about 30 years.

***Last Phase:*** After Raman's personal visit, the contact between the two academies became closer. In the beginning of the 1960s, Gyorgy [George] Szigeti — an ordinary member of the HAS was elected an honorary fellow of the Indian Academy of Sciences to which Rusznyak responded as follows: 'I was pleased to learn that [Szeigeti has been elected as member of the IAS]....I consider this recognition is a further step in making the scientific relations between our scientists and Academies closer'. Obviously, the contact between Raman and Hungarian scientists were more than simple honours.

The last available document on Raman-Hungarian connection is his letter to Dr. Janoshoz [John] Horvath, in which Raman thanked for a copy of a paper on *"The Internal Structure of Physical Fields"*.

### *The Summary*

George de Hevesy who was invited by Raman for the Readership in Chemistry at the Indian Institute of Sciences, Bangalore, did not come to India as he preferred to stay in Copenhagen. He was of the opinion that he could not broaden his knowledge in India.

Raman though outside Europe and America was a part of the international scientific community. Raman's deep contacts with the Hungarian Scientific Community began due to Ortvay's visit to India in the middle of the 1930s and continued for the following three decades. These contacts brought the two scientific academies closer.

Raman's lecture based on reminiscence on the discovery of the Raman effect delivered in Hungary has some contradictory statements to the publications in *Nature.* This indicates that the sources based on reminiscence need careful evaluation by the historians.

## C. V. Raman's Dutch Connections

There are a number of biographies about C. V. Raman, who in 1930 brought the Nobel Prize in Physics to the 'East side of the Suez' and also brought Indian science to the international scene. Though different aspects of his life have been elaborated, his contacts with Dutch scientists and an invitation for the Zeeman Chair are almost unknown.

### *Life and Times of Raman*

Raman lived in Calcutta for 25 years, where he started his career as a young scientist, founded an Indian School of Physics and won the Nobel Prize. That was the 'Golden Period' of his life. Due to his popularity, he was offered the directorship of the Indian Institute of Science (IISc). Soon after his arrival administrative controversies broke out, the details of which have been given by Venkataraman and Subbarayappa.

Raman had been humiliated. He would have preferred to leave the Institute if he had got the chance. In fact such a chance came in his life. He was asked to take the Zeeman Chair at the University of Amsterdam. Before we give the details, it will be appropriate to give a short biography of Pieter Zeeman and his contacts with Raman.

### *Pieter Zeeman (1865-1943)*

The extracted biographical data of Zeeman's life are taken from well-known references. Zeeman who together with H. A. Lorentz (1853-1928) was awarded the Nobel Prize in 1902, is known for the discovery of the Zeeman effect. It deals with the splitting of spectral lines in magnetic fields and was later recognised as a consequence of the spin of the electron. The effect provides information on the mechanism of light radiation and on the nature of matter, i.e. it reveals the intimate structure of the atom and behaviour of its components.

Zeeman was born in a small village in Holland. After finishing his schooling he entered the University of Leiden. In 1894 he finished his Ph.D. and later became 'Privatdozent' (extra-mural lecturer) at the same place, where he discovered the above mentioned effect in 1896.

In 1908 Zeeman became the Director of the Physics Laboratory. As precision measurement in the field of electromagnetism is rather sensitive to vibrations a special laboratory was built for him in 1923, to perform vibration-free experiments. He worked here from 1897 until his retirement in 1935.

Zeeman's scientific work had profound implications in the theory of relativity, investigations of the magnetic resolution of spectral lines of certain noble gases, study of hyperfine structure and Zeeman effect of the strong spectral lines of rhenium.

### *Raman-Zeeman Contact*

In 1924, following an invitation from the British Association for the Advancement of Science Raman went to Canada. From there he travelled to the United States, where he was invited by the Nobel Laureate R. A. Millikan (1868-1953) to stay at the California Institute of Technology, Pasadena. Raman met Zeeman during this visit. Zeeman recalled, 'I enjoy remembering our meeting in Philadelphia' (Zeeman to Raman, dated 11 July 1931).

Raman's first letter to Zeeman dated back to 12 June 1931, in which he invited the latter to become an honorary fellow of the Indian Association for the Cultivation of Science. On 11 July 1931 Zeeman replied: '. . . It was a great pleasure for me to receive your letter. I accept with authensiasm (enthusiasm) the Foreign Membership of a Society on which your name sheds a special lusture. Will you be so kind as to interpret my feelings of gratitude to the Council and members of the Society.' Nearly four years later Raman's second letter followed in which he asked Zeeman to accept the Fellowship of the Indian Academy of Sciences, Bangalore which was founded in April 1934.

In 1937 Raman visited different uni-versities in Bologna, Vienna, Berlin, Copenhagen, Amsterdam and Liege. During his stay in Amsterdam, Raman was asked to take the prestigious Zeeman Chair as his letter to a British physicist O. W. Richardson (1879-1959) shows. It follows: '... Among... many interesting experiences of the tour, was an offer I received to take up the Professorship of Physics at the Amsterdam University vacant by the retirement of Prof. Zeeman. I am considering the offer and have been allowed time to make my decision.' (Raman to Richardson, dated 8 November 1937).

It is a tradition in some of the European countries that a person to be asked for a chair, is allowed to determine the material conditions under which he will like to work. These include salary, research laboratories, workers and other special allowances which are needed for his research work. Raman, who already had good contact with Western scientists must have known about that. But for this particular Zeeman Chair he needed more information. So he wrote to Zeeman on 10 January 1938: 'As you may probably be aware, I have written accepting generally the call of the Faculty of Amsterdam to be your successor and have now to state the terms of appointment which would be agreeable to me. In this connection, I am urgently in need of information on the following points (about the type of appointment – permanent or not, salary, scholarships and annual grants for material and journals) regarding the position held by you, and shall be most highly obliged if you can kindly give the same.'

Zeeman, who wanted to have a worthy successor, was convinced that Raman was a suitable candidate. He wrote: 'It gives me great pleasure that you have written accepting generally the call of the Faculty of Science of Amsterdam University, to be my successor. I will now give you the informations you ask about the position held by me. . . . Of course I will give you all advices you will want.' (Zeeman to Raman, dated 28 January 1938). Zeeman had written a long letter, in which he gave details about his salary, laboratory conditions and his assistants.

### *International Reputation and Local Consideration*

Raman was not only in contact with Zeeman, but also with Clay, Michels and Brouwer. Brouwer was the Dean of the Physics Department at the University of Amsterdam. The correspondence between Raman and some of the professors at the University of Amsterdam shows that the scientists were in favour of Raman's selection. On 23 February 1938 Raman wrote to Clay: 'I hope by this time, the Dean of the Faculty (Dr. Brouwer) would have received my letter of the 26th January, stating my wishes (...) and that the Faculty and the Curatorium would have supported them. I shall be much obliged if you can kindly write me a few lines as soon as the Curatorium has made its decision in the matter.'

At the initial stage there were some doubts whether Raman would continue Zeeman's work. If he started an entirely new programme, the apparatus and laboratory which was placed at his disposal would be of no use. With regard to this problem Raman wrote to Clay on 16 March 1938, '. . . There are still many important problems in light-scattering, spectroscopy, magnetism and magneto-optics in the solution of which I am interested, and in calling me to Amsterdam, your University may feel fully assured that the equipment collected by Professor Zeeman will be fully employed.' His case was strengthened as Clay was willing to collaborate with Raman as indicated in one of the letters. Thus this objection was swept away and the Curatorium wanted to support Raman for the Chair. However, Clay knew that there were people with a different opinion, and wrote 'I think the opposition will not have enough force against our unanimous decision' (Clay to Raman, undated letter).

Although most of the physicists in Amsterdam University preferred Raman, there were some who wanted to have a Dutchman as Zeeman's successor. For example: '. . . It is my opinion (strictly personal opinion!) that the vacancy left by Zeeman can only be fulfilled by a foreigner in the case no fellow countryman can be found that can be considered a serious candidate. For this reason I contacted the physicists outside Amsterdam, to learn their opinion on this matter. They gave me the names of Goudsmit, de Groot and Casimir and they feel that from these three names a recommendation of two persons could well be made.' (van der Waals to Zeeman, dated 11 March 1938, translated from Dutch). Although the Curators believed that Raman was an excellent scholar and an attractive offer for the university they wrote to Zeeman, '. . . we are of the opinion that such an appointment also has its risks and its drawbacks for the education. We would be willing to put these aside, in the case we had the certainty that no Dutch citizen would be available, who, on the basis of his performances, or, in case he would be young, with regard to the future, could be considered worthy to fulfil this chair' (Curators of the University to Zeeman, dated 25 April 1938, translated from Dutch). The authorities argued that teaching might suffer as Raman would not be able to teach in Dutch.

Unfortunately, circumstances were not in favour of Raman and his advocates. His supporters were equally disappointed as the letter shows. It follows: 'Curatorium fears insurmountable difficulties to carry through your appointment in the municipality. The burgomaster means, he cannot take the responsibility of an echec (failure) of your candidature. On the other hand the faculty decided not to change its opinion, but cannot hope, this changes anything, because the Curatorium only has the right of the nomination' (Clay to Raman, dated 8 July 1938). Raman in his last letter thanked Clay, Michels, and Brouwer as: 'I can never forget the honour of the invitation of your Faculty and their enthusiastic support of my appointment' (Raman to Clay, dated 19 July 1938).

Although Raman was unconditionally supported by the faculty and Zeeman the final decision of the Curatorium was to search for a Dutch scientist. Besides the municipality and a few scientists in The Netherlands, some other European scientists were not in favour of Raman. One of the founders of quantum mechanics W. Pauli (1900-58) wrote, 'I am happy that Raman does not come to Amsterdam, . . .' (Pauli to Uhlenbeck, dated 27 July 1938, translated from German).

It was well known among European scientists that definitely this position was for a Dutch only. Pauli observed, '... In case Goudsmit does not accept and a non-Dutchman can be considered, subjectively I think it will be correct to appoint K. W. Meissner. ... Do you think that it makes sense to write to Zeeman or Goudsmit in this case?' (Pauli to Uhlenbeck, dated 27 July 1938, translated from German).

Finally the Zeeman Chair was offered to the Dutch physicist S. A. Goudsmit (1902-78), who together with G. E. Uhlenbeck (1900-88) discovered the spin of the electron. Although it was a great honour to succeed Zeeman, Goudsmit did not accept the offer as he was afraid that due to the tension between Germany and its neighbouring countries a war could break out in Europe at any time. He preferred to continue his work in the United States.

A. J. Kox who is Pieter Zeeman Professor of History of Physics at the University of Amsterdam wrote, 'The procedure to find a successor to Zeeman dragged on for about 5 years: from his [Zeeman] retirement in 1935 to the appointment of C. J. Gorter in 1940' (private communication). C. J. Gorter (1907-80) was known for his work in the field of super conductivity, the loss of electrical resistance at temperatures close to absolute zero.

### *Summary*

Due to his outstanding status among the Western scientific community, Raman was invited for the prestigious Zeeman Chair at the University of Amsterdam. He was supported by Pieter Zeeman and the faculty of physics, but the local government was opposed to him and by all means wanted to have a Dutch for the chair. The case for Raman was rejected with the argument that education of the students would suffer since Raman did not know Dutch language. The authorities might have given him a chance if he would have been younger.

## Raman and American Scientists

In 1928 C. V. Raman and Kariamanikam Srinivasa Krishnan (1898-1961) observed that if monochromatic light is passed through a transparent medium, thereafter the scattering light is accompanied by other colours. This phenomenon was later named as Raman effect. The effect helps to find out the molecular structure of substances. In 1930 Raman was awarded the Nobel Prize for his work on "light scattering and the discovery of the effect" named after him. Raman was the first Asian to receive this honour. This made him extremely popular. During Raman's lifetime and there after a number of biographies appeared. However, none of them explores his contacts with the American scientific community. The following communication is intended to fulfil this gap.

### *Raman's Visit to USA, His Contacts and the Honour by the Franklin Institute*

It is a well-known story that in 1907, the young C. V. Raman after finishing his education and competing the Finance Services Examinations came to Calcutta as a bank officer. During his spare time he did research at the Indian Association for the Cultivation of Sciences (IACS) and was offered a Professorship due to his popularity as a researcher. After some consideration, in 1917, he accepted the "Palit Professor Chair" of the University of Calcutta. First time in his life, in 1921, he went to Oxford (England) at the Congress of British Universities to represent the Calcutta and Banaras Hindu Universities.

In the 1924 Annual Report of the IACS, before informing about his participation in the International Congress of Mathematician held in Toronto in August 1924, Raman reported that:

> "He received an invitation from the British Association for the Advancement of Science [BAAS] to attend the meeting to be held at Toronto in Canada in August and to be opener of a discussion on the scattering of light".

The report of the BAAS shows that Raman delivered a lecture on light scattering research being carried out in his laboratory. The BAAS and Calcutta University gave him a substantial grant that enabled him to travel to Canada and then proceed to America.

### *Raman, Arthur Holly Compton and Light Quanta*

In 1923 the American physicist A. H. Compton (1892-1962) observed that the x-rays scattered by the free (loosely bounded) electrons experience a change in wavelength. This effect was later named as the Compton effect. Just a year later at the BAAS meeting he presented the experimental results that were interpreted in terms of light quanta – a concept disputed in those days. His countrymen William Duane of Harvard University and Raman took active part in the discussion. Particularly Duane who could not reproduce Compton's results did not believe Compton. In his memoirs, Compton recalled that Raman said to him, *"Compton, you're a very good debater; but the truth isn't in you"*. The authors Roger H. Stuewer and A. Sur interpreted Raman's statement as evidence that he did not accepted Einstein's light-quantum hypothesis.

After Toronto meeting Raman left for the USA and stayed with Robert A. Millikan (1868-1953).

### *C. V. Raman and the Nobel Laureate Robert A. Millikan*

It is not quite clear, how Raman came in contact with Millikan. However, *The New York Times* of November 22, 1970 hints that Millikan encouraged Raman to come to the USA. In September (1924), at the Centenary of the Franklin Institute, he represented the IACS. Between September 20, 1924 and December 16, 1924, Raman was appointed as a Research Associate and Visiting Professor at the California Institute of Technology. During this period, he also met scientists Irving Langmuir (1881-1957), Albert W. Hull (1880-1966), William D. Coolidge (1873-1975) and other staffs of General Electric Company.

It was entirely different experience for the Americans to have an Indian physicist, because, in general, the Indians were seen as persons related to religion and philosophy. It is clear from the statement of President of the Institute Clinton K. Judy who introduced Raman as follows: "Most Hindu coming to this country talk on philosophy, and it is a distinct novelty to have one who is more in accord with Western scholarship".

*The Pas Star News* (presently Pasadena, California) on November 12, 1924 announced Raman's lecture on the musical instruments as follows:

> "Raman stands out as one of the most productive scientists of the Orient. He has already done a surprising amount of high-grade scientific work himself and has stimulated a great deal more among his students. His publications on the mechanical theory of stringed instruments have made him an internationally known authority upon the subject about which he is speaking".

About five weeks later again on December 19, 1924, *The Pas Star News* wrote:

> "Prof. C. V. Raman, noted Indian scientist...., yesterday addressed an enthusiastic audience of more than 300 teachers, students and graduates of the California Institute of Technology on the subject of *'The scattering of light and its relation to atomic and molecular structure'*".

And further:

> "His lecture was illustrated with many experiments, given in such a simple and direct manner that they could be easily understood by less scientific audience than that present. In one demonstration, the scientist gave a remarkable view of the setting sun, which he obtained by using liquid encased in a square glass receptacle in the receptor of a projector instead of a scale".

The above descriptions written shortly after the lectures show that there were many audiences and Raman's lectures were well attended. This is in contrary to the observation of the Norwegian physicist Svein Rosseland's (1894-1985) conversation with S. Chandrasekhar (1910-1995), who once recalled: *"Apparently Raman was not too happy that he was not generally known in the United States. He was even more disappointed that so very few came to his lectures".*

Another American scientist from the University of California Ernest Orlando Lawrence (1901-58) also had correspondence with Raman. For instance, on February 9, 1932 he thanked Raman for reprints of his paper on the spin of photon, which was published in *Nature.* He informed Raman that his name is in their mailing list and the latter will get the reprints whenever he (Lawrence) will publish.

With Millikan, Raman's contact remained in tact for long time. In the beginning of 1940, Millikan and his co-workers Henry Victor Neher (1904-99) and William H. Pickering (1910-present) came to Bangalore to perform experiments on cosmic rays. They also delivered 4 lectures. Millikan's first communication of January 26, 1940, was on the history of cosmic rays and their measurement. *The Hindu* of February 4, 1940 wrote an article on *"The mystery of cosmic rays — Prof. Millikan on the investigations".*

A few years later, that is, on January 5,1945 Raman wrote a letter to Millikan and introduced K. L. Ramaswamy who was visiting the USA for his chemical business. Due to some circumstances, Ramaswamy was unable to meet Millikan. The latter, on June 9, 1945 sent the following message for Raman: *"Please extend to Sir C. V. Raman and his whole family my greetings. Mrs. Millikan and I still treasure greatly the memory of the two or three weeks which we spent under his hospitable roof'.* Obviously, Raman had cordial relations with Millikan. As we shall see below, it was not the case with his contemporary W. H. Zacheriasen - an X-ray physicists at the University of Chicago.

### *W. H. Zacheriasen, C. V. Raman and Diffuse Spots in the Laue X-RAYS Photographs*

In the end of 1930s and the beginning of 1940s some diffuse spots were observed by American, Indian, British and French scientists independently. From India C. V. Raman and P. Nilakantan (1910-1964) from the Indian Institute of Sciences were the two persons who observed the phenomenon. Due to the question of priority and the theoretical interpretation of the spots, there was controversy between the first three groups.

Unfortunately, too less is known about Raman's partner P. Nilakantan. The fact is, while the controversy was going on, in the beginning of 1940s he visited Zacheriasen. About the visit the latter wrote as follows to the theoretical physicist Max Born (1882-1970) - who was supporting the British group and opposing Raman:

> "You may be interested to learn that I yesterday had a visit from Dr. Nilakantan who collaborated with Raman. Although he was very pleasant person, he is quite as stubborn as his teacher and is still insisting that their explanation is the only correct one".

Due to the Second World War, Zacheriasen was forced to leave his field of research. However, Raman was in better position. To make his theory of lattice dynamics known and to counter his critics in the USA, Raman sent the *Proceedings of the Indian Academy of Science* to Leonard Benedict Loeb, who on February 25, 1942 replied that *"I have received the complimentary copy of the symposium of papers on the 'quantum theory of X-ray reflection'"*. Loeb stated that although these papers were somewhat outside his own field, yet he read them with considerable interest. In order to make them more generally available to the Department he has turned the volume over to the department library.

In the following years, *"Born-Raman lattice dynamics controversy"* continued, but Americans were not involved in it.

It seems, the American scientific community was not influenced by the controversy and decided to honour Raman with the Franklin Medal.

### *The Franklin Medal for C. V. Raman*

On March 12, 1941 Indians got the news that the Franklin Institute of Philadelphia, USA has honoured Sir C. V. Raman with Franklin Award. In the recent years the other scientists to get this honour were Albert Einstein (1879-1955), R. A. Millikan and A. H. Compton. (A Newspaper clip; copy with the author).

Raman was awarded the Franklin Medal in *"recognition of his many brilliant contributions to Physical Science and of his leadership in the renaissance of scientific work and scientific education that has occurred in India during the last thirty years"*. The Selection Committee was of the opinion that Raman has trained and inspired more than one hundred young scientists who now occupy strategic positions in the scientific and educational life of India. And further, it observed that nearly every institution in India devoted to research and education in science has benefited by Raman's influence and support.

The available documents show that officially, in May 1941, Raman was supposed to get the Franklin Medal and Diploma of Honorary Membership of the Franklin Institute. *The Indian Express* o/July 15, 1942 informed its readers that due to the Second World War, Raman could not go to USA to receive the medal. It was handed over to the British Ambassador Lord Halifax in Washington, who transmitted it to India. In the presence of small gathering at Mysore Residency, Arthur Hope -Governor of Madras decorated Raman. Other persons present were Lt.-Col. Fraser, J.C. Ghosh—Director of the India Institute of Sciences, Bangalore.

This honour did not remain the only one. As we shall see below, the American scientific community took interest in Raman's scientific achievements and in the last part of his life, he was honoured with the Fellowship of another American Society.

### *American's Interest in Raman's Scientific Work*

Raman largely worked in the fields of musical acoustics, light scattering, crystal dynamics, ultra sonic waves and the physiology of vision. It will be shown below that at all stages the American's scientific community took interest in Raman's work.

***Raman Effect and Robert William Wood (1868-1955):*** After the discovery of the Compton effect, in 1923, P.A. Ross (USA) tried to find similar effect in the case of visible light. He experimented with paraffin using Lummer-Gehrcke interferometer of resolving power 360, 000 and a wavelength of 546,2 nanometers. But he was not successful. Also according to the Indian astrophysicist Meghnad Saha (1893-1956), unsuccessful experiments to verify Kramers-Heisenburg theory (of dispersion and scattering of light) were carried out at Niels Bohr's laboratory at Copenhagen. Surely, Raman was aware of these results. *The. Statesman,* which announced Raman discovery on February 29, 1928 after describing Raman's results wrote: "*Shortly after the publication of Prof. Compton's discovery, other experimenters sought to find out whether a similar transformation occurs also when ordinary light is scattered by matter and reported negative results*".

At last the Indian physicists in Calcutta discovered the effect. However, their results were met with scepticism in Germany and the USA. In Germany at the University of Munich the physicists remained unsuccessful in producing Raman' results and even on theoretical basis the physicist Georg Joos (1894-1959) thought that the intensity of the light is too low to be observed. So far as the American R.W. Wood was concerned, the editor of *Nature* described his reaction as below:

> "He [Editor] received a letter from the Professor [Raman] referring to certain spectroscopic lines and putting forward what seemed to be an impossible theory. So incredible was Professor Raman's discovery, that before feeling prepared to publish it in *Nature* - ...He [Sir Richard] consulted Professor R.W. Wood of Baltimore who happened to be in London at the time. After reading Professor Raman's letter, Professor Wood declared, "I don't believe it!" Three weeks after the letter appeared in *Nature,* Professor Wood visited Sir Richard and said, 'Raman is right'".

In the Compton effect only the increase in wavelength takes place and also it depends on the angle of incidence. Whereas in the case of Raman effect both the increase and decrease in wavelength are observed and also it is independent of observation angle. Clearly, the second effect shows that a quanta (later named as photon) can take or give energy to a molecule. Probably, due to the generality of the effect, Wood hailed Raman's discovery as *"one of the most convincing proofs of the quantum theory of light which we have at the present time".*

In the beginning of 1933 Raman left Calcutta and came to the Indian Institute of Sciences, Bangalore. Just about 3 years later, he did a marvellous work in the field of ultrasonic, that is, the sound waves which cannot be heard.

## *Raman-Nath Diffraction and the American Reaction*

In 1932 the multiple diffraction of monochromatic light by the ultrasonic waves was observed by Peter Debye and Francis Weston Sears in the USA, and independently by Rene Auguste Lucas and Pierre Biquard in France. Richard Bar (1892-1940) and his colleague at Zurich (Switzerland) modified the experimental technique and studied the phenomenon in detail. In a sequel in the *Proceedings of the Indian Academy of Science,* Bangalore, Indian physicists Raman and Nagendra S. N. Nath -from the Indian Institute of Sciences, developed a theory and gave the explanation for the observed effects. About this work and the reaction of others *The Madras Mail,* on May 1,1936 wrote: *"An important scientific discovery - Results of research at the Indian Institute of Science - Diffraction of light waves. Raman received letters of congratulation from Europe and USA for Raman-Nath diffraction."*

After that Raman studied the properties of crystal and diamonds. His theory of lattice dynamics led to a long controversy with Max Born. As mentioned before, its detail are given by different authors.

Raman devoted the last phase of his scientific life to the studies on the physiology of vision.

## *C. V. Raman, George Wald and the Physiology of Vision*

Between 1960 and 1970, Raman wrote a number of papers and a monograph on the physiology of vision. Raman was convinced that*"his later work was even more grander and would have earned him a second Nobel Prize if only the academic world could comprehend it".*

Reading of Raman scientific papers related to this field shows that he hardly made use of existing literature. In the papers only once a list of books is recommended. In 1968, in the monograph *"The Physiology of Vision"* Raman seems to justify the omission of others work as follows: *"The aim of the studies was to obtain an insight into the subject by independent study without being influenced by ideas and belief inherited from the past".*

There are different opinions about the quality of this work. The editor S. Ramaseshan observed that the others working with complicated modern instruments *"felt, quite justifiably, that Raman's elementary experiments, ... were too simplistic for this complex field".* Partially due to his theories and partially due to ignoring the work of others, one of the renowned American bio-chemist George Wald had dislike for Raman.

Shortly after starting this new topic, Raman sent the *Memoirs of the Raman Research Institute* on the perception of light and colour to George Wald and his wife Ruth Hubbard - who were working in the Biological Laboratories of the Harvard University. G. Wald though not quite agreed with Raman's ideas, on April 18, 1961 wrote to Raman that:

> "I read it with great interest and enjoyed very much its clarity and directness. I am very happy also that vision has come to interest you to this degree, since I am spending most of my life with it and am happy to have much distinguished company".

In the same communication Wald informed Raman that at some points the former did not agree with. According to his [Wald's] years long work; pigment serves not as a photosensitive pigment in the blue receptors in eye, but as a filter. The pigments in human and primate retinas help to compensate the chromatic aberration of the eye, which is large in the blue region and tends to lower visual image resolution.

Raman promised to write on the role of the chemical xanthophyll ($C_{40}H_{56}O_2$ ) in the human vision in his letter of April 28, 1961 to Wald. In the same communication he also wrote that:

> "I am looking forward eagerly to receiving the publications of Dr. Ruth Hubbard and of yourself that you have sent. Some of them I have probably not read already and I have no doubt that the collected papers of your both on the subject would be most helpful to me in my further work in this field".

At least according to Raman's own statement, he was aware of Wald's work, however, he did not mention in his publications.

On June 1, 1961 Raman thanked Wald for the 11 reprints he received. After that the communication ceased.

Raman in between had spent a few years on the physiology of vision. Donald L. Fuller - Scientific Attache of the USA Ambassador in Delhi, on December 31, 1964 wrote a letter to Frederick Seitz - President of the National Academy of Sciences and informed the latter that at the occasion of the 30th session of the Indian Academy of Sciences at Poona, Raman delivered a lecture on December 25, 1964. *The Hindustan Times,* dated December 26,1964 wrote about Raman's lecture on *"Vision and the Nature of Light"*.

Immediate reaction of the American Embassy and writing a letter by a high official on a holiday, particularly December 31, clearly shows, how serious was Raman's work for him. The *"Analysis and Distribution Branch"* sent to various departments (including the famous CIA - Criminal Investigation Agency) a letter that was accompanied by four pages text entitled *"Raman explores nature of light and vision"*.

It will be worth while to reproduce in detail D. L. Fuller's letter of December 31, 1964, as it gives glimpse of Raman's conclusions. It reads:

> "India's only Nobel Laureate in science, Dr. Raman is seventy six years old and perhaps the only Indian scientist at that age still engaged in active research. Dr. Raman was discussing his most recent investigations on the relation between the physical nature of light and the physiological sensations excited by its incidence on the retinae of the eye. He said that his work in the past year had thrown new light on the subject of vision, which completely destroyed old theories. According to the new theories he has pronounced he maintains that the perception of light by the human eye is essentially controlled by the number of light corpuscles or quantas that reach the retina of the eye; that the material in the eye that absorbs light does not exist in the 'rods and cones of the eye' but it exists in the portions on and behind the retina; and that the colour perception of the human eye is controlled by a very small area only a millimetre in diameter in the fovea of the human eye. He also

> claimed that he had developed new techniques for the study of human visual sensations and the structure and functions of the retinae of human eyes".

Wald, who probably had forgotten the whole story, received a letter from F. Seitz. The latter on February 8, 1965 wrote to Wald as follows:

> "I wonder if the accompanying report from our Embassy in New Delhi concerning Dr. Raman's work on 'Vision and the Nature of Light' makes any significant sense. For a number of years Raman's work has run on the whole somewhat at cross gain with much of traditional science".

Wald who was not quite happy with the past experience lost no time and on February 10, 965 replied to Seitz. After informing him about the *Memoir of the Raman Research Institute,* No. 133 on *"Perception of light and colour"*, and another *Memoir* on *"The role of the retina in vision"* from the year 1962, he wrote:

> "These are most extraordinary documents in which Raman goes at these things as though no one had ever examined them before. I find nothing that even resembles an interesting contribution. I have the impression that Raman is so dominant figure in India, and surely in his own Institute, that no word of criticism reaches him. It is a sad thing that this very distinguished physicist should be publishing this nonsense in his old age".

The main reason for the criticism was somewhere else. Namely, the negligence of his work by Raman, as is clear from the following statement: *"I had back a very courteous letter assuring me that he knew all about my work and valued it; but he paid no attention to it whatever".*

It seems Wald was informed about "Born-Raman controversy on lattice dynamics theory". At this stage, he brought Max Born in the game as follows:

> "You might be interested in knowing that another great physicist, Max Born, (... ), recently published a

> really beautiful and penetrating essay on human colour vision in the *Zeiss Journal.* I have been in correspondence with him since. He writes me that he has put colour vision behind him; yet he does have continuing interest, and if you are thinking of having a visitor to our symposium, he'd be a good one".

Just two years later, that is, in 1967, H. K. Hartline from the Rockfeller University in New York in the financial matter wanted to help Raman, as a letter from Ward Morehouse - Director of the University of the State of New York, to Wald indicates. Wald being a recognised expert in the physiology of vision was again asked by Morehouse for his opinion. The latter had met Raman in Bangalore and was impressed from his theories. He wrote to Wald on June 16, 1967 as follows:

> "I [Ward Morehouse] have no scientific competence in this field but am anxious to have some idea of the relative scientific significance of his more recent work, because, if it is as significant as Raman himself suggests that it is — or even in substantial measure so — it may be worth making concerted efforts to find ways and means of helping him expand his work in Bangalore — at the present time, almost entirely confined to what he himself, now at a venerable age — can do".

Unfortunately, Wald's reply is not to be found in the archive. But it is not difficult to imagine that it was certainly not positive.

Wald's last letter in this connection is of December 14, 1981. One Indian historian X asked Wald to comment on Raman's work. To which the latter replied on January 8, 982 politely as follow:

> "As you see, my impressions do no differ greatly from your own. I would hesitate however to make the content of this correspondence public. With Raman's death these last emanations died also, and should be allowed to rest forgotten".

However, in other quarters in the USA, even in the late-1960s, about 80 years old Raman still had his fans. The last honour came from them, as we shall see below.

### *Raman's Research on Musical Instruments and Catgut Acoustical Society of America*

The Catgut Acoustical Society came into existence in 1963. It was due to the efforts of Carleen M. Hutchins, Frederick A. Saunders, John C. Schelleng and Robert E. Fryxell, who were working on string instruments like violin.

On August 30, 1968 Carleen M. Hutchins - later Secretary of the Society, informed Raman (who had worked in the same field in the first two decade of the twentieth Century and that work is still being referred) that very often people in their group refer to his monograph (presumably, *"On the mechanical theory of vibrations of bowed strings and of musical instruments of the violin family, with experimental results - Part I"*, *Bull. IACS* 15 (1918) 1-158, which he sent to F. H. Saunders years ago. She requested Raman to accept the Honorary Membership of the Society.

On November 23, 1968 Raman thanked for this honotir. He also revealed that his work on the bowed string instruments was done between 1914 and 1918, and due to his call as Professor at the University of Calcutta and the intensification of his interest in optics brought halt to further studies of the violin family instruments.

Soon followed another letter of December 6, 968 from CM. Hutchins with the following remarks:

> "One thing that has concerned many of us for a long time is that we feel, insufficient attention has been paid to your very remarkable researches on the violin string, and we most certainly hope that as the work of the society organises, this condition may be remedied".

In one of the letters, the Editor of the *Newsletter* of the Society - Robert E. Fryxell on February 7, 1969, thanked Raman for accepting the membership. He also sent Raman the *Neivsletter* and reprints of papers of members of the Society. He requested Raman to send papers or any comments on the work of the members. *"I and all of our members would be highly gratified if you, with your great insight into the intriguing problems of stringed instruments, would occasionally feel inclined to send a 'letter to the editor' with your views"*, wrote Fryxell.

In the same year one of the members of the Society - Arthur H. Benade was in India. He was asked to enquire and if possible to purchase complete collection of Raman's published work on violin acoustics.

On June 23, 1969 in a letter to Raman, Benade wrote:

> "On a more personal note, let me pass on the greetings of my father, Professor J. M. Benade who was for so many years at Forman Christian College in Lahore. He has often spoken of your hospitality when he and my mother called upon you a few years ago in Bangalore. I myself have still very vivid memories of a beautiful public lecture you once gave at the Punjab University about 1937.1 can describe some of what I saw, and can say what particular things I learned at this lecture, which was one of the formative influences of my professional career as a physicist."

Further, he told Raman that about six years ago he met Professor S. Bhagavantam who visited the Case Physics Department for a week for lectures. During private talk Benade told his guest about an impressive lecture of Raman, which the young 12 years old Benade had heard and after so many years was able to give its details. However, Benade did not recognise that Raman's assistant on that particular day was his guest himself. In the end Benade wrote: *"I hope you will accept this brief account as an expression of my respect for you as a great physicist, and impressive lecturer."*

On July 4, 1969 Benade thanked Raman for his June 27, 1969 letter, the monograph and the list of publications in acoustics.

After Raman expired, in the fall of 1971 CM. Hutchins wrote to the authorities of the Raman Research Institute and asked for permission to reproduce his papers *"Vibrations of bowed strings and instruments of the violin family" Bulletin IACS* 15 (1918) 1-158 and *"Experiments with mechanically played violins", Proc. IACS* 6 (1920).

In fact these two and one more paper *"On the 'Wolf Note' in bowed strings instruments"* were reprinted by the Society.

From the above discussion we see that Raman had contacts with the individual as well as Institutions and Societies. He also personally visited America. This gave him chance to know the political and educational aspects.

***Raman's Views on the American Political and Industrial System***

There are at least two incidences in record showing Raman's discrimination in the USA due to his colour and race. The one deals with Raman and Compton's servant and the other with Dean Gale at the University of Chicago, who simply ignored Raman in the Faculty Club.

The authors S. Ramaseshan and C. R. Rao have quoted Raman's reaction as follows: "As in India, there are many stupid fools in every country. I would like to remember the United States as the country of Jefferson and Franklin, Walt Whitman and Thoreau, Edison and Graham Bell, or my own friends Millikan and Compton".

Raman was a great admirer of American educational, industrial and political systems. Though, India is a democratic land, but still Raman had problems with Indian system. On the very first day of Indian Independence Day, i.e. August 15, 1947, he expressed his views to *The Indian Express* as follows:

> "Looking round and sizing up the situation, it seems to me that the real danger before our country in the days to come is the crushing down of individual freedom and initiative by the steam roller of government authority.... already visible from taxation and other bills".

On January 3, 1948 Raman suggest the freedom of individual as in the USA. On the model of American system, he suggested that in India the Government, Industrial and scientific institutions should come together to establish industry.

He did not minimise the value of foreign assistance in industrialising the country. However, he stated that the industrial and economic progress of Indian could be firmly established only on the basis of self-help and self-reliance.

On July 26, 1948 while addressing a press conference he said, *"The scientists must be free from Governmental interference if they were to do their best. This was one of the reasons for the United States' scientific achievements"*. (Newspaper clip with author; Original in the *archive* of Raman Research Institute, Bangalore).

According to *The Hindu* from September 13, 1948 Raman went to America as a representative of the *Advisory Council of the International Bank of Reconstruction* and also to attend *the First International Congress of Crystallographers* at Harvard. *The Hindu* wrote further:

> "He (Raman) visited on invitation of several famous Companies like the American Optical Company at South Bridge and the Bell Telephone Company at Merry Hill near New York. He spent some days at the Bureau of Standards in New York, one of the largest institutions in the world engaged in fundamental scientific research, where nearly 2000 scientists are engaged in research and delivered a lecture at the institution".

After returning back he delivered three lectures in Bangalore. On October 10, 1948 a newspaper published a short review under the title, *"America Today, Sir C. V. Raman's Impression"*. Raman praised the American for punctuality, enthusiasm and hard work. He observed that:

> "The average American evinces enthusiasm even for the hardest kind of work, and this is because there is practically unlimited scope of reward from private enterprise-which according to the distinguished scientist, is the real secret behind American abundance".

And further:

> "The vast majority of the American citizens live a full life, in an atmosphere of complete freedom, thus calling into play each of one's natural gifts and faculties. This,..., is yet to be become as true in India as it is already so in America".

Raman who was worried about the going on development in India, in the end of 1949, while addressing Jaipur Convocation stated that India is today as the US 100 years ago. Again he repeated his criticism that country cannot become great by borrowing millions of dollar or sending their students in foreign countries for training. He observed that after 100 years of education, other countries have conquered Indian spiritually, intellectually and culturally.

So far as the USA was concerned, he stated:

> "I have watched the United States and how it has reached the present position. Fifty years ago, the United States was in a particular position. Its students were sent out in shiploads to other countries to study and bring back knowledge. To day, America stands almost, certainly in the very front rank in educational and scientific progress. We all know it as the most powerful nation, financially, economically and politically. ...The source of that strength, .., was unquestionably not in the action of one or two but hundreds of wealthy men, who having made immense money under the system of private enterprise,..'.'.

From above we see that Raman believed in a democratic system. Most probably, his pro USA statements made him a sympathetic scientist among the American scientific community.

### *Summary*

Raman was a lecturer par excellence. The high quality scientific work at the initial stage and the Nobel Prize made him a scientist special from the non-European countries. Due to these reasons the Americans took interest in his work at each stage.

Raman, though from a different continent and with different clothes, was seen at the California Institute of Technology as a man *"in accord with Western scholarship" due* to his physical researches.

The appreciation and criticism of his work by the Americans show that he was accepted as an integral part of the American scientific community. Though the racial issue cannot be neglected, on the whole, we see that in this particular case the boundaries of the natural sciences were broader than the racial issue.

Raman saw the American political system as an ideal model. According to his interpretation, it offers an individual the freedom and chance to come further. In particular, Raman was fascinated by the American political policies towards education and industrialisation in which the private institutions and persons played important role.

In the last phase of his life, Raman started ignoring the work of his contemporaries. It was against the rules of the game and affected Raman's status as a scientist.

## Raman's Election to the Royal Society

These are well-known facts that in 1907 Raman came to Calcutta as a bank officer and in the following ten years, in his spare time, accomplished his research at the Indian Association for the Cultivation of Science. In 1917, he was offered Professorship at the University of Calcutta. Until the end of 1921, i.e. the year of his nomination to the Fellowship of the Society, his fields of research were musical acoustics and optics.

Raman's nomination certificate to the Royal Society shows that he was nominated by the following Fellows of the Royal Society: Sidney G. Burrard (1860-1943), John Evershed (1864-1956), Gilbert T. Walker (1868-1958), George C. Simpson (1878-1965), Charles S. Middlemiss (1859-1945), Alfred W. Porter (1863-1939) and Edwin H. Barton (1858-1925). The nominators sent a list of publications by Raman and about his scientific achieve-ments. They stated that: 'Although trained entirely in India (he) has made consider-able additions to our knowledge of sound and light, having published about fifty memoirs.

The chief are: 'Experimental investigations on the maintenance of vibration'; 'The dynamical theory of bowed strings'; 'Vibrations of bowed strings and of musical instruments of the violin family'; 'On Kaufmann's theory of the pianoforte hammer', 'On the photo-graphic study of impact at minimal velocities'; 'On Hertz's theory of impact'; 'Photometric measurement of the obliquity factor of diffraction'; 'The curvature of lines in diffraction spectra'; 'Colours of the striae in Mica'; 'The diffraction figures due to an elliptic aperture'; 'The colours of mixed plates' (Nomination certificate).

Raman's name was proposed in November 1921 and he was elected as a Fellow of the Royal Society on 15 May 1924.

## Raman's Resignation from Royal Society

In 1924 the first Asian Nobel Laureate in the field of Physics — C. V. Raman (1888-1970) was elected as the fourth Indian for the Fellowship of the Royal Society of London. Raman is the only Indian FRS who resigned from the Fellowship of the Society. The documents regarding this issue were obtained from the archive of the Society.

C. V. Raman is known for the discovery of the effect named after him. The effect deals with change in frequency of the monochromatic light, after scattering through a medium. For his work on light-scattering and the discovery of the effect, he was awarded the Nobel Prize in 1930. Before that, another great honour came to him in the form of his election to the Fellowship of the Royal Society, London. Various biographies of Raman exist which deal with different aspects of his life.

## Raman's Resignation from the Fellowship

Raman was associated with the Society for a long period (44 years) and resigned from the Fellowship in March 1968. About his resignation, R. S. Krishnan, a respected Indian scientist and a close associate of Raman, wrote: 'Nearly two years ago (i.e. in 1968), Prof. Raman had sent a paper describing his new findings on the physiology of human vision for publication in the *Proceedings of the Royal Society of London*. This was returned with some unfavourable remarks by a referee. He got so annoyed about it that he sent in his resignation from the Fellowship of the Royal Society which he held for 45 years.'

In Raman's biography, the author G. H. Keswani also refers to the above statement.

In order to check the correctness of this version, I enquired of the Information Officer of the Royal Society and was informed that, 'the library holds referee's reports on papers submitted for publication . . . checked through all the referees' reports for papers submitted in 1967 and 1968, and there is nothing by Raman amongst them' (Broad, C., Information Officer, Royal Society, London, Private commun., dated 3 December 1999). This clearly shows that the information given by Krishnan is not correct.

Wali gives another version regarding the resignation. He quotes a talk with the famous astrophysicist and Nobel Laureate S. Chandrasekhar as follows: 'I believe, I heard the story from P. M. S. Blackett. Apparently, *The London Times* had an article on Fellows of the Royal Society who had received the Nobel Prize, and it did not mention Raman.

Raman blamed the omission on the Society and wrote to Blackett (who was President of the Royal Society at that time) saying that unless a satisfactory explanation was forthcoming, he would resign his fellowship. Blackett wrote back saying that it was a *London Times'* article; the Society had no part in it. . . . Blackett's response, how-ever, did not satisfy Raman. He resigned anyway; he was not satisfied with the explanation'.

As Wali did not refer to the issue of *The Times* (London), it is obvious that he has not verified Chandrasekhar's statement. In order to check the truth about this version, browsed *The Times* issues from January 1967 to 8 March 1968, i.e. the time period in which the suspected list of 'The Fellows of the Royal Society who won the Nobel Prize' might have appeared.

To the best of our knowledge such a list has not been found. Also the 'Catalogue of P. M. S. Blackett's papers and correspondence' in possession of the Royal Society Library does not contain any entry about Raman. Obviously, there was no communication between Blackett and Raman.

The next source to find the truth is in Raman's resignation letters. In the following paragraphs the content of Raman's letter which he wrote to the Secretary of the Society (but not to Blackett as Wali mentioned), are reproduced.

In the first letter dated 9 March 1968 Raman wrote to D. C. Martin – the Executive Secretary of the Royal Society that, 'I am writing to inform you that I have decided to withdraw from the Royal Society.

I have taken this decision after careful consideration of all the circumstances of the case. I would request that my resignation be accepted and my name removed from the list of the Fellows of the Society'.

Just after four days, i.e. on 13 March 1968 Raman wrote a second letter to D. C. Martin. It reads: 'I am writing in continuation of my letter No. 132 dated the 9th March 1968, informing you of my resignation of the Fellowship of the Royal Society.

I desire that this resignation should take effect immediately. Further, if the Yearbook of the Royal Society for 1968 has not yet been printed, I would request that my name be left out from the list of the Fellows . . . .'

Raman's own letters give hardly a clear picture of his action. The last reliable source left with is the record of the Royal Society.

On page 96 of the Council Minutes dated 4 April 1968 it has been recorded: 'Reported intimation in a letter dated 9 March 1968 from C. V. Raman of his decision to withdraw from the Royal Society and his request that his resignation be accepted and his name removed from the list of Fellows and, in a letter dated 13 March, of his desire that his resignation should take effect immediately. Resolved – That Sir C. V. Raman's request be accepted.'

The date of acceptance of Raman's resignation is in accord with that given by Kochhar.

Like Raman's letters, the record of the Society does not give a clear picture about Raman's resignation. But the fact remains that his resignation was accepted by the Society.

Though Raman was no more a member, after his death due place was given to him in the *Memoirs of the Fellows of the Royal Society*. The author S. Bhagawantam who knew Raman for more than 30 years, also did not mention anything about this incident.

Raman was elected as the Fellow of the Royal Society, London for his achieve-ments in the field of acoustics and optics. Raman did not resign when his paper was rejected by the referee of the *Proceedings of the Royal Society of London*.

The primary sources like Raman's resignation letters and the available record of the Society did not give a definite answer to the puzzle. Under these circumstances, Raman's resignation remains a mystery.

9

# Raman's Impact on Science

Professor Raman bought his ticket to Europe in 1929 to attend the Nobel Prize awarding ceremony in 1930, indeed a year earlier before he was declared for the prize. Such was the confidence of this great man, that after seeing the effect in February 1928 and declaring it in a conference on 16th March, 1928, he had no doubt in his mind that he was going to be recipient of Nobel Prize in physics in 1930! Surprisingly physics world was in unison with his claim. In the history of Nobel Prize, nobody was awarded Nobel Prize so quickly after a major contribution. On average it takes a decade to recognise the merit of any discovery. But in Raman's case it was an exception and sometimes we have been puzzled by the fact, how come Raman was so confident about his winning in 1930 when revolutionary contributions in physics discovered much before Raman effects have not been awarded till that time! That includes Heisenberg (who discovered the famous uncertainty principle in quantum mechanics and also credited for Matrix operator approach in quantum mechanics. He was awarded Nobel in 1932. Raman defeated Heisenberg by 6 to 1, Schrodinger (Famous Schrodinger equation that led first theoretical foundation of quantum mechanics. He was awarded Nobel in 1933 with PM Dirac) and PM Dirac (The man who founded relativistic quantum mechanics and led the foundation of interaction of light with electrons)! Indeed, Raman defeated Schrodinger, Dirac and Heisenberg in 1930 who were also nominated for Nobel Prize in physics for the year of 1930.

## The History of the Discovery

### *Science College 1928*

Before we break the puzzle, we will walk down the lane of 210 Bow Bazaar Street in Calcutta where Prof. CV Raman was carrying out his experiments on scattering of light by liquid from 1918, after the foundation of Indian cultivation of science in the same year. It was the glorious time for Calcutta University-in its newly founded post graduate physics department, faculty includes Sir C. V. Raman, S. N. Bose, M. N. Saha and S. K. Mitra. Later in their careers, all of them would be elected as a fellow of Royal Society. For a brief period of two decades, Calcutta was the most intense site for fundamental research in science outside Europe. Even in Europe, except for centres of excellence like University of Gottingen in Germany, University of Oxford and Cambridge, London University and So bourn University in Paris, Calcutta University has no parallel. When we were looking at what was going on in MIT, Harvard and Princeton University between 1910-30, we really felt proud that for a brief period, research in cultivation of science in Calcutta, exceeded the standard of these famous University chain in USA. Unfortunately we could not keep the standard up because of socio-economical dynamics between science and the society. Continuation of excellence in science needs Buddhist model-Dharma (the belief in their own standard of science), Buddha (the great teachers of science) and Sangha (The university system and its students who will be the next generation of teachers). We never had a shortage of students or teachers but our Sangha, University system has continuously faltered. Not that Neheru didn't take enough initiative to fund money for science. Indeed he did. Council of Industrial and Scientific Research (CSIR), Defence Research and Development Organisation (DRDO), Indian Institute of Technology (IIT), Indian Institute of Science (IISc), Department of Atomic Energy (DAE) and Indian Space Research Organisation (ISRO) are all 'dreams come true story' for Neheruvite socialism. But none of the organisation could repeat a Raman story! Reason is deeply lying in Neheruvite socialism itself. Today MIT, Stanford, Princeton are centre of excellence in Science and technology because it receives huge grant to develop new technology from defence organisations (DARPA) and contractors like Boeing, Lockheed Martin (company that manufactures F16/18), General dynamics, etc. Where as in India, from its beginning, DRDO is crippling to develop new science and technology thanks to the fact that greedy Generals and defence ministers were more interested to pocket billions of dollars worth of Russian commission for arms sale rather than proliferating commercialisation of defence research like in UK and USA. During Second World War all the greatest technologies were developed by commercial companies who generally hold a much higher degree of accountability of delivery. Quite naturally, DRDO/DAE has no accountability in delivery and as a consequence, most of scientists in DRDO/DAE are more interested in trading stocks than doing research. Strength of fundamental research in an institute can be gauged from the excellence of its mechanical workshop-and not by its latest state of the art instruments. That's why once former director of IIT-Kharagpur shouted his frustration in convocation — "IIT has every equipment to do state of art research but for last four decades we have not produced any innovation that is worth mentioning to the world like Prof. Raman did proudly on 28th February in 1928!"

## *Why a Second Raman in India is Unlikely?*

Indian scientists neglected the most important teaching of Raman that his student K S Krishnan wrote in his diary — "Professor always tells me that it is not good for a scientists to be out from the laboratory for a long time and doing theoretical research only". This has exactly happened to Indian science, it has moved from laboratory to theoretical hypothesis. Reason is simple. In general defence and medical fields are greatest consumer of latest discoveries in Physics and Chemistry. Due to lack of defence and medical development, there is no outlet for Indian discoveries and innovations. In USA, story is opposite. Venture capitalists are wielding their dollars to convert even the simplest innovation from MIT and Stanford to gold. Quite naturally in USA, thinking of the scientists are always occupied by commercial landscape and in India for a long time, scientists lacked objectives other than publishing papers. This has led to gradual degradation of the position of scientists in Indian society. We can not imagine that Tagore is raising fund for research of Prof. J. C. Bose in this century. Indeed, in his own words to King of Tripura, Tagore took pride to be a beggar for Prof. J. C. Bose. Quite naturally, when anyone opted for Physics instead of Engineering in 1991, his parent thought he has gone out of his mind. Due to the reduced status of the scientists in the society in the subcontinent, only the students who can not get through Engineering schools are studying science! The trend has affected the quality of science in India.

### *Indigenous Set-up from Workshop of Howrah!*

So, it is extremely important to understand what Raman and his group was doing by building their own equipments from numerous unskilled workshops of Howrah. Strong sunlight is passed through a big aperture of a telescope and then focused on a hole to collimate the light-to make it a straight pencil beam. Raman and his students were using coloured crystal and grating to make the beam monochromatic (means light with only one wavelength) — a very rudimentary technique. Then this beam was allowed to pass through liquid.

Typically, if a spectrometer (an optical instrument that breaks the light into all of its colours or wavelengths) is placed at 90 degree angle of the beam and from beam and liquid cross section, a faint scattered light can always be found which is typically 1/1000 times weaker than the original beam if the liquid is very pure without any solid particles. However, this faint beam has same wavelength as that of original beam that has fallen on the liquid. So it is as if, light has been scattered by the molecules. In classical theory of electromagnetism, the scattered and incident light should have same spectrum. Or in more simple words, green light will scatter green only; blue light will scatter blue only!

### *Raman Could not Understand Raman Effect in 1922!*

In 1922, one of Raman's PhD student Ramanathan observed a faint green glow in the scattered light when the original beam was blue. This is exception to what his group knew at that time. However, he was carrying out experiments on effect of magnetic anisotropy of the liquid and was never expecting anything like this kind of green faint light. He actually saw the Raman Effect but he thought it is fluorescent.

A phenomena where light absorbs a colour say blue and then emits a characteristic colour say green). However this light was highly polarised and can not be from fluorescent. Raman and Krishnan saw this phenomenon as well, but due to the lack of knowledge of quantum scattering, they turn their suspicion on impurity of the incident blue beam. However this spurious green light remained a mystery till Compton announced his epoch making experimental results that X-ray scattered by electron has an interesting property which can be explained only through the newly developed subject of quantum mechanics. Compton proved that wavelength of the X-ray get modified by both the bound and free state of the electron. Something that can be explained only if light is considered as a particle like photon colliding with certain energy with electron and electron is altering the energy of the photon as a result of collision!

### *Inspired by Compton Effect*

Raman immediately got interested in Compton Effect and indeed set up an experimental arrangement to observe Compton Effect as early as in 1923 using an entirely different concept. In December 1927, Compton was awarded Nobel Prize in Physics. In the same day, the news was published in evening chronicle of Calcutta. As per K S Krishnan's diary, Professor grabbed the paper and run into the laboratory.

> "But look here Krishnan, if this is true of X-rays, it must be true of light too. There must be an optical analogue to the Compton Effect. We must pursue it.."

K. S. Krishnan was actually involved in the study of magnetism but Raman told him to dig the faint green scattered light that they have failed to explain for a long time. Raman was sure, since X-ray is nothing but an electromagnetic wave, similar phenomena should also happen in liquid in visible domain since electrons are loosely bound in liquid! And he wanted to see the end of the enigma of feeble green scattering. On 16th March 1928, while explaining this new effect for the first time, he announced:

> Early this year, however, a powerful impetus to further research was provided when I conceived the idea that the effect was some kind of optical analogue to the type of X-ray scattering discovered by Professor Compton, for which he recently received the Nobel Prize in Physics. I immediately undertook an experimental re-examination of the subject in collaboration with Mr. K. S. Krishnan and this has proved very fruitful in results.

### *Re-examination of a Green Light!*

The 'experimental re-examination' started in January 1928. During the same month, Venkateswaran was studying the phenomenon of light scattering in highly viscous and magnetic liquid. While experimenting with glycerin, he made the same observation again — that the blue filtered sunlight scattered in a highly purified sample of the liquid was green instead of the usual blue. Tests with different filters transmitting narrow regions of the solar spectrum showed that in every case the scattered light was different in colour from that of the incident beam. Moreover, the scattered radiation appeared to be polarised.

As we saw before, Raman was sure that he is observing optical equivalent of Compton Effect and prevailed upon Krishnan to undertake a thorough investigation of the phenomenon, drawing him away from the theoretical problems he was busy with at the time. Since sunlight was the principal incident source they were using and since Venkateswaran, a part-time worker at the laboratory could only devote time early in the morning or late in the afternoon, the responsibility of carrying on with the experiments fell on Krishnan's shoulders.

The Raman Effect was discovered on 28 February 1928. It was a tireless pursuit lasting about four to five weeks and in the end was a great experimental discovery, yet to be matched in contemporary Indian science. Krishnan kept a record of the events in the form of a diary. The diary contains an elaborate day-to-day account of the quest that ultimately led to this discovery. We reproduce below the transcribed text of the original diary [Source — Diary of K.S. Krishnan by D.C.V. Mallick].

## History of the February 1928: through K. S. Krishnan's Diary

Sunday, 5 February 1928

For the last three or four days I have been doing some experimental work on the fluorescence of organic vapours. For a long time past I haven't done any systematic experimental work; in fact, the last experiment I did was the one on the magnetic double refraction of nitric oxide, in the summer of 1926. Since then, I have been exclusively confined to my desk excepting for a short period of about a week last March when I set up the X-ray tube for investigating X-ray scattering by gases, which however was left uncompleted, first because we had some interesting problems in magnetism (viz. anisotropy of crystalline nitrates and carbonates), and second, because, Dr. Sethi who was to work in our laboratory during the summer holidays on X-diffraction in liquids at high temperatures, had no spare Shearer tube to work with. As Professor says, it is not quite healthy for a scientific man to be out of touch with actual experimental facts for any length of time and it was specially to keep myself busy with some experimental work that Professor asked me to take up the subject, though the period has been extremely fruitful regarding my scientific output — in fact all our work on electric and magnetic double refraction, magnetic anisotropy of crystals, diffraction by metallic screens, and the series of three papers modifying the Langevin theory of electric and magnetic double refraction, the Lorentz-Debye theory of refraction and dielectric polarisation and the Ramanathan theory of light scattering and the Phil. paper on the theory of the Maxwell effect in liquids.........

This diary is awesome. It shows mindset of K. S. Krishnan that he is still under impression that the unwanted green light is fluorescence and not something like Compton Effect as Ranan was insisting. It also shows he was working on theoretical magnetism and Professor pulled him out of his theoretical work and put him to investigate what he thinks equivalent of optical Compton Effect. His deep respect for professor can not be unnoticed in this diary.

> ...Still one must agree with Professor that it is not quite healthy for a scientific man to be out of touch with actual experimenting for any length of time. It was mainly with a view to start immediately some experimental work that I took up (at the suggestion of Professor the general problem of the fluorescence of organic vapours; rather than from the pressing nature of any specific problem in the subject awaiting experimental solution, which usually draws a man to a new field. In fact the paper on the experimental evidence for the anisotropy of the polarisation field, which I proposed to write jointly with Ramachandra Rao, and which we partially wrote together when he was here for the Science Congress last month, is not yet completed.

He does not look convinced by Raman's explanation that this might be optical equivalent of Compton's effect. Indeed, he still thinks it is a fluorescence attributed to anisotropic magneto-optical property of the liquid.

> I have also spent a week or more on trying to give a theory of the Jamin effect, and also in finding out whether in the photographs taken long ago by Professor of thin soap bubbles placed between crossed nicols, there is any evidence of double refraction of the film. The latter two will require some more time. However I have thought it best to leave off the desk straight way and begin the experimental work; and accordingly for the last three or four days I have been devoting all my time to fluorescence. Also the subject

> promises to open out a wide field for research, since at present there is no theory of fluorescence which could explain even the outstanding facts.

Later on there was controversy on Raman's Nobel as to whether Krishnan had legitimate claim to it since he observed the phenomenon first. This diary proves the conception that Krishnan first saw the effect is not correct. Indeed, they were re-investigating a phenomenon seen by Ramanathan and Venkateshwaran based on Raman's assumption that something like Compton effect is in play.

> Studied anthracene vapour. It exhibits strong fluorescence; which does not seem to show any polarisation when viewed through a double image prism. Professor has been working with me all the time. Received today the proof of our Phil. Mag. paper on the theory of the Maxwell effect. Recently Professor has been studying with Mr. Venkateswaran the fluorescence exhibited by many of the aromatic liquids in the near ultraviolet region present in sunlight and the fluorescence of some of the liquids was found to be polarised. However in view of the fact that the fluorescence of anthracene vapour does not show any polarisation Professor has asked me to verify again his observations on the polarisation in some of the liquids. Monday, 6 February 1928 When Professor went to Bangalore about a fortnight back in connection with the meeting of the Indian Institute of Science I had been to the station and in the course of our conversation told him that Dr. A. L. Narayanan suggested to me that I might write to the Madras University for exemption from the three year limit for applying for the Doctorate and asked him, if he might happen to meet the Syndicate members at Madras to consult them on the matter. Professor told me today that he called on the Vice Chancellor Sir Venkataratnam but couldn't meet him. However he says that Sir Venkat has written to him a very nice letter inviting him to deliver a lecture under the

> auspices of the University. That would give him an opportunity to write to Sir Venkataratnam and that he would refer to my case. He took from me a detailed account of my academic career. Incidentally Professor mentioned that if the University arranged for a regular course of lectures instead of a single lecture he would like to take me with him...

K. S. Krishnan never received his M.Sc. degree through examinations because he was too busy in research from the beginning. By 1928, Raman is the best known physicist of the country and he came forward to rescue his student. Understanding the local Bengali politics which was always against his group, would not allow K. S. Krishnan to get a formal degree in master in science from Calcutta University, he pulled his weight to get a MSc degree in Physics from Madras University for K. S. Krishnan. It is worthwhile to notice that there was no Bengali student in Raman's group despite he was in Calcutta and Palit professor of Physics. In India, the tradition of power struggle in science between Tamil Bramhins and Bengalis is continuing till today. 95 per cent of the Indian scientists are either Tamil or Bengali or Marathi!

> Tuesday, 7 February 1928
>
> Tried to verify the polarisation of the fluorescence exhibited by some of the aromatic liquids in the near ultraviolet region. Incidentally discovered that all pure liquids show a fairly intense fluorescence also in the visible region, and what is much more interesting all of them are strongly polarised; the polarisation being the greater for the aliphatics than for the aromatics. In fact the polarisation of the fluorescent light seems in general.
>
> ...to run parallel with the polarisation of the scattered light, i.e. the polarisation of the fluorescent light is greater the smaller the optical anisotropy of the molecule. When I told Professor about the results he wouldn't believe that all liquids can show

> polarised fluorescence and that in the visible region. When he came into the room, I had a bulb of pentane in the tank blue with violet filter in the path of the incident light, and when he observed the track with a combination of green and yellow filters he remarked 'you don't mean to suggest, Krishnayengar all that is fluorescence!'. However when he transferred the green yellow combination also to the path of the incident light he couldn't detect a trace of the track. He was very much excited and repeated several times that it was an amazing result. One after another the whole series of liquids were examined and every one of them showed the phenomenon without exception. He wondered how we missed discovering all that five years ago.

This is the most interesting part of the diary. Look at the last sentence. Raman agreed that they have neglected the faint green scattered light for a long time. Not only him, other workers in Europe also saw the same polarised fluorescent but nobody had vision of Raman to identify the phenomenon as a separate effect similar to Compton Effect.

> After meals at night Venkateswaran and myself were chatting together in our room when Professor suddenly came to the house (at about 9 p.m.) and called for me. When we went down we found he was very much excited and had come to tell me that what we had observed this morning must be the Kramers-Heisenberg effect we had been looking for all these days. We therefore agreed to call the effect modified scattering rather than fluorescence. We were talking in front of our house for more than a quarter of an hour when he repeatedly emphasised the exciting nature of the discovery.

So for the first time Krishnan was convinced by Raman that the effect they have seen is not fluorescence but new scattering phenomena!

Wednesday, 8 February 1928

Took some preliminary measurements of the polarisation of the modified scattering by some typical liquids. Thursday 9 February 1928 Set up this morning the big telescope and made preliminary arrangements for observing the effect with vapours. Before the arrangements were complete Professor left for the College for his lecture. In the afternoon tried Ether vapour and it was surprising that the modified radiation was very conspicuous. Tried a number of others in quick succession without however the same success.

When Professor came from the College at about three, I announced to him the result, and there was still enough sunlight for him to see for himself. He ran about the place shouting all the time, that it was a first rate discovery, that he was feeling miserable during the lecture because he had to leave the experiment, and that however he was fully confident that I wouldn't let the grass grow under my feet till I had discovered the phenomenon in gases. He asked me to 'call in everybody in the place to see the Effect' and immediately arranged in a most dramatic manner, with the mechanics to make arrangements for examining the vapours at high temperatures. Told Mr. Sogani that it was for him now to make his temperature influence on the Compton effect as great a success. Evening was busy preparing the hot bath and I didn't go out. When Professor returned after his walk he told me that I ought to tackle big problems like that and asked me to take up the problem of the experimental evidence for the spinning electron after this work was over. Told Mr. Venkateswaran about the discovery and was discussing the problem with us, in the course of which he said that the phenomenon should be called the Raman-Krishnan Effect. Mr. Venkateswaran or somebody will call it by that name. Incidentally he remarked that nothing was now

> beyond my reach referring to the Fellowship of the Royal Society and that I might probably get the Fellowship before I got my Doctorate. He instanced in a manner most flattering to me, the case of Ramanujan who was only a B.A. when he got the Fellowship.

Last paragraph is getting interesting. Raman wanted to call this newly discovered phenomenon as Raman-Krishnan Effect though unfortunately Krishnan was left out! By 12th February, Raman boosted his student that his latest invention is worthy of giving him a seat in Royal society though he didn't receive his doctorate yet. Also, it shows Raman as an inspiring guide who can install high ambition in his student to achieve only the best! Also it shows Raman was methodical. It can be seen in liquid, it must be observed in gas. So Raman was clear. Krishnan has to carry out his experiments to its logical conclusion.

> 10-15 February 1928
>
> Studied a number of vapours. Though a number of them showed the effect nothing definite could be said regarding the polarisation of the modified scattering
>
> Thursday, 16 February 1928
>
> Studied today pentane vapour at high temperature and it showed a conspicuous polarisation in the modified scattering. We sent a note today to *Nature* on the subject under the title 'A new type of secondary radiation'.
>
> Friday, 17 February 1928
>
> Professor confirmed the polarisation of fluorescence in pentane vapour. I am having some trouble with my left eye.

Krishnan works so intensely and so passionately, he nearly harmed Cornea of his eye. Constant exposure to strong radiation leads to temporary blindness.

Raman demonstrated the effect before the distinguished member of the cultivation of science on 28th February. Also, this diary proves beyond doubt that K. S. Krishnan just worked as instructed and Raman had the original idea. So, K. S. Krishnan can not be said to have discovered the effect since Raman conceived it first. Not only that, even after Raman explained to him what to except, from diary it is clear that Krishnan didn't have enough understanding of Compton effect because Magnetism was his subject and Quantum mechanics was last in his imagination.

We learned in great details how Raman and his group observed a green light instead of blue light in the scattered spectrum. So what? Even if it is new, how it can be so great that it has to be merited above Schrodinger's equation?

### *How Raman Effect Changed the Organic Chemistry*

Answer lies in understanding vibrational spectroscopy of organic compounds that is typically observed in infrared domain (IR). Study of infrared spectroscopy in 1930s was nearly impossible since Infrared spectrometry is extremely difficult and till today, it is under-developed subject. However, Raman scattering opens a new area in spectroscopy where information embedded in IR spectroscopy can also be obtained from Raman spectroscopy but from its UV-VIS (ultraviolet-visible) study which is a developed subject. But why IR spectroscopy is so hot?

Simple to understand. All the chemical bonding in organic and inorganic substances is essentially a kind of small vibrational string that holds together two atoms. This bonding can only be understood from its vibrational spectrum that is typically in IR domain.

Hence discovery of Raman Effect gave unprecedented powerful tool to understand structure of bonding in the molecules which was otherwise impossible to carry out using IR spectroscopy directly! It won't be prudent to say, early development of organic chemistry before the discovery of NMR (Nuclear Magnetic Resonance), owes its progress to Raman spectroscopy.

### *Raman Lasers and Amplifier: Longest Lasting Active Research Topic in Physics*

In recent decades, Raman scattering become important phenomena with the discovery of Raman scattering in optical fibre that gave birth to two very important discovery of last decade. Fibre Raman laser and Fibre Raman amplifier. Both the devices outperformed its traditional competitors for various reasons. Right now all the long distance trans-oceanic fibre optic cable are using Raman amplifier to amplify its signal because it has much better signal to noise ration over its traditional rival Erbium Doped Fibre Amplifier (EDFA). Eventually Raman amplifier will replace all the optical amplifiers over next two decades in Fibre optic networks — or backbone of our communication system. Unlike photoelectric or Compton Effect, Raman scattering remains an ever green subject to build new device using non-liner optics of Raman scattering. Its remains the most potent effect to be utilised in building future all optical computing or Quantum informatics. In terms of diversity of applications and potential for future use, Raman Effect is only compared to discovery of laser and Nuclear Magnetic Resonance (NMR) in the last century.

However, we will be able to appreciate Raman Effect a lot better if we go through a little bit of basics of Vibrational spectroscopy.

## Understanding Raman Effect

### *Basic of Vibrational Spectroscopy*

Understanding the region of the infrared spectrum which is of greatest interest to organic chemists is the wavelength range 2.5 to 15 micrometers (μ). In practice, units proportional to frequency, (wave number in units of cm-1) rather than wavelength are commonly used and the region 2.5 to 15 μ corresponds to approximately 4000 to 600 cm-1.

Absorption of radiation in this region by a typical organic molecule results in the excitation of vibrational, rotational and bending modes, while the molecule itself remains in its electronic ground state.

Molecular asymmetry is a requirement for excitation by infrared radiation and fully symmetric molecules do not display absorbances in this region unless asymmetric stretching or bending transitions are possible.

For the purpose of routine organic structure determination, using a battery of spectroscopic methods, the most important absorptions in the infrared region are the simple stretching vibrations. For simple systems, these can be approximated by considering the atoms as point masses, linked by a 'spring' having a force constant *k* and following Hooke's Law. Using this simple approximation, the equation shown below can be utilised to approximate the characteristic stretching frequency (in cm-1) of two atoms of masses m and $m_2$, linked by a bond with a force constant k:

Where $\mu = m_1m_2/(m_1+m_2)$ (termed the 'reduced mass'), and c is the velocity of light. The stretching vibrations of typical organic molecules tend to fall within distinct regions of the infrared spectrum, as shown below:

(cm-1 means, how many lines within one centimetre space of spectrograph. In wavelength (μm)=10000/cm-1)

- 3700-2500 cm-1: X-H stretching (X = C, N, O, S)
- 2300-2000 cm-1: C X stretching (X = C or N)
- 1900-1500 cm-1: C X stretching (X = C, N, O)
- 1300-1800 cm-1: C-X stretching (X = C, N, O)

Since most organic molecules have single bonds, the region below 1500 cm-1 can become quite complex and is often referred to as the 'fingerprint region': that is, if you are dealing with an unknown molecule which has the same 'fingerprint' in this region, that is considered evidence that the two molecules may be identical.

Because of the complexity of the region below 1500 cm-1, in this review, we will focus on functional group stretching bands in the higher frequency region. You should note that for many of these bands, the IR spectrum may give equivocal structural information; quite often the absence of a band is as informative as the presence of a particular band.

- Alcohols and amines display strong broad O-H and N-H stretching bands in the region 3400-3100 cm. The bands are broadened due to hydrogen bonding and a sharp 'non-bonded' peak can often be seen at around 3400 cm.
- Alkene and alkyne C-H bonds display sharp stretching absorptions in the region 3100-3000 cm. The bands are of

medium intensity and are often obscured by other absorbances in the region (i.e. OH).

- Triple bond stretching absorptions occur in the region 2400-2200 cm. Absorptions from nitriles are generally of medium intensity and are clearly defined. Alkynes absorb weakly in this region unless they are highly asymmetric; symmetrical alkynes do not show absorption bands.
- Carbonyl stretching bands occur in the region 1800-1700 cm. The bands are generally very strong and broad. Carbonyl compounds which are more reactive in nucleophilic addition reactions (acyl halides, esters) are generally at higher wave number than simple ketones and aldehydes, and amides are the lowest, absorbing in the region 1700-1650 cm.
- Carbon-carbon double bond stretching occurs in the region around 1650-1600 cm. The bands are generally sharp and of medium intensity. Aromatic compounds will typically display a series of sharp bands in this region.
- Carbon-oxygen single bonds display stretching bands in the region 1200-1100 cm. The bands are generally strong and broad. You should note that many other functional groups have bands in this region which appear similar.

With this basic knowledge of IR spectroscopy, we move forward to understand Raman spectroscopy which helps to unfolds these bonding discussed above. Indeed, our very life forms on the earth is dependant on above covalent bonding and therefore, it won't be a bad idea to learn more about them.

### *Raman Spectroscopy in 2005*

Today Raman spectroscopy has become much more sophisticated and much simpler to measure. Major technological advances have transformed Raman spectroscopy from telescopes and visual observation to a highly sensitive spectroscopic technique. The first technological advance was the laser. The sun is pretty bright, but it is sending its energy in all directions and over a very broad range of wavelengths. The Raman Effect is observed as a shift in energy of a photon and the shift can be related to a vibrational state of the sample. To observe the shift one needs all of the photons to be a very narrow band of energies. Otherwise, you'll never be able to distinguish the shifted ones from the source photons. The laser produces quasi-monochromatic light that forms a very narrow band of frequencies. Lasers also produce this light in a small concentrated beam that is very intense.

A second technological advance that has revolutionised Raman spectroscopy is the Charge Coupled Device (CCD). The CCD is millions of times more sensitive than the eye and is able to record a complete Raman spectrum in less than a second. Let's look back at the history of Raman spectroscopy to understand the advantage that the CCD affords. Not long after Raman's first experiments scientists started using a photographic plate to record the Raman spectrum. This provided the first hardcopy of a Raman spectrum. The problem was that it didn't have a softcopy version that could be used for data analysis and spectral manipulation.

Early Raman spectroscopy was also like shooting in the dark. The plates were exposed for hours to get a spectrum and you didn't know if the optics were properly aligned until the plate was developed. The next big advance was the photomultiplier tube. This is a sensitive optical transducer that converts photons into electrons. They are sensitive enough to detect a single photon and a whole technology of "single photon counting" grew around them. Now a Raman spectroscopist could set his instrument to view an energy where Raman scattering should be observed and with an electronic display optimise the optical alignment. When computers became commonly available it was possible to have them record this electronic signal and produce a software file that contained the spectrum. This software file could be manipulated to remove artifacts that otherwise can distort Raman spectra.

## Raman and his Belief

Raman never liked to waste his time. Time was most precious diamond to him. Whenever he was approached by such questions on religion, he switched over the topic — you must have a better topic to discuss. In general, he thought discussing about religion is a waste of time which is so valuable otherwise.

Once he was persistently asked about to comment on God. He was not replying. But after sometimes, he got irritated and told him, if God is there find him in the Universe with a telescope and don't waste your time in speculation!

No doubt he was a confirmed atheist. But he never deviated from his conservative Ayaar tradition. We believe just to feel comfortable in social life. In that sense, Raman was a legend and a living proof that one can be a deeply rooted atheist and conservatively traditional at the same time.

A journalist once asked him, "What do you feel about the long and eventful period of your scientific work and achievements?" Raman replied promptly, "I have no time to think of the past and I am not inclined to do so. I spend my life as a scientist. My work gives me satisfaction."

As he was completing his 82 year Raman organised a week-long conference of the members of the Academy in September 1970. On that occasion he invited young scientists to present papers on different subjects.

Every year he used to deliver a popular science lecture on the Gandhi Jayanthi Day. In 1970, he spoke on the new theories about hearing and the eardrum. This was his last lecture.

A few days before his 83 birthday Raman suffered a mild heart attack. But there was quick recovery. He never dreamt of a life without work. He had told his doctor, "I wish to live a hundred per cent active and fruitful life."

Raman, a seeker of truth throughout his life, passed away on the 21st of November 1970.

Radhakrishnan, his younger son, became the Director of the Raman Research Institute.

Without much encouragement, Raman had entered the field of science in his early years. Deeply attracted by the secrets of sound and light, he marched ahead in the world of science. By his achievements and self respect he earned an honoured place for India in the world of science. He laid the foundations of a scientific tradition in India by building up institutes for research, by publishing science journals and by encouraging young scientists. Truly he was the 'Grand Old Man of Indian Science'.

Raman possessed the curiosity of a little boy to know new things, and the intuition of a great genius in understanding the secrets of Nature. The life of this great scientist was truly the life of a great seer.

## The Nobel Citation on Raman

Your Majesty, Your Royal Highnesses, Ladies and Gentlemen.

The Academy of Sciences, has resolved to award the Nobel Prize in Physics for 1930 to Sir Venkata Raman for his work on the scattering of light and for the discovery of the effect named after him.

The diffusion of light is an optical phenomenon, which has been known for a long time. A ray of light is not perceptible unless it strikes the eye directly. If, however, a bundle of rays of light traverses a medium in which extremely fine dust is present, the ray of light will scatter to the sides and the path of the ray through the medium will be discernible from the side. We can represent the course of events in this way; the small particles of dust begin to oscillate owing to electric influence from the ray of light, and they form centres from which light is disseminated in all directions. The wavelength, or the number of oscillations per second, in the light thus diffused is here the same as in the original ray of light. But this effect has different degrees of strength for light with different wavelengths. It is stronger for the short wavelengths than for the long ones, and consequently it is stronger for the blue part of the spectrum than for the red part. Hence if a ray of light containing all the colours of the spectrum passes through a medium, the yellow and the red rays will pass through the medium without appreciable scattering, whereas the blue rays will be scattered to the sides. This effect has received the name of the "Tyndall effect".

Lord Rayleigh, who has made a study of this effect, has put forward the hypothesis that the blue colours of the sky and the reddish colouring that is observed at sunrise and sunset is caused by the diffusion of light owing to the fine dust or the particles of water in the atmosphere. The blue light from the sky would thus be light-scattered to the sides, while the reddish light would be light that passes through the lower layers of the atmosphere and which has become impoverished in blue rays owing to scattering. Later, in 1899, Rayleigh threw out the suggestion that the phenomenon in question might be due to the fact that the molecules of air themselves exercised a scattering effect on the rays of light.

In 1914 Cabannes succeeded in showing experimentally that pure and dustless gases also have the capacity of scattering rays of light.

But a closer examination of scattering in different substances in solid, liquid, or gaseous form showed that the scattered light did not in certain respects exactly follow the laws which, according to calculation, should hold good for the Tyndall effect. The hypothesis which formed the basis of this effect would seem to involve, amongst other things, that the rays scattered to the sides were polarised. This, however, did not prove to be exactly the case.

This divergence from what was to be expected was made the starting point of a searching study of the nature of scattered light, in which study Raman was one of those who took an active part. Raman sought to find the explanation of the anomalies in asymmetry observed in the molecules. During these studies of his in the phenomenon of scattering, Raman made, in 1928, the unexpected and highly surprising discovery that the scattered light showed not only the radiation that derived from the primary light but also a radiation that contained other wavelengths, which were foreign to the primary light.

In order to study more closely the properties of the new rays, the primary light that was emitted from a powerful mercury lamp was filtered in such a way as to yield a primary light of one single wavelength. The light scattered from that ray in a medium was watched in a spectrograph, in which every wavelength or frequency produces a line. Here he found that, in addition to the mercury line chosen, there was obtained a spectrum of new sharp lines, which appeared in the spectrograph on either side of the original line. When another mercury line was employed, the same extra spectrum showed itself round it. Thus, when the primary light was moved, the new spectrum followed, in such a way that the frequency distance between the primary line and the new lines always remained the same.

Raman investigated the universal character of the phenomenon by using a large number of substances as a scattering medium, and everywhere found the same effect.

The explanation of this phenomenon, which has received the name of the "Raman effect" after its discoverer, has been found by Raman himself, with the help of the modern conception of the nature of light. According to that conception, light cannot be emitted from or absorbed by material otherwise than in the form of definite amounts of energy or what are known as "light quanta". Thus the energy of light would possess a kind of atomic character. A quantum of light is proportionate to the frequency of rays of light, so that in the case of a frequency twice as great, the quanta of the rays of light will also be twice as great.

In order to illustrate the conditions when an atom emits or absorbs light energy, we can, according to Bohr, picture to ourselves the atom as consisting of a nucleus, charged with positive electricity round which negative electrons rotate in circular paths at various distances from the centre. The path of every such electron possesses a certain energy, which is different for different distances from the central body.

Only certain paths are stable. When the electron moves in such a path, no energy is emitted. When, on the other hand, an electron falls from a path with higher energy to one with lower energy — that is to say, from an outer path to an inner path - light is emitted with a frequency that is characteristic of these two paths, and the energy of radiation consists of a quantum of light. Thus the atom can give rise to as many frequencies as the number of different transitions between the stable paths. There is a line in the spectrum corresponding to each frequency.

An incoming radiation cannot be absorbed by the atom unless its light quantum is identical with one of the light quanta that the atom can emit.

Now the Raman effect seems to conflict with this law. The positions of the Raman-lines in the spectrum do not correspond, in point of fact, with the frequencies of the atom itself, and they move with the activating ray. Raman has explained this apparent contradiction and the coming into existence of the lines by the effect of combination between the quantum of light coming from without and the quanta of light that are released or bound in the atom. If the atom, at the same time as it receives from without a quantum of light, emits a quantum of light of a different magnitude, and if the difference between these two quanta is identical with the quantum of light which is bound or released when an electron passes from one path to another, the quantum of light coming from without is absorbed. In that case the atom will emit an extra frequency, which either will be the sum of or the difference between the activating ray and a frequency in the atom itself. In this case these new lines group themselves round the incoming primary frequency on either side of it, and the distance between the activating frequency and the nearest Raman-lines will be identical with the lowest oscillation frequencies of the atom or with its ultrared spectrum. What has been said as to the atom and its oscillations also holds good of the molecule.

In this way we get the ultrared spectrum moved up to the spectral line of the activating light. The discovery of the Raman-line has proved to be of extraordinarily great importance for our knowledge of the structure of molecules.

So far, indeed, there have been all but insuperable difficulties in the way of studying these ultrared oscillations, because that part of the spectrum lies so far away from the region where the photographic plate is sensitive. Raman's discovery has now overcome these difficulties, and the way has been opened for the investigation of the oscillations of the nucleus of the molecules. We choose the primary ray within that range of frequency where the photographic plate is sensitive. The ultrared spectrum, in the form of the Raman-lines, is moved up to that region and, in consequence of that, exact measurements of its lines can be effected.

In the same way the ultraviolet spectrum can be investigated with the help of the Raman effect. Thus we have obtained a simple and exact method for the investigation of the entire sphere of oscillation of the molecules.

Raman himself and his fellow-workers have, during the years that have elapsed since the discovery was made, investigated the frequencies in a large number of substances in a solid, liquid, and gaseous state. Investigations have been made as to whether different conditions of aggregation affect atoms and molecules, and the molecular conditions in electrolytic dissociation and the ultrared absorption spectrum of crystals have been studied.

Thus the Raman effect has already yielded important results concerning the chemical Constitution of substances; and it is to foresee that the extremely valuable tool that the Raman effect has placed in our hands will in the immediate future bring with it a deepening of our knowledge of the structure of matter.

Sir Venkata Raman. The Royal Academy of Sciences has awarded you the Nobel Prize in Physics for your eminent researches on the diffusion of gases and for your discovery of the effect that bears your name. The Raman effect has opened new routes to our knowledge of the structure of matter and has already given most important results.

I now ask you to receive the prize from the hands of His Majesty.

10

# Raman Effect, the Revolutionary Achievement

## Stokes and Anti-stokes Scattering

There are two types of Raman scattering, Stokes Scattering and Anti-stokes Scattering. The interaction of light with matter in a linear regime allows the absorption or simultaneous emission of light precisely matching the difference in energy levels of the interacting electrons.

The Raman effect corresponds, in perturbation theory, to the absorption and subsequent emission of a photon via an intermediate electron state, having a virtual energy level. There are three possibilities:

- no energy exchange between the incident photons and the molecules (and hence no Raman effect),
- energy exchanges occur between the incident photons and the molecules. The energy differences are equal to the differences of the vibrational and rotational energy-levels of the molecule. In crystals only specific phonons are allowed (solutions of the wave equations which do not cancel themselves) by the periodic structure, so Raman

scattering can only appear at certain frequencies. In amorphous materials like glasses, more phonons are allowed and thereby the discrete spectral lines become broad,

- molecule absorbs energy: Stokes scattering. The resulting photon of lower energy generates a Stokes line on the red side of the incident spectrum,
- molecule loses energy: anti-Stokes scattering. Incident photons are shifted to the blue side of the spectrum, thus generating an anti-Stokes line.

These differences in energy are measured by subtracting the energy of the mono-energetic laser light from the energy of the scattered photons. The absolute value, however, doesn't depend on the process (Stokes or anti-Stokes scattering), because only the energy of the different vibrational levels is of importance.

Therefore, the Raman spectrum is symmetric relative to the Rayleigh band. In addition, the intensities of the Raman bands are only dependent on the number of molecules occupying the different vibrational states, when the process began. If the sample is in thermal equilibrium, the relative numbers of molecules in states of different energy will be given by the Boltzmann distribution:

$$\frac{N_1}{N_0} = \frac{g_1}{g_0} e - \frac{\Delta E_v}{kT}$$

Where:

$N_0$: number of atoms in the lower vibrational state

$N_1$: number of atoms in the higher vibrational state

$g_0$: degeneracy of the lower vibrational state (number of orbitals of the same energy)

$g_1$: degeneracy of the higher vibrational state

$\Delta E_v$: energy difference between these two vibrational states

$k$: Boltzmann's constant

$T$: temperature in kelvins

Thus lower energy states will have more molecules in them than will higher (excited) energy states. Therefore, the Stokes spectrum will be more intense than the anti-Stokes spectrum.

## Distinction with Fluorescence

The Raman effect differs from the process of fluorescence. For the latter, the incident light is completely absorbed and the system is transferred to an excited state from which it can go to various lower states only after a certain resonance lifetime. The result of both processes is essentially the same: A photon with the frequency different from that of the incident photon is produced and the molecule is brought to a higher or lower energy level. But the major difference is that the Raman effect can take place for any frequency of the incident light. In contrast to the fluorescence effect, the Raman effect is therefore not a resonant effect. In practice, this means that a fluorescence peak is anchored at a specific excitation frequency, whereas a Raman peak maintains a constant separation from the excitation frequency. Another, related distinction is that Raman scattering is a coherent process, whereas fluorescence is not. This means that the measured intensity is the square of a coherent sum of scattering amplitudes. In practice, this means that different paths to the excitation of the same mode may interfere, leading to Fano effects: asymmetries in the shape of the scattering peaks.

## Selection Rules

The distortion of a molecule in an electric field, and therefore the vibrational Raman cross section, is determined by its polarisability.

A Raman transition from one state to another, and therefore a Raman shift, can be activated optically only in the presence of non-zero polarisability derivative with respect to the normal coordinate (that is, the vibration or rotation):

$$\left|\frac{\partial \alpha}{\partial Q}\right| > 0$$

Raman-active vibrations/rotations can be identified by using almost any textbook that treats quantum mechanics or group theory for chemistry. Then, Raman-active modes can be found for molecules or crystals that show symmetry by using the appropriate character table for that symmetry group.

## Stimulated Scattering and Amplification

Raman amplification can be obtained by using Stimulated Raman Scattering (SRS), which actually is a combination of a Raman process with stimulated emission. It is interesting for application in telecommunication fibres to amplify inside the standard material with low noise for the amplification process. However, the process requires significant power and thus imposes more stringent limits on the material. The amplification band can be up to 100 nm broad, depending on the availability of allowed photon states.

SRS is one of the processes which impedes the laser coupling of ICF capsules.

## Spectrum Generation

For high intensity CW (Continuous Wave) lasers, SRS can be used to produce broad bandwidth spectra. This process can also be seen as a special case of four wave mixing, where the frequencies of the two incident photons are equal and the emitted spectra are found in two bands separated from the incident light by the phonon energies. The initial Raman spectrum is built up with spontaneous emission and is amplified later on.

At high pumping levels in long fibres, higher order Raman spectra can be generated by using the Raman spectrum as a new starting point, thereby building a chain of new spectra with decreasing amplitude. The disadvantage of intrinsic noise due to the initial spontaneous process can be overcome by seeding a spectrum at the beginning, or even using a feedback loop like in a resonator to stabilise the process. Since this technology easily fits into the fast evolving fibre laser field and there is demand for transversal coherent high intensity light sources (i.e. broadband telecommunication, imaging applications), Raman amplification and spectrum generation might be widely used in the near future.

## Applications

Raman spectroscopy employs the Raman effect for materials analysis. The frequency of light scattered from a molecule may be changed based on the structural characteristics of the molecular bonds. A monochromatic light source (laser) is required for illumination, and a spectrogram of the scattered light then shows the deviations caused by state changes in the molecule.

Raman spectroscopy is used as a tool to detect high-frequency phonons, magnons and electronic excitations.

Raman spectroscopy is also used in combustion diagnostics. Being a completely non-intrusive technique, it permits the detection of the major species and temperature distribution inside combustors and in flames without any perturbation of the (mainly fluid dynamic and reactive) processes examined.

Stimulated Raman transitions are also widely used for manipulating a trapped ion's energy levels, and thus basis qubit states.

Raman amplification is used in optical amplifiers.

Raman lidar is used in atmospheric physics to study aerosol vertical distribution.

## The Experiment

At the time of the discovery, the 40-year-old Raman held the Palit Chair for physics at Calcutta University. His research, however, was conducted at the Indian Association for the Cultivation of Science (IACS) in Calcutta, which was established by Mahendra Lal Sircar in 1876 as the first basic research centre in India. Educated entirely in India, Raman made his first trip to London in 1921, where his reputation in the study of optics and especially acoustics was already known to the English physicists J. J. Thomson and Lord Rutherford, who gave him a warm reception. Raman's speciality had been the study of the vibrations and sounds of stringed instruments such as the violin, the Indian veena and tambura, and the uniquely Indian percussion instruments, the tabla and the mridangam.

But it was the return trip from London to Bombay aboard the *S.S. Narkunda* that would change forever the direction of Raman's future. During the fifteen-day voyage, his restless and probing mind became fascinated with the deep blue colour of the Mediterranean. Unable to accept Lord Rayleigh's explanation that the colour of the sea was just a reflection of the colour of the sky, Raman proceeded to outline his thoughts on the matter while still at sea and sent a letter to the editors of the journal *Nature* when the ship docked in Bombay. A short time later Raman was able to show conclusively that the colour of the sea was the result of the scattering of sunlight by the water molecules.

Ironically, it was exactly the same argument that Rayleigh had invoked when explaining the colour of the sky — the blue was the result of the scattering of sunlight by the molecules in the air. Raman was now obsessed with the phenomenon of light scattering. His group in Calcutta began an extensive series of measurements of light scattered primarily by liquids but also by some solids. As a result, Raman was able to explain the blue colour observed in the ice of Alpine glaciers.

Analysis of light scattered by a liquid is not an easy task, and much of the early work in Calcutta was done by the visual observation of colour rather than precise measurements of the light's wavelength.

The violet light of the solar spectrum is isolated with a violet filter and passed through the liquid sample. Most of the light emerging from the liquid sample is the same colour as the incident violet beam: the so-called Rayleigh scattered light. However, Raman and K. S. Krishnan were able to show that some of the scattered light was a different colour, which they could isolate by using a green filter placed between the observer and the sample. The advantage of using a visual observation is that several substances can be studied quickly. In his first report to *Nature*, titled "A New Type of Secondary Radiation," Raman indicated that approximately 60 different liquids had been studied, and all showed the same result-some scattered light had a different colour than the incident light. "It is thus," Raman said, "a phenomenon whose universal nature has to be recognised."

The Raman Effect is a very weak effect; only one in a million of the scattered light particles, or photons, actually exhibits the change in wavelength. This explains, in part, why the effect was not discovered earlier. In all of the early light-scattering studies, the excitation source was sunlight, which Raman has described as being plentiful in Calcutta, but it still lacked the desired intensity. The acquisition in 1927 by the IACS of a seven-inch (18 cm) refracting telescope enabled Raman to condense the sunlight and create a more powerful light source for his studies. By early-1928, mercury arc lamps were commercially available, and he switched to this even more intense light source. Raman knew that visual and qualitative observations alone would not be sufficient information. He methodically set out to measure the exact wavelengths of the incident and Raman scattering by replacing the observer with a pocket spectroscope. He ultimately replaced it with a quartz spectrograph with which he could photograph the spectrum of the scattered light and measure its wavelength. These quantitative results were first published in the *Indian Journal of Physics* on March 31, 1928.

## Raman Effect as the Physicist's Tool

The significance of the Raman Effect was recognised quickly by other scientists. Professor R. W. Wood of Johns Hopkins cabled *Nature* to report that he had verified Raman's "brilliant and surprising discovery ... in every particular. It appears to me that this very beautiful discovery which resulted from Raman's long and patient study of the phenomenon of light scattering is one of the most convincing proofs of the quantum theory." Raman had also recognised that his discovery was important to the debate in physics over the new quantum theory, because an explanation of the new radiation required the use of photons and their change in energy as they interacted with the atoms in a particular molecule. Raman also knew that there was a more important result, remarking in his 1930 Nobel Prize address that "... the character of the scattered radiations enables us to obtain an insight into the ultimate structure of the scattering substance."

In the first seven years after its discovery, the Raman Effect was the subject of more than 700 papers in the scientific literature, mostly by physicists who were using the technique to study the vibration and rotation of molecules and relating those phenomena to the molecular structure. Then, as noted by Raman biographer G. Venkataraman, there was a decline in interest, as "the first bloom of novelty had worn off and physicists were satisfied that they understood the origin of the effect." At the same time, chemists became interested in the Raman Effect as an analytical tool. In James Hibben's words, "The Raman Effect became the adopted child of chemistry."

## Raman Effect as a Chemist's Tool

By the late-1930s the Raman Effect had become the principal method of non-destructive chemical analysis for both organic and inorganic compounds. The unique spectrum of Raman scattered light for any particular substance served as a "fingerprint" that could be used for qualitative analysis, even in a mixture of materials. Further, the intensity of the spectral lines was related to the amount of the substance. Raman spectroscopy could be applied not only to liquids but also to gases and solids. And unlike many other analytical methods, it could be applied easily to the analysis of aqueous solutions. It was a ubiquitous technique, giving information on what and how much was present in a plethora of samples.

The use of Raman spectroscopy as a basic analytical tool changed sharply after World War II. During the war, infrared spectroscopy was enhanced by the development of sensitive detectors and advances in electronics. Infrared measurements quickly became routine operations, while Raman measurements still required skilled operators and darkroom facilities. Raman spectroscopy could no longer compete with infrared until another development in physics — the laser — revived Raman spectroscopy in a new form beginning in the 1960s.

## Laser and Raman Spectroscopy

Raman understood the need for more intense light sources to amplify the effect and observation of the scattered light. The laser provided an even more intense source of light that not only could serve as a probe exploring the properties of the molecule but could also induce dramatically new effects. With the development of the

Fourier Transform (FT) technique and the application of computers for data handling, commercial FT-Raman spectrometers became available in the late-1980s, resulting in resurgence in the use of the original Raman Effect. The new Raman spectroscopy has been used to monitor manufacturing processes in the petrochemical and pharmaceutical industries. Illegal drugs captured at a crime scene can be analysed rapidly without breaking the evidence seal on the plastic bag. Chemists can watch paint dry and understand what reactions are occurring as the paint hardens. Using a fibre-optic probe, they can analyse nuclear waste material from a safe distance. Photochemists and photobiologists are using laser Raman techniques to record the spectra of transient chemical species with lifetimes as small as $10^{-11}$ seconds. Surface-enhanced Raman spectroscopy is used for studying surfaces and reactions on surfaces. And, according to Kathy Kincade, Raman spectroscopy "has the ability to provide specific biochemical information that may foreshadow the onset of cancer and other life-threatening illnesses."

In his 1928 talk in Bangalore, Raman concluded, "We are obviously only at the fringe of a fascinating new region of experimental research which promises to throw light on diverse problems relating to radiation and wave theory, X-ray optics, atomic and molecular spectra, fluorescence and scattering, thermodynamics, and chemistry. It all remains to be worked out."

Seventy years later scientists are still actively working out the results and practical applications of Raman's deceptively simple experiment.

# 11

# Views on Raman

***Albert Einstein***

Dr. C. V. Raman was the first to recognise and demonstrate that the energy of a photon can undergo a partial transformation within matter. I still recall vividly the deep impression that this discovery made on all of us, who at the time, attended the colloquium in Berlin.

***Ashutosh Mukherjee***

I shall fail in my duty. If I were to restrain myself in my expression of the genuine admiration. I feel for the courage and spirit of self sacrifice with which Mr. Raman has decided to exchange a lucrative official appointment for a university professorship, which I regret to say, does not carry even liberal emoluments. This one instance encourages me to entertain to hope that there will be no lack of seekers after truth in the temple of knowledge which it is our ambition to erect.

***C. Rajagopalachari***

Let us honour C. V. Raman, one of our eminent men who has raised India in international status and who adds to the honour of every title or honour bestowed on him.

### *Dr. M. K. V. Bappu*

Raman belonged to the restricted fold, whose members gained inspiration from the beauty of their surroundings. The blue of the ocean, the plumage of the birds, floral colours and the symmetry of crystals gave him a feeling of intense rapture, and the inspiration to ponder over their origins and characteristics. Likewise the canopy of stars as seen on a clear moonless night must have stirred the imagination of one who was so much impressed by natural splendour. Indeed in one of his writing he has described astronomy as "a river of knowledge which flows to the earth and fertilizes the fields of learning and culture".

### *Dr. S. Radhakrishnan*

Dr. Raman was a great teacher. His knowledge was not confined to Physical Science. In this over specialised his world, breadth of knowledge was remarkable. He combined highest intellectual integrity with a winning warmth of heart. His latter feature sometimes comes out in his utterances, which are delightfully free and frank. He was our most illustrious scientist, who continued for many years to guide the scientific progress of India.

### *Lord Rutherford*

Sir Venkata Raman is one of the leading authorities in Optics, in particular on the phenomenon of the scattering of light. In this connection he is govern that the lights colour could be changed by scattering. This had been predicted sometime before, but in spite of search, the change had not been found. The 'Raman Effect' must rank among the best three or four discoveries in experimental physics in the last decade, it has proved and it will prove, an instrument of great power in the study of the theory of solids.

### *Prof. Bhagwantam*

He (Raman) was a self-made man and had always set an example to his associates and students, of hard work, indomitable will and total dedication to science, which he practised during his entire life time, was so intense and so much to the exclusion of all other interests that in tune with the traditions of Indian scholarship, one would be justified in calling him a real Rishi.

Nature was the object of his worship. We should not fall into the trap of regarding him (Raman) as just a successful scientist like what we generally regard other successful scientists or successful businessmen and successful politicians. Men like him are not thrown up every day and if the rugged contours and sharp corners of this giant did not compromise with the soft spoken ways of the successful world, we can only describe the phenomenon by stating that "it is no reproach on Everest that one cannot play golf on it."

### *Prof. K. Ramanathan*

Prof. Raman's scientific achievements, infections and enthusiasm for science attracted motivated young men from all parts of the country. He trained them in scientific research and instilled self-confidence in them. When they went out into the world, they could grow on their own and create schools of research in universities or entering scientific services in Government, invigorate and improve them by research arid development. Raman himself remained till the last day of his life and dedicated life, the wide-eyed child of Nature, inquisitive about all aspects and phenomena of Nature and their inner workings. May the example and memory of Prof. Raman's life and work, his courage, his faith in young men and women, and his ceaseless quest for Truth be an inspiration to the young people of our country.

### *Prof. M. G. K. Menon*

Prof. Raman showed the true humility of a scientist when he spoke about others whom he regarded highly and admired such as Newton, Rayleigh, Einstein, Rutherford and so on. Among the great men of science these stood out as towering singularities. And these were the men whom Prof. Raman hoped to emulate in some way. Prof. Raman himself was in the line of the great classical scientists — a dwindling band. The richness of his life and of his discoveries and his outstanding qualities have covered the canvas of Indian science in dominating fashion for over half a century — a richness for which Indian science will ever be grateful.

12

# Lectures and Letters

## LECTURES

### On the Molecular Scattering of Light

#### *The Colour of the Sea*

In the history of science, we often find that the study of some natural phenomenon has been the starting-point in the development of a new branch of knowledge. We have an instance of this in the colour of skylight, which has inspired numerous optical investigations, and the explanation of which, proposed by the late Lord Rayleigh, and subsequently verified by observation, forms the beginning of our knowledge of the subject of this lecture. Even more striking, though not so familiar to all, is the colour exhibited by oceanic waters. A voyage to Europe in the summer of 1921 gave me the first opportunity of observing the wonderful blue opalescence of the Mediterranean Sea. It seemed not unlikely that the phenomenon owed its origin to the scattering of sunlight by the molecules of the water. To test this explanation, it appeared desirable to ascertain the laws governing the diffusion of light in liquids, and experiments with this object were started immediately on my return to Calcutta in September, 1921. It soon became evident, however, that the subject possessed a significance extending far beyond the special purpose for which the work was undertaken, and that it offered unlimited scope for research. It seemed indeed that the study of light-scattering might carry one into the deepest problems of physics and chemistry, and it was this belief which led to the subject becoming the main theme of our activities at Calcutta from that time onwards.

### *The Theory of Fluctuations*

From the work of the first few months, it became clear that the molecular scattering of light was a very general phenomenon which could be studied not only in gases and vapours but also in liquids and in crystalline and amorphous solids, and that it was primarily an effect arising from molecular disarray in the medium and consequent local fluctuations in its optical density. Except in amorphous solids, such molecular disarray could presumably be ascribed to thermal agitation, and the experimental results appeared to support this view. The fact that molecules are optically anisotropic and can orientate freely in liquids was found to give rise to an additional type of scattering. This could be distinguished from the scattering due to fluctuations in density by reason of its being practically unpolarised, whereas the latter was completely polarised in the transverse direction. The whole subject was critically reviewed and the results till then obtained were set out in an essay published by the Calcutta University Press in February 1922.

The various problems requiring solution indicated in this essay were investigated with the aid of a succession of able collaborators. It is possible to mention briefly only a few of the numerous investigations which were carried out at Calcutta during the six years 1922 to 1927. The scattering of light in fluids was studied by Ramanathan over a wide range of pressures and temperatures with results which appeared to support the "fluctuation" theory of its origin. His work also disclosed the remarkable changes in the state of polarisation which accompany the variations of intensity with temperature in vapours and in liquids. Liquid mixtures were investigated by Kameswara Rao, and furnished optical proof of the existence in such systems, of simultaneous fluctuations of density, composition, and molecular orientation. Srivastava studied the scattering of light in crystals in relation to the thermal fluctuations of density and their increase with temperature. Ramdas investigated the scattering of light by liquid surfaces due to thermal agitation, and established a relation between surface-tension and surface-opalescence. He also traced the transition from surface-opalescence to volume-opalescence which occurs at the critical temperature. Sogani investigated X-ray diffraction in liquids, in order to connect it with their optical behaviour, and test the application of fluctuation theory to X-ray scattering.

### *The Anisotropy of Molecules*

As stated above, the state of polarisation of the light scattered in fluids is connected with the optical anisotropy of the molecules. Much of the work done at Calcutta during the years 1922 to 1927 was intended to obtain data concerning this property and to establish its relations with various optical phenomena. Krishnan examined a great many liquids, and by his work showed very clearly the dependence of the optical anisotropy of the molecule on its chemical Constitution. Ramakrishna Rao studied the depolarisation of scattered light in a very large number of gases and vapours, and obtained information of high importance for the progress of the subject. Venkateswaran studied the scattering of light in aqueous solutions to find the influence on it of electrolytic dissociation. Ramachandra Rao investigated liquids having highly elongated molecules and also highly polar substances over a wide range of temperatures, and discovered the influence of molecular shape and molecular association on the depolarisation of scattered light in liquids.

The interpretation of the observations with liquids involved the development of a molecular theory of light-scattering in dense media which was undertaken by Ramanathan, myself, and Krishnan. A revised opalescence formula was derived which differed from that of Einstein and yielded results in better agreement with observation. Krishnan and myself also published a series of investigations showing how the optical anisotropy of the molecules deduced from light scattering could be utilised to interpret the optical and dielectric behaviour of fluids, and also the electric, magnetic, and mechanical birefringence exhibited by them. The conclusions derived from these studies enabled a connection to be established between the molecular anisotropy observed in fluids and the optical, electric, and magnetic aeolotropy exhibited by solids in the crystalline state.

### *A New Phenomenon*

The investigations referred to above were in the main guided by the classical electromagnetic theory of light, the application of which to the problems of light-scattering is chiefly associated with the names of Rayleigh and of Einstein. Nevertheless, the possibility that the corpuscular nature of light might come into evidence in scattering was not overlooked and was in fact elaborately discussed in the essay of February 1922 which was published at least a year before the well-known discoveries of Compton on X-ray scattering. While our experiments in the main appeared to support the electromagnetic theory of light, evidence came to hand at a very early stage of the investigations of the existence of a phenomenon which seemed to stand outside the classical scheme of thought. The scattering of light in transparent fluids is extremely feeble, much weaker in fact than the Tyndall effect usually observed in turbid media. It was experimentally discovered that associated with the Rayleigh-Einstein type of molecular scattering, was another and still feebler type of secondary radiation, the intensity of which was of the order of magnitude of a few hundredths of the classical scattering, and differed from it in not having the same wavelength as the primary or incident radiation. The first observation of this phenomenon was made at Calcutta in April 1923 by Ramanathan who was led to it in attempting to explain why in certain liquids (water, ether, methyl and ethyl alcohols), the depolarisation of scattered light varied with the wavelength of the incident radiation. Ramanathan found that after exhaustive chemical purification and repeated slow distillation of the liquid in vacuum, the new radiation persisted undiminished in intensity, showing that it was a characteristic property of the substance studied and not due to any fluorescent impurity. Krishnan observed a similar effect in many other liquids in 1924, and a somewhat more conspicuous phenomenon was observed by me in ice and in optical glasses.

### *The Optical Analogue of the Compton Effect*

The origin of this puzzling phenomenon naturally interested us, and in the summer of 1925, Venkateswaran attempted to investigate it by photographing the spectrum of the scattered light from liquids, using sunlight filtered through colour screens, but was unable to report any decisive results. Ramakrishna Rao in his studies on the depolarisation of scattering during 1926 and 1927 looked carefully for a similar phenomenon in gases and vapours, but without success. This problem was taken up again by Krishnan towards the end of 1927. While his work was in progress, the first indication of the true nature of the phenomenon came to hand from a different quarter. One of the problems interesting us at this time was the behaviour in light-scattering of highly viscous organic liquids which were capable of passing over into the glassy state. Venkateswaran undertook to study this question, and reported the highly interesting result that the colour of sunlight scattered in a highly purified sample of glycerine was a brilliant green instead of the usual blue. The phenomenon appeared to be similar to that discovered by Ramanathan in water and the alcohols, but of much greater intensity, and, therefore, more easily studied. No time was lost in following up the matter. Tests were made with a series of filters transmitting narrow regions of the solar spectrum and placed in the path of the incident beam, which showed that in every case the colour of the scattered light was different from that of the incident light, and was displaced from it towards the red. The radiations were also strongly polarised. These facts indicated a clear analogy between the empirical characters of the phenomenon and the Compton effect. The work of Compton had made familiar the idea that the wavelength of radiation could be degraded in the process of scattering, and the observations with glycerine suggested to me that the phenomenon which had puzzled us ever since 1923 was in fact the optical analogue of the Compton effect. This idea naturally stimulated further investigation with other substances.

The chief difficulty which had hitherto oppressed us in the study of the new phenomenon was its extreme feebleness in general. This was overcome by using a 7-inch refracting telescope in combination with a short-focus lens to condense sunlight into a pencil of very great intensity. With these arrangements and using complementary light-filters in the path of the incident and scattered beams, as was done by Ramanathan in 1923, to isolate the modified radiations, it was found that they could be readily observed in a great many liquids, and that in many cases they were strongly polarised. Krishnan, who very materially assisted me in these investigations, found at the same time that the phenomenon could be observed in several organic vapours, and even succeeded in visually determining the state of polarisation of the modified radiations from them. Compressed gases such as $CO_2$ and $N_2O$, crystalline ice, and optical glasses also were found to exhibit the modified radiations. These observations left little doubt that the phenomenon was really a species of light-scattering analogous to the Compton effect.

### *The Spectroscopic Characters of the New Effect*

Thanks to the vastly more powerful illumination made available by the 7-inch refractor, the spectroscopic examination of the effect, which had been abandoned in 1925 as indecisive, now came within the reach of direct visual study. With a Zeiss cobalt-glass filter placed in the path of the incident beam and one or other of a series of organic liquids as the scattering substance, a band in the blue-green region was observed by me in the spectrum of the scattered light, separated by a dark interval from the indigo-violet region transmitted by the filter. Both of these regions in the spectrum became sharper when the region of transmission was narrowed by the insertion of an additional filter in the incident beam. This suggested the employment, instead of sunlight, of the highly monochromatic radiations given by a mercury arc in combination with a condenser of large aperture and a cobalt-glass filter.

With these arrangements the spectrum of the scattered light from a variety of liquids and solids was visually examined, and the startling observation was made that the spectrum generally included a number of sharp lines or bands on a diffuse background which were not present in the light of the mercury arc.

The quartz mercury lamp was so powerful and convenient a source of monochromatic illumination that, at least in the case of liquids and solids, photographing the spectrum of scattered light was found to present no extraordinary difficulties. The earliest pictures of the phenomenon were in fact taken with a portable quartz spectrograph of the smallest size made by the firm of Hilger. With a somewhat larger instrument of the same type, Krishnan obtained very satisfactory spectrograms with liquids and with crystals on which measurements of the desired precision could be made, and on which the presence of lines displaced towards the violet was first definitely established. The experimental difficulties were naturally greater in the case of gases or vapours, though they could be lessened by working with the substance under pressure. With an improvised instrument of large aperture (F/1.8), Ramdas obtained the first spectrograms with a gaseous substance (ether vapour) at atmospheric pressure.

In interpreting the observed phenomena, the analogy with the Compton effect was adopted as the guiding principle. The work of Compton had gained general acceptance for the idea that the scattering of radiation is a unitary process in which the conservation principles hold good. Accepting this idea it follows at once that, if the scattering particle gains any energy during the encounter with the quantum, the latter is deprived of energy to the same extent, and accordingly appears after scattering as a radiation of diminished frequency. From thermodynamic principles, it follows that the reverse process should also be possible. Adopting these ideas, the actual observations could be interpreted, and the agreement of the observed displacements with the infrared frequencies of the molecules made it clear that the new method opened up an illimitable field of experimental research in the study of the structure of matter.

### *Interpretation of the Effect*

It appears desirable to emphasise that though the conservation principle of Compton is useful in interpreting the effects disclosed by experiment, it is by itself insufficient to explain the observed phenomena. As is well known from studies on molecular spectra, a gaseous molecule has four different species of energy of increasing orders of magnitude, namely those corresponding to translatory motion, rotation, vibration, and electronic excitation. Each of these, except the first, is quantised and may be represented by an integer in an extended sequence of quantum numbers. The aggregate energy of a molecule may, therefore, assume any one out of a very large number of possible values. If we assume that an exchange of energy occurs in the collision between the molecule and the quantum, and limit ourself to the cases in which the final energy of the molecule is less than that of the incident quantum, we arrive at the result that the spectrum of the scattered light should contain an immense number of new lines and should in fact rival in its complexity the band spectrum of the molecule observed in the emission or absorption of light. Nothing more different from what is actually observed can be imagined than the foregoing picture. The most conspicuous feature revealed by experiment is the beautiful simplicity of the spectra of even complicated polyatomic molecules obtained in light-scattering, a simplicity that is in striking contrast to the extreme complexity of their emission or absorption spectra. It is this simplicity that gives to the study of light-scattering its special significance and value. It is clear that the effect actually observed was not and could not have been foreseen from an application of the conservation principles.

The general principle of correspondence between the quantum and classical theories enunciated by Niels Bohr enables us, on the other hand, to obtain a real insight into the actual phenomena. The classical theory of light-scattering tells us that if a molecule scatters light while it is moving, rotating or vibrating, the scattered radiations may include certain frequencies, different from those of the incident waves. This classical picture, in many respects, is surprisingly like what we actually observe in the experiments. It explains why the frequency shifts observed fall into three classes, translational, rotational and vibrational, of different orders of magnitude. It explains the observed selection rules, as for instance, why the frequencies of vibration deduced from scattered light include only the fundamentals and not the overtones and combinations which are so conspicuous in emission and absorption spectra. The classical theory can even go further and give us a rough indication of the intensity and polarisation of the radiations of altered frequency. Nevertheless, the classical picture has to be modified in essential respects to give even a qualitative description of the phenomena, and we have, therefore, to invoke the aid of quantum principles. The work of Kramers and Heisenberg, and the newer developments in quantum mechanics which have their root in Bohr's correspondence principle seem to offer a promising way of approach towards an understanding of the experimental results. But until we know much more than we do at present regarding the structure of molecules, and have sufficient quantitative experimental knowledge of the effect, it would be rash to suggest that they afford a complete explanation of it.

### *The Significance of the Effect*

The universality of the phenomenon, the convenience of the experimental technique and the simplicity of the spectra obtained enable the effect to be used as an experimental aid to the solution of a wide range of problems in physics and chemistry. Indeed, it may be said that it is this fact which constitutes the principal significance of the effect. The frequency differences determined from the spectra, the width and character of the lines appearing in them, and the intensity and state of polarisation of the scattered radiations enable us to obtain an insight into the ultimate structure of the scattering substance. As experimental research has shown, these features in the spectra are very definitely influenced by physical conditions, such as temperature and state of aggregation, by physico-chemical conditions, such as mixture, solution, molecular association and polymerisation, and most essentially by chemical Constitution. It follows that the new field of spectroscopy has practically unrestricted scope in the study of problems relating to the structure of matter. We may also hope that it will lead us to a fuller understanding of the nature of light, and of the interactions between matter and light.

### *Some Concluding Remarks*

From a physical point of view, the quantitative study of the effect with the simplest molecules holds out the largest hope of fundamental advances. The beautiful work of McLennan with liquefied gases, and of R. W. Wood and Rasetti are pioneer investigations in this field which command the highest admiration. The quantitative study of the effect with crystals of the simplest possible chemical Constitution is naturally of great importance. The case of the diamond, which has been investigated by Ramaswamy, Robertson, and Fox, and with especial completeness by Bhagavantam, is of special interest. Very surprising results have been obtained with this substance, which may be the pathway to a fuller understanding of the nature of the crystalline state. I should also like to draw attention to the work of Krishnamurti, who has traced a remarkable dependence of the intensity of the spectral lines observed in scattering on the nature of the chemical bond, and followed the transition from the homopolar to the heteropolar type of chemical combination. Krishnamurti's observation that the paramagnetism of crystals apparently influences the observed intensity of the displaced lines is one of the most remarkable ever made in this new field of research.

## The Role of the Retina in Vision

### *Introduction*

Our sense-organs are the gateways through which a knowledge of the external world reaches us. The relationships which exist between our sensory impressions and the nature of the stimuli which excite those impressions are thus matters of great importance. For, they furnish us with indications regarding the processes by which the stimuli received by the sense-organs are transformed into sense-impressions. Studies on the perception of stimuli of the simplest character are particularly important, since their results are most readily analysed and understood.

Light which appears as a sharply-defined line in the spectrum is the simplest type of radiation. It is appropriate therefore that we recognise the sensations excited by monochromatic lights of various colours as the primary or fundamental visual sensations. Likewise, when a continuous spectrum of radiation is dispersed by a prism into a band of colour, each strip which the eye can distinguish as being different in hue from the strips on either side can be regarded as a primary or fundamental visual sensation. Hence the primary visual sensations are as numerous as the hues which can be distinguished from each other in the spectrum by the eye under the most favourable conditions of observation.

We may here usefully recall various facts of observation. It is known that as many as 250 different hues in the spectrum can be distinguished under appropriate conditions. The spectral shift which results in an observable change of hue is less than 20 A over the greater part of the spectrum and as little as 10 A in some parts. It is also known that the addition of white light in any desired proportion to a pure spectral colour does not change the observed hue. Quantitative studies have further established that the power of the eye to discriminate between the hues of adjacent regions in the spectrum is not sensibly diminished even when the colours are diluted by considerable additions of white light to the fields under comparison.

The facts of experience stated above are just what we would expect to find if the colours of homogeneous light are the primary or fundamental colour sensations. That such a relationship exists is not in the least surprising. For, our organs of vision would be of little use to us, if the external stimuli and the sensations which they excite are not very simply related to each other. We are, therefore, entirely justified in concluding that the basic or primary sensations with which physiological optics has to concern itself are those produced by the radiations which are recognised by the physicist as simple and homogeneous. These sensations stand in a category by themselves and they are clearly distinguishable from the sensations excited by compound or heterogeneous radiation.

The basic problem in physiological optics is thus to find an answer to the question, how does the apparatus of human vision function and enable us to distinguish the colours of monochromatic lights from each other with the degree of precision actually observed?

### *The Nature of the Visual Process*

Geometrical optics and the wave-theory of light form an appropriate basis for a consideration of the propagation of light in refractive media. Thus, they enter into the realm of physiological optics when we consider the functioning of the cornea and the crystalline lens and the formation of images of external objects on the retina. But when we reach the retina, wave-optics ceases to be relevant, and Einstein's concept of light as consisting of discrete energy-quanta or photons necessarily takes its place. For, the wave-theory is incapable of giving any acceptable explanation of such phenomena as the emission or absorption of light and the transformations of light-energy. Hence, we must lay aside the ideas and language of the wave-theory and think of light as a stream of photons, if we are to make any progress towards an understanding of the facts of human vision.

Homogeneous light may be described as a stream of radiant energy consisting of units or quanta which are all identical. The quanta increase progressively in magnitude as we move up the spectrum from the red towards the violet end. The colour of the perceived light also changes progressively in the same circumstances. We are, therefore, justified in associating the sensation of colour experienced in homogeneous light with the energy carried by the individual photons or light-quanta. The other sensation excited by light, viz., its luminosity, is determined by the number of photons traversing any given area per unit of time. Thus, the two physiologically experienced sensations of colour and luminosity excited by homogeneous light are connected respectively with the two specifiable properties of the radiation in the language of the quantum theory.

A fuller insight into the nature of the visual process is furnished by quantitative data of two different sorts which are available regarding the sensations excited by homogeneous light. These data are represented in the form of the curves known respectively as "the luminous-efficiency curve" and "the hue-discrimination curve" of the visible spectrum. The luminous-efficiency curve exhibits the results of a comparison of the visual luminosity of the different parts of the visible spectrum for a constant energy-flux. The hue-discrimination curve represents determinations of the smallest difference of spectral position necessary to give an observable difference in colour between two fields of illumination, the luminosities of which are equal.

The data of observation represented in the hue-discrimination curve are particularly significant. In the entire range of the visible spectrum, a change in the energy of the photon of 1 per cent is sufficient to give a perceptible change of colour. Indeed, this statement underestimates the power of the visual mechanism to perceive differences of colour. Except near the ends of the spectrum where the luminosity is low, a change of one-half of 1 per cent in the energy of the photon is everywhere detectable. In the blue-green region, a change of one-fifth of 1 per cent and in the orange-yellow, of one-sixth of 1 per cent reveals itself by an alteration of the observed colour.

The facts of experience stated above are most readily understood if vision is assumed to result from the acceptance of the energy of the photon by the retina and its immediate transference without addition or subtraction to the centres of perception. We do not have to assume that all the photons incident on the retina are thus dealt with. A considerable proportion, especially in daylight vision, may be expected merely to pass through the retina and suffer absorption by the pigmented choroid coat behind it. The energy of the other photons may be expected to be used up in producing thermal effects or photochemical changes in the substance of the retina. The photons thus disposed of cannot be effective in vision. The observed precision of the colour sense over the entire visible spectrum precludes any such possibility.

The distribution of visible luminosity in the continuous spectrum of radiation emitted by a hot body differs greatly from the distribution of energy in it. This difference is a characteristic property of human vision and arises from the enormous differences between the luminous efficiencies of homogeneous radiation in the different parts of the spectrum. The efficiency exhibits a pronounced maximum in the green and falls off rapidly as we proceed away from it either towards the red or towards the violet end of the spectrum, but more rapidly so in the latter case.

Indeed, the luminosity of the violet end of the spectrum is very low. These differences in the ability of photons of different energies to excite the sensation of luminosity are ascribable to the differences in the probability of their energies being taken over by the retina and transmitted to the centres of perception as indicated above. On this basis, we should expect to find noticeable relationships between the variations of luminosity and of colour in the different parts of the spectrum, and this is actually the case. We shall return to these topics later.

### *The Spectral Sensitivity of the Retina*

A technique of observation has been devised and used by the author which is both simple and effective and which enables an observer to see a greatly enlarged picture of his own retina in the act of functioning. The technique enables highly important information regarding the structure of the retina and its sensitivity to light in different areas and in different parts of the spectrum to be obtained.

We may first briefly explain the technique and how it works. By screening the eye from an external illumination for a short period which need not exceed a few minutes, it is possible greatly to increase the sensitivity of the retina to light. This improvement may be made spectrally selective, in other words, restricted to any desired part of the spectrum by using an appropriately chosen colour filter and holding it before the eye for a suitable interval of time. Accordingly, when the filter is removed and a brightly lit white surface is viewed by the observer, he sees on it a picture of his own retina which exhibits the selective responses of its different areas to the parts of the spectrum which had been screened off by the filter before its removal. This picture, of course, is fugitive. But it may be recalled as often as desired by putting back the filter and then removing it from before the eye.

A series often drawings of the retina showing the effects observed with different colour-filters in the manner explained above are reproduced in the accompanying colour plates. The colour-filters were prepared by dyeing gelatine films on glass with different water-soluble dyes to an appropriate depth of colour and then washing and drying the film. The commercial names of the colouring matters used are entered against each figure. We shall proceed to comment briefly on the effects noticed with the different filters.

It is significant that a rhodamine filter, which cuts off the green sector of the spectrum without weakening other regions, gives no observable effect following its removal. This indicates that the sensitivity of the retina to the green which is the most luminous part of the spectrum is not sensibly enhanced by its being screened off from the eye for a brief period.

Very striking and beautiful effects are observed using a filter dyed with methyl-violet. The density of the filter and the accompanying changes in the strength of the absorption and the extent of cut-off in the spectrum greatly influence the observed results. In all cases, the foveal area and the foveolar depression are conspicuous features, the colour which they exhibit varying with the density of the filter. A lightly-dyed filter cuts off the yellow and orange sectors and weakens the green of the spectrum. With such a filter, the foveal region appears green, while yellow and orange are the dominant colours elsewhere in the field. A halo of orange-red hue appears encircling the foveal disc.

Using filters whose absorption is at the violet end of the spectrum and which accordingly appear yellow or orange by transmitted light, the retina exhibits a blue glow following the removal of the filter. With filters which cut off the red of the spectrum and allow the rest to pass through freely, a rose-red glow appears covering the entire field following the removal of the filter. The fovea is either not seen at all or is only very dimly visible in the retinal picture in these cases. Filters which appear green or greenish-blue by transmitted light usually exhibit a cut-off at both ends of the visible spectrum. If the cut-off covers the yellow and orange regions of the spectrum, the retinal picture shows the fovea very clearly as an yellow ring with a bright yellow spot at the foveola. With the more deeply coloured filters, the foveal region appears also encircled by a halo or haloes.

A variety of blue filters may be prepared by dyeing gelatine films on glass. All such filters cut off the yellow and orange regions of the spectrum, and hence when they are used, the fovea is invariably seen in the picture, the colour which it exhibits and the colour of the surrounding field varying with the nature of the spectral cut off by the filters. Very similar effects may also be observed using commercially available blue glasses. If such a filter cuts out the green, yellow and red sectors completely, its transmission is a clear deep blue of low intensity. When a filter of this kind is held against the eye against a bright background and then suddenly removed, a multi-coloured picture flashes into view in which the fovea with the foveola at its centre appears as a bright disc surrounded by a less luminous field and further encircled by a halo. This picture slowly fades away.

### *Observations with Polarised Light*

The use of a polaroid in combination with a colour filter in observations of the kind described above reveals some highly significant facts. It may be stated at once that the special effects observed with polarised light are restricted to the foveal area on the retina. They are seen with filters transmitting the violet and blue sectors of the spectrum and are unobservable with filters which do not transmit those parts of the spectrum. The use of filters which transmit other parts of the spectrum besides the blue and the violet serves only to dilute the observed effects and make them less readily observable.

We shall now proceed to state what is actually observed. Placing a blue filter in front of the eye, a bright field of illumination is viewed; after a few minutes, a polaroid is placed in front of the filter. A dark brush shaped like a dumbell crossed by a bright brush of similar shape then springs into view in the foveal area of vision. This picture slowly fades away. The polaroid is then suddenly removed, the blue filter remaining in place. *The brushes then reappear, but turned through a right angle, in other words, the bright brush takes the place of the dark brush and* vice-versa. This again duly fades away. The observations may be repeated as often as desired.

Observations of the same nature may also be made with the polaroid alone but without any colour-filter. Putting the polaroid in front of the eye, we observe the well-known phenomenon of Haidinger's brushes, a feeble yellow brush crossed by a blue brush appearing in the foveal area of vision. When this has faded away, the polaroid is suddenly removed. The brushes then reappear but with the yellow brush and the blue brush interchanged in their positions.

Another significant result emerges when the brightness of the field against which these brushes are viewed is varied. The polaroid and the blue filter should be used together so that the brushes are seen with the maximum clarity. Their fading-away is obviated by the simple device of oscillating the polaroid in its own plane through a right angle, so that the brushes remain continually visible, though constantly shifting their position. When the brightness of the field viewed by the observer through the polaroid-filter combination is progressively diminished. It is found that the visibility of the brushes vanishes when the level of illumination is reduced to the point at which the blue colour of the light becomes inconspicuous. In other words, the phenomena exhibited in polarised light are confined to the photopic levels of illumination and disappear when we pass into the scotopic range.

### *The Visual Pigments: Xanthophyll*

We shall now proceed to make use of the facts and results set forth in the preceding pages to establish the chemical identity of the colouring matters present in the retina which enable it to function as a receptor of vision in the photopic range of illumination. The functioning of the retina in the lowest or scotopic levels of illumination will not be dealt with here.

Xanthophyll is a plant pigment of very wide occurrence. Its chemical name is dihydroxy-á-carotene and its chemical formula is $C_{40}H_{58}O_2$; it is dextrorotatory and has no vitamin-A activity. The spectral properties of xanthophyll are similar to those of á-carotene. Xanthophyll is sensibly transparent for all wavelengths greater than 520 mµ; the absorption-strength becomes sensible at 500 mµ and rises very steeply beyond 490 mµ; it reaches a pronounced maximum at 477 mµ and this is followed by a second and even more pronounced maximum alt 448 mµ. It falls off at shorter wavelengths and after exhibiting a third and minor maximum at 420 mµ goes down steeply to small values beyond 400 mµ.

Like all the carotenoid pigments, xanthophyll exhibits in its structure a long chain of conjugated carbon-carbon double bonds, to which it owes its power to absorb light in the visible region of the spectrum. It may be remarked that this absorption appears only in the violet and blue sectors of the spectrum. The presence of xanthophyll in the retina is unquestionable. Indeed, the yellow colour of the *macula lutea* has long been known and that it is due to xanthophyll was established by extraction and the study of its absorption spectrum, notably by Wald. What we are now concerned with is to demonstrate that xanthophyll is the visual pigment which enables the eye to perceive light and colour in the violet and blue sectors of the spectrum. Several items of proof are forthcoming which will be set out in proper order.

The absorptive properties of xanthophyll account satisfactorily for the observed features of colour and luminosity in the spectrum. The region between 490 and 440 mµ usually marked out as the blue sector in the spectrum is also the region where the absorption of xanthophyll rises steeply from very small values to maximum strength. The region beyond 440 mµ designated as the violet sector of the spectrum is also the region where the absorption of xanthophyll having passed its zenith drops down to small values.

The wavelengths at which the absorption-curve of xanthophyll exhibits its steepest gradients are also the wavelengths at which the hue-discrimination curve in the spectrum exhibits the most pronounced dips, in other words, the wavelengths at which the spectral shifts necessary to produce an observable change of colour reach their minimum values. The very steep rise in absorption at 490 mμ corresponds exactly with the conspicuous dip of the hue-discrimination curve at 490 mμ. The second and much less conspicuous dip of the hue-discrimination curve at 440 mμ also coincides in its position with the steep fall of the absorption of xanthophyll after it has reached its maximum value.

The effects observed with polarised light are a conclusive demonstration that xanthophyll is the visual pigment for the blue and violet sectors of the spectrum. They are explained as follows: Xanthophyll has long-chain molecules containing an alternation of single and double bonds; they can absorb light and function as a visual pigment only if the light is polarised with the electric vibrations parallel to the chain-structure of the molecules. On the slopes of the foveal area, the nerve fibres have a radial setting. In that region, therefore, the xanthophyll molecules lie parallel to the nerve fibres and also have a radial setting. Hence, in the foveal area, a bright brush is seen in the same plane as the electric vector of the incident light and a dark brush in the transverse direction. That the brushes are visible only in the blue and violet sectors of the spectrum and not elsewhere is readily intelligible. For, the absorption of light by xanthophyll appears only in the former regions and not elsewhere.

That the brushes reappear turned through a right angle following the removal of the polaroid has already been mentioned. This is a further proof that we are here concerned with a physiological phenomenon and not with an effect of physical origin. When the polaroid is kept before the eye long enough, the sensitivity of the foveal region to light is enhanced in the region of the dark brush and diminished in the region of the bright brush. Hence, when the polaroid is taken out, the brushes are seen again but with the dark and bright brushes exchanged in their positions.

Xanthophyll functions as a visual pigment only under photopic conditions. It is therefore to be expected that the brushes observed in polarised light over the area of foveal vision disappear when the illumination is reduced from the photopic to the scotopic level.

### *The Visual Pigments: Hemeproteins*

The observations with colour filters described earlier make it evident that the pigments which enable the retina to function in the red and green sectors of the spectrum are different. However, it is also clear from those observations that there is an overlap of the regions of the spectrum in which the two pigments function and that they cooperate in the perception of light and colour in the regions of such overlap. It is in these regions that the spectral colours of yellow and orange are perceived.

That the pigments which enable us to perceive the green and the red of the spectrum are hemeproteins of the ferrous and ferric types respectively is indicated by various considerations. In the first place, the absorption of light by these pigments appears in just those regions of the spectrum where they are needed to account for the observed facts of vision. Ferroheme exhibits a pronounced maximum of absorption around 550 mμ. Likewise, the luminous efficiency in the spectrum exhibits a highly pronounced maximum around 550 mμ. Accordingly, we are justified in recognising ferroheme as the visual pigment which functions in the green sector of the spectrum. Ferriheme behaves differently. Its absorptive power is much weaker than that of ferroheme in the green but is much stronger in the red. Hence, we are led to assign to ferriheme the role of the visual pigment which functions at the red end of the spectrum.

As is well known defects and anomalies in the perception of red and green in the spectrum are fairly common. It is very significant that these defects and anomalies are congenital and that they are transmitted from generation to generation according to the laws of heredity. Further, whereas the condition of night-blindness arising from dietary deficiency can be rapidly cured by an adequate addition of vitamin A to the food consumed, the defects of photopic colour-vision cannot thus be dealt with. These facts very clearly indicate that the visual pigments which enable us to perceive the green and the red of the spectrum are products of biological activity in the human body itself and that they are not plant products which have entered the retina by way of the articles of food consumed.

Having thus set aside the possibility of the carotenoids being the visual pigments for the green and the red, We naturally turn to the other great class of pigments of biological origin, viz. those in which the chromophore is a tetrapyrrolic group with a metallic atom located at its centre. Thus, by a simple process of exclusion, we are led to the identification of our visual pigments as hemeproteins, as already indicated. Heme is ubiquitous and we need therefore have no hesitation in assuming its presence in the retinal structures. The analogy with the activity of chlorophyll in the green leaves of plants indicates that heme which is a powerful absorber of light is also capable of transferring the energy absorbed to the retinal structures and thus enabling it to be perceived. Heme is also fairly stable chemically. Though a substantial fraction of the incident photons may be used up in effecting photochemical changes, enough would be left over to make vision in daylight both possible and efficient.

### *Defects and Anomalies of Colour Vision*

The characteristics of the rare condition known as tritanopia may be explained as arising from the absence of the pigment xanthophyll from the retina. The defects and anomalies of colour vision more commonly met with appear in the part of the spectrum between the termination of the blue and the extreme red end. The recognition that the heme pigments in the ferrous and ferric states are the mediators of vision in these regions makes these defects and anomalies explicable. Indeed, it is also possible to elucidate in detail the results of quantitative studies of those defects and anomalies. The subject has" been fully discussed in an earlier memoir by the author. It will therefore suffice here to indicate broadly the approach developed in that publication.

As has already been explained, ferroheme is the visual pigment functioning in the green and ferriheme in the red; in the region of overlap of the absorption spectra of the two pigments, homogeneous light exhibits the various intermediate colours. The precise sequence of the luminosity and colour observed would evidently depend on the proportions of ferroheme and ferriheme functioning in the retina. The proportion in which iron is present in the ferrous and ferric states would presumably be determined by some regulating biochemical mechanism. Any malfunctioning of that mechanism would result in an alteration of the proportion in one direction or the other. This is the clue to the explanation of the observed deviations from the normal in the perception of light and colour.

If ferriheme be totally absent in the retinal pigment, the observer would fail to perceive the red end of the spectrum and the latter would therefore appear distinctly shortened. This is the state referred to as protanopic vision in the literature of the subject. If, on the other hand, the ferriheme is present in excess of the normal proportion, the region in which the two pigments function jointly would extend further towards the green. In consequence, the regular sequence of colour normally seen between the green and the red would tend to disappear. Ultimately, green and red would merge and be indistinguishable. This is the condition known as deuteronopia. Both in protanopia and in deuteronopia, the rapid change of hue appearing at 490 mμ would be observable. In both cases also, the colour progression from the green to the red would be unobservable, but for wholly different reasons.

Protoanomalous and deuteranomalous vision may be considered as intermediate states between the normal condition and the conditions of protanopia and deuteronopia respectively. The luminosity and hue discrimination curves determined by observation for these anomalous types of vision are in satisfactory accord with the results to be expected on that basis.

## Convocation Address

[*It is no small honour to be asked to address the Convocation of a University in India, and certainly it is a unique experience for me, at any rate, to be called upon to address a University Convocation at one place a second time*].

I know poverty and misery and I quite appreciate by personal experience what it is to be poor, what it is to have no clothes, what it is to have no books, what it is to struggle through life, what it is to walk through the streets without an umbrella, without conveyance along miles in dusty wards, I have been through it all and I can understand the difficulties that most of you graduates have to face up today. I'm speaking from a long experience of 60 years. Please do not imagine that all the 60 years are milk and roses. To be able to accomplish something I want to tell you that you have to go through such experience.

I admit, success in life is not always to the intelligent or the strong and it is to some extent a bit of a gamble, but nonetheless those who have got their minds right and those who know their job will sooner or later, sooner perhaps than later make their way in life. But they should not be disappointed if they do not they have to face up life and take it as they find it. This is the kind of philosophy that I have learnt by experience, and I make a free gift of it to you all.

What I say is this that the great things in life are not really great things in life. The Nobel Prize, the F.R.S. and the like, many of them leave a bitter taste in the mouth. What I love is to enjoy the common things of life. I am happy that I am still able to sleep at night provided I have three miles walk in the evening. I am still able to enjoy a good lunch or a good dinner. I am still able to look at the blue sky and like it. I still like to walk in the open fields and like the smell of the Ragi or the Jowar. I feel a younger man when I see the Babul flower and say God has given us these wonderful things. That is the real philosophy of life to appreciate what we see round us.

We think that happiness consists in going to pictures and seeing thrilling films and techni-colour dramas. Not at all, the great things in life are the God-given things which cost nothing. What you need is the desire to appreciate them. If you have your minds and hearts open, you have around you things which give you joy. There is the butterfly jumping about in flourishing colours on all sides. Look at this wonderful thing that God has given for our enjoyment.

We have to love nature ad appreciate nature and appreciate her wonderful gifts, her marvellous ingenuity, her resourcefulness, her infinite variety. It is the same thing that has inspired me all my life. I study science not because anything is going to happen to me but because I feel it is a kind of worship of this great Goddess, Nature of which we are a part. That has been my inspiration as a man of science. I feel now that is one thing that can always make a man happy, the small things in life not only in nature - our old friends, old music and the things that we have around us. Many a time I would like to go back to them.

It may be a sign of cynicism, but 1 would like to go back to the common things of life. A glass of cold water, for example, gives us vigour and freshness. (Dr. Raman so saying drank a glass of cold water amidst laughter). I can assure you there is no pleasure in this world for a healthy man, then after a vigorous exercise or doing something hard just to go home and have a glass of cold water. If you have lost the capacity to appreciate that, you may as well drink a cup of hemlock, as Socrates had to do.

I have another word to say. We all speak of patriotism. What is patriotism? I want you to think it over and in the last analysis bring down patriotism to a physical term. I have thought over the problem. Patriotism as well as a number of things boil down to the love of the earth. We are of the earth. When we die we return to the earth, dust to dust, ashes to ashes, the human body whether cremated or buried returns to earth. Seeta was of earth and returned to earth. This good earth sustains us. On earth grows green grass, which the cow cats and which a vegetarian like myself as well as a non-vegetarian gets milk from. Ultimately it is the earth and the things that grow upon it that sustain us and feed us and make human life possible. I think ultimately the love for the land means the love of the earth which has borne us and which sustains us. I want you to appreciate the meaning of love of earth.

The love of mother earth should be shown by tending her. If she is ruthlessly raped and destroyed, we shall also die with her. The tremendous problem of lack of food in the country boils down to this that we have left the love of earth to ignorant people who know nothing of the advance of science. We educated people who understand science, do not love mother earth. Knowledge of science will make us create anything, but unless we have that vision, that desire to love mother earth, we shall not make any advance.

I think it is a duty laid on every educated man to create something, to see something grow. I say this not as a part of the 'grow more food campaign', I have not been paid to do propaganda for it. I am telling you about it in the same spirit that a famous Roman did. When once Rome was in danger the people wanted to have him as a dictator to save Rome. When they went to him they found him ploughing the land with his own hands and tending his farm. After he became a dictator he went back to the land and said, these plants I have grown, I give them water, I give them labour and they repay. We should work in this spirit.

The more you help a man, the less grateful he is to you. It is, however, our duty to help fellow beings and we should not expect them to show any gratitude in return. If they do show, we are very happy and more fortunate. The plant on earth will never fail to repay any attention that we bestow on it. We must go back to earth and regard it as our supreme duty to do something to produce the things on which we live.

It is a great privilege to see such a great body of young people, women and men alike who are entering the pathways of life after, a course of study in colleges and university and to be allowed to speak to them and making a heart to heart speech gives me great pleasure.

I never believe in manuscript eloquence or in after dinner speeches carefully prepared 24 hours beforehand. I always believe in standing up in front of my audience, appreciate the situation and speak to them heart to heart. I have no desire at all to inflict unwanted advice on you. I want you to think over what I have told you and see if some little thing that I have said may prove the seed of some great achievement on your part, sustain you, encourage you, elevate your hearts above and so push you on in life that you may rise triumphant over all the difficulties and all the troubles that are the common lot of the common man in India today.

(Loud and prolonged applause).

## Why the Sky is Blue

[*Prof. C. V. Raman's lecture on "WHY THE SKY IS BLUE" delivered on December 22/1968 at the Foundation Stone-laying ceremony of the Community Science Centre, Ahmedabad*].

When I was asked to choose a scientific subject for my lecture I had no difficulty at all in choosing the subject of "Why the sky is blue." Fortunately, nature has been kind today; as I look up and see, the sky is blue; not everywhere, as there are many clouds. I chose this subject for the simple reason that this is an example of something you do not have to go to the laboratory to see. Just look up, look at the sky. And I think it is also an example of the spirit of science. You learn Science by keeping your eyes and ears open and looking around in this world. The real inspiration of science, at least to me, has been essentially the love of nature. Really, in this world, wherever we see, we see all kind of miracles happening in nature. To me, everything I see is something incredible something absolutely incredible. We take it all for granted. But I think the essence of the scientific spirit is to look behind and beyond and to realise what a wonderful world it is that we live in. And everything that we see presents to us not a subject for curiosity, but a challenge, a challenge to the spirit of man to try to understand something of this vast mystery that surrounds us.

Science continually attempts to meet this challenge to the spirit of man. And the great problem today, which Dr. Sarabhai has addressed himself to, is how to rouse the younger generation of our country to meet this great challenge before us, once again to build up India into a great centre of knowledge and learning and endeavour. Well, I wish you all success. Now let me turn back to my problem "Why the sky is blue."

> I raised this question because it is an easy subject. I only have to look up and see that the sky is blue. But why is it blue? The interesting point is that it is easy to answer that question in a casual way. If you ask a Botanist, why are leaves green?

He murmurs, 'Chlorophyll'. Finished. You see, all scientific questions can be disposed of in that summary fashion, in one or two words. You can surely pass your examinations with that kind of answer, but that is not the real answer. As I said before, the scientific challenge of nature is to think, not only to discover but to think, to think continually and to try to penetrate this mystery: "Why is it blue?" That is a very interesting problem, because two things are there. The sky is there and I am here. I see it is blue. It is the human brain and the human mind as well that are involved in this problem. Now suppose we put this problem before the young people. Don't read any book about it, don't ask your teacher. Let us sit down and try to think but this problem: why is the sky blue. Look at it as if it is a completely new scientific problem about which nobody has troubled himself before. You sit down and think it out and you will find it a most exciting thing to ask yourself that question and see if you can discover the answer for yourself. Now I will put it to you in this way. The best way to answer a question is to ask another. At night, we all see the stars. On a fairly clear night you see the stars twinkling in the sky. Why are the stars not visible in day time? Please ask yourself this question. Well, the reason obviously is that the earth, as a modest lady, has hidden herself under a veil. The sky is a veil which she has thrown around us. We cannot see the stars during the day, because the veil hides the stars. And what is this veil? The veil obviously is the atmosphere of the earth. The same veil which at night is so transparent that we can see the faintest star and the milky way, is covered up in day-time.

Obviously, it is the atmosphere which is the veil. And we see the sky as blue only because we have not got other thicker veils like these clouds. You see for example, those clouds high in the blue sky. Obviously therefore, for the sky to be really blue, there must be nothing else, no clouds and perhaps no dust. The clearer the sky is, the bluer it is. So the sky is not always blue; it is sometimes blue and sometimes not blue at all. So that the mere looking at the sky enables us to understand the condition of the atmosphere.

Let me say one thing more. Obviously, the sky and the atmosphere are lit up by the sunlight. Sunlight is passing through this great column of air and obviously it is the atmosphere, something that is transparent and invisible at night, that is seen to us by the light — sunlight — passing through the atmosphere.

Now I want you to ask yourself another question. I don't know if any of you have had the curiosity to look at the clear sky on a full-moon night. You know that moonlight is only the sunlight incident on the moon and is diffused or reflected. I don't know if arty of you have really watched the sky on a clear full-moon night. You will be astonished to find that the sky is not blue.

It appears pale, you just see some light and you see some of the stars even under the full-moon sky, but the sky is not blue. Why is it that the sky which appears blue in sunlight, does not appear blue in moonlight? The answer obviously is: the illumination is far less powerful. You don't require to be much of a mathematician to calculate the ratio of the intensities of full-moon light and sunlight. I present it to some young mathematician to sit down and work out. How big is the moon? What should be the brightness of moonlight? It is a little astronomical problem. Rough arithmetic would tell you that moonlight is something like half a millionth part as bright as sunlight; you would, think, it is terribly small. But moonlight, when it is there seems- very bright though it is only half a millionth part of the brightness of sunlight. Why does it look so bright? Well, the eyes have got accustomed to much lower levels of illumination.

So moonlight appears very bright, but not so bright, as to veil all the stars. But the sky, it does not appear blue. So this comparison of Sunlight and moonlight brings to our notice a very remarkable fact. It is an absolutely fundamental aspect of human vision that to perceive colour, you must have a high level of illumination. The sky is blue, merely because sunlight is brilliant; moonlight is much less brilliant and so you don't perceive colour. This is a principle which perhaps is not so widely appreciated as it ought to be. Colour is only perceived at high levels of illumination. The higher the illumination the brighter are the colours. You go down to low levels of illumination, say, a millionth part, half a millionth or a hundred thousandth part of sunlight, the sense of colour disappears. Now this is a very fundamental fact of human vision, which simply comes out of nothing else but just observation and thinking, that's all. I can go on giving any number of illustrations. Perhaps the most striking illustration emerges when you look at the stars or such objects as the Orion nebula through small telescopes. Let me say here and now, my belief that there is no science so grand, so elevating, so intensely interesting as astronomy. It is amazing to see how many people high up have never seen the sky through the telescope. I want to tell them something which is absolutely incredible: Nothing more than a pair of binoculars, a good pair of binoculars is needed to educate oneself in the facts of astronomy. I think a man who does not look at the sky even through that modest equipment — a pair of binoculars -- cannot be called an educated person, because he has missed the most wonderful thing and that is the universe in which he lives. You must have a look at if. You don't see much of it, but you see a little and even this little is enough to elevate the human soul and make us realise what a wonderful thing this world is.

I come back now to the problem of the blue sky I want to pose to you a very difficult question. Why is it that we perceive the blue colour only under intense illumination in sunlight, and not in moonlight? I will by pass that and come back to the question: Why is the sky blue? Well, we all know that white light is composed of all the colours in the spectrum. You divide white light into various colours; you start with deep red at one end, light red, orange, yellow, green, blue and violet, so on, the whole range of colours. When I look up at the sky, I see only the blue; what has happened to the rest of the spectrum? This is the basic question. The question becomes is very pressing one when I remark that when we actually spread out sunlight into a spectrum, the blue part of it is the least intense part. Less than 1/40th of the whole energy of the brightness of the sunlight appears in the blue of the spectrum and we see only that 1/40th part. You don't see the rest of the spectrum. It has simply vanished. It is not there at all. You can look very very hard and try to see if you can see any red or yellow or green in blue sky. We don't see it. The blue has just masked the rest of the spectrum. This is a very remarkable fact. If you watch the sky on some occasions, you get great masses of white clouds, what they call, the cumulus clouds not huge things, just little bunches. It is a beautiful sight to see the blue sky, and these little masses soaring above. I have derived great satisfaction in just doing nothing at all and looking at these masses of clouds and the blue sky. The interesting point is precisely when you have the clouds moving about that the sky is bluest. What it means is that these cumulus clouds in the, course of their formation just cleaned up the rest of the atmosphere. They take up the dust particles and concentrate them on the white clouds. The rest is left nice and clean. You see the beautiful blue view against the brilliant white, it is a very lovely sight. A sight for the Gods; only you don't bother to look at it because it is so common. You may ask me, how is the cleaning process accomplished? Now here is a wonderful story. When I ask the young people, "what is the cloud?" "Oh I sir, it is steam". The usual answer you get is that the cloud is steam, but it is nothing of the sort. The cloud consists of particles and what looks to us as great masses of white clouds are just droplets of water. Water is heavy but why does it not fall down? We find it floating in the air I You see that is another problem. Already I am going from one problem to another. We ask ourselves, what is a cloud? Why is it floating in the air? The moment you ask the question, "Why the sky is blue?" you go deeper and deeper into some of the deepest problems of Physics. Now the interesting point is this you cannot have a cloud unless you have dust particles about which it can form.

There must be particles of some sort, may be very small, may be very large. They call it in learned language 'Nuclei'. If there is no dust in the air, there will be no cloud and no, rain. You see, how from the blue sky, we have got on to the origin of rain, rain fall and so on. One thing leads to another. That is the essence of science. You must go deeper where it leads you. You cannot go thus far and no further. The moment you raise a question, another question arises, then another question, so on and so on. Ultimately, you find that you have to travel the whole field of science before you get the answer to the question: Why the sky is blue? So I told you this fact about the clouds. Well, I should say the cloud cleans up the atmosphere. Cloud forms and then leaves the atmosphere clean, comparatively free from dust particles and other nuclei and that is why the sky is blue. So we come down at last to getting some kind of answer to the problem. The sky is blue because the atmosphere is clean and free from dust and all nuclei. The clearer it is, the bluer it looks, provided there is enough light. So you come somewhere near the answer to the question. What is it you are able to see? The fact is that when we see a blue sky, we see the atmosphere of the earth, the gases of the atmosphere, they diffuse the light and we see the blue light of the sky. But still we are far from the answer.

I told you that blue is only 1/40th part of the sunlight. What happens to the rest of the light, the sunlight? That is the question. Now this question can be answered in the following fashion. You look at the white cloud and look at the blue sky. You can compare them with the help of a pocket spectroscope and you find strangely enough that you have to look very very carefully before you' find any difference in the spectrum of the blue sky and the spectrum of the white cloud. White cloud is certainly very much brighter. But so far as spectrum is concerned, you see in the blue sky and in the cloud the same spectrum. It also starts with the red end and goes on till the blue. But in one case you see the blue, in the other case you see the white. And with great trouble, you look very carefully; you see that there is some difference in the relative brightness. You can see the yellow and the red, not so bright relatively. Mind you, it is a mental calculation.

You see the relation of brightness between the blue part of the sky, the blue part of the spectrum and the violet part and the rest of the spectrum. Relatively to the red, the yellow and the green, the blue and violet are stronger in the scattered light, in the diffused light of the blue sky. Still you are very far from the answer. It does not explain why don't we see the rest of the spectrum. Actually in the blue sky the green and the yellow and the red are still there, they are still far brighter, perhaps not so perhaps not 40 times but perhaps ten times brighter than the blue. Then why do we see the blue and why don't we see the rest? Here again you come across an extremely difficult question to answer. The actual brightness of the blue part of the spectrum in skylight is still much smaller than the brightness of the rest of the spectrum but we don't perceive that part of the spectrum.

Now this is very simple and very surprising. But there is a nice little experiment which, perhaps one day, will be shown at the Science Centre Which will enable you to see at least that it is not an exceptional phenomenon. It is one of the most fundamental facts of human vision that the blue part of the spectrum in spite of its weakness dominates the spectrum in certain conditions and plays a role tremendously far more important than its actual brightness warrants. Now the experiment is the following. It is a very easy experiment. You take water and put a little copper sulphate in it and then put excess ammonia in it. You will get a solution called *cuprammonium*. If it is very strong it will transmit only deep violet light. Put it in a cell. You go on adding water in the cell and look at the colour of the bright lamp and see that the following thing happens. The deep violet changes into blue. The blue changes to a lighter blue and so on. But till the, very last, it remains blue. In the spectrum of the light, the solution is transmitting red light, green light, not of course yellow.

Lot of light comes through the spectrum and the blue is still only a minor part to the whole. Whatever light comes through the spectrum you cannot see and you cannot even imagine any other colour coming through. And the reason for it is as follows. If you examine the transmitted light through a spectroscope you will find that the yellow part of the spectrum is diminished by the influence of cuprammonium. It absorbs and cuts out the small part of the width of the specturm, but a very important part and that very important part is the yellow of the spectrum. Never mind how it absorbs the yellow part and controls the colour.

The light is blue simply because the yellow is absorbed and the blue comes into vision. If you take the whole spectrum and if you reduce the strength of the yellow part of the spectrum, at once you find the blue part of the spectrum and the blue colour dominates. This is again a fact of physiology. If you want any colour whatsoever to be showy, you must take out the yellow. Take for example that red carpet, which has been spread in my honour, I suppose. You look at it through a spectroscope. I can tell you beforehand, there will be no yellow in it at all. To get any colour, red, green or blue, you must take out the yellow. Yellow is the deadly enemy of colour.

All other colours I mean. Look at the green leaf. All the leaves are green, not because of the presence of chlorophyll — the chlorophyll has a strong absorption of red no doubt. But the real factor which makes the colour green is the fact that the yellow is taken off. Chlorophyll has enough absorption of the yellow to reduce the strength of yellow. Well, I examined silks for this. Bangalore is a great place for silk manufacture. I managed to purchase about 25-30 blouse pieces. I got them to verify the proposition that all brilliant colours require the suppression of the yellow region of the spectrum. Look at the rice field. It is wonderful. Look at the rice field with a spectroscope.

It looks very much like the spectrum of the blue sky. But the only visible difference you can actually see at a glance between the blue sky and the green rice field is that the blue part of the spectrum has been cut off and that is produced by the so-called carotenoid pigments that are present here, which cut off the blue; the rest of the spectrum looks almost alike. But if you look very carefully, you will see that in the colour of the rice field, you do not get the yellow. The removal of yellow is essential, before you can perceive the leaves as green. You see always this predominance of the yellow. On the contrary, if the yellow is taken off, the blue dominates. If you don't take off the yellow, the yellow dominates. The two are contradictory and they are enemies to each other.

The fact is that you can divide — the physical explanation is deeper still — you can divide the whole spectrum into two parts. The division is just where the blue ends; that part of the spectrum extending to green, yellow, orange and red amounts only to yellow. The other parts of the spectrum summed up amounts to blue. Now if you take off this or reduce this you get the other. This is the real explanation of the blue colour of the sky and is very significant. You reduce — not that you abolish — the intensity of the yellow in the spectrum and of course of the green and the red. It is the reduction of the yellow of the spectrum that is to say the predominance of the blue which is responsible for the blue light of the sky. Well, one can carry further and say that it is the reduction of yellow that is basic.

And why is it reduced? So here comes the second part of it. I could have started with that and said "why is the sky blue?" "Oh, the scattering of light by the molecules of the atmosphere". I could have dismissed the whole lecture in one sentence. I could have said just as the botanist says "why is it green?" "Just chlorophyll". I could have said "why is the sky blue?" "Scattering of light by the molecules of the atmosphere." One sentence. "Then sir" you would ask me, "why all this lecture?" Because, my young friends, I want you to realise that the spirit of science is not finding short and quick answers. The spirit of science is to delve deeper — and that is what I want to bring home to my audience — and deeper. Don't be satisfied with the short and ready quick answers. You must never be content with that; you must look around and think and ask all sorts of questions; look round the problem and search, and search and go on searching. In the course of time you will find some of the truth, but you never reach the end.

The end, as I told you, is the human brain, but that is very far away yet. This is the spirit of science. I should give you an illustration of how by pursuing a simple question, I can go on talking to you as if I have just begun, the real subject of my lecture: "Why the sky is blue". "The sky is blue because the illumination of the sky light is due to the scattering of light by the molecules of the atmosphere". Now this is a discovery which came rather slowly. The person who first stated this explanation was the late Lord Rayleigh.

I think that dreams are the best part of life. It is not the realisation, but the anticipation; I am going to make a discovery tomorrow, that makes a man of science work hard, whether he makes the discovery or not. And this is what I want to emphasise once again. Science is essentially and entirely a matter of the human spirit. What does a poet do? What does a painter do? What does a great sculptor do? He takes a block of marble, chips, goes on chipping and chipping. At the end of it, he produces the dream in the marble. We admire it. But, my young friends please remember what a tremendous amount of concentrated effort has gone in to producing that marble piece.

It is the hope of realising something which will last for ever which we will admire for ever that made him undertake all that work. Essentially, I do not think there is the least difference whatever between the urge that drives a man of science to devote his life to science, to the search for knowledge and the urge that makes workers in other fields devote their lives to achieving something. The greatest thing in life is not the achievement but it is the desire to achieve. It is the effort that we put in, that ultimately is the greatest satisfaction.

Effort to achieve something in the hope of getting something; let it come or not come, but it is the effort that makes life worth living and if you don't feel the urge towards the search for knowledge, you can never hope to be a man of science. You can perhaps get a job in some of the departments, get a nice, comfortable salary, in which you don't have to do anything except to wait for the monthly cheque; but that is not science. The real business of a scientific man is to try to find something real and to look forward to the acquirement of knowledge.

Having said all this, may I again come back to the blue sky? I have not finished yet. In fact, to tell you the honest truth, I have only just begun my lecture. Why is it that the molecules of the air scatter light? The obvious thing is this, as I told you, the long waves in the spectrum — I am using the language of wave optics — the long waves of the red, yellow and the green are scattered less in the diffused light and the rest quite strongly, with the result that the eye perceives this and not that. Now why is that? The answer is very obvious. The molecules of the atmosphere are extremely small in size, incredibly small compared with what is the standard of comparison, the wave length of light. The same thing you notice, for example, if you look at a big lake.

The wind blows on the waves and you have a piece of cork or wood floating on it. You see the wood trembling. Why? Because the size of the wood is comparable with the size of the waves. But suppose you had a big boat going on the lake; I don't know how big the boat can be but you see that the big boat is not disturbed so much as the small particle. It is the relationship between the size of the disturbance and the size of the particle that determines the effect the waves produce on the particles and vice versa, the effect produced by the particles on the waves. This is the basic principle which results in the scattering of the shorter waves by preference. You can show that by any number of experiments in the laboratory; for that, you don't require molecules of air. You require just some water and put in it some substance like bit of soap. You can also make the experiment with smoke; particles small enough will scatter the shorter waves by preference.

But you don't get the real rich blue colour unless the particles are extremely small. And as I have already indicated, you must have adequate illumination. Unless the illumination is strong enough, the sensation will be just the palest of pale blues. Now I have come from the scattering of blue sky to the study of molecules. And there the subject begins and it goes on. In fact. I started the subject in the year 1901. What I told you was known pretty well except the vision part of which I have spoken about. That is my most recent work, but what I spoke about molecules and so on was all known in 1921. At that time, we thought it was finished. Today, we know that the faculty of vision and the quality of vision play an immense role in the subject.

The subject of my lecture is not the blue of the sky, but as you must have all understood by this time it is the spirit of science. What is science? And how can we in this country hope to advance science? How can we try to really make ourselves worthy of our ancestors in the past? That is the real topic of my lecture. It is only the peg to hang the subject upon. Well, the story begins there. The question is how does light interact with molecules and what happens with molecules and what are molecules and so on. Science never stops. It is going on. The more you find, the more appears that you have to find. That is the attraction of science, provided you are not distressed too much by other people getting in front of you. Don't bother about them. The real point is that it is an endless quest and every new discovery opens new paths for discovery. New questions arise requiring new answers.

But then, I cannot give this lecture without making some reference at least as to how all this I am talking about is united up with meteorology all the time. But the real interest in the subject is not in meteorology at all. The real interest in the subject is the scattering of light which is the most powerful weapon we have today for understanding the ultimate nature of the molecules of the air. You can count the molecules. You can make the experiment in the laboratory. It is an experiment which every student of science ought to have seen.

You take a glass bottle, a flask and a cork and get all the dust out of it and send a beam of light, it may be sunlight, it may be any thing else but see that the beam of the light goes through the air. You can see the air. The air is not such a transparent, colourless gas; it is not invisible. You can make air visible by means of this scattered light. This is a very simple experiment and ought to be seen by every student of science at least once in his life time. You can see air. You can see any gas. You can see any vapour, by the strength of the light diffused by the individual particles. And the more particles you have, the stronger the diffusion. From the strength of the diffusion, you can actually count the number of molecules. I use the word counting, not like one, two, three, four; it is a sort of different type of counting. When I was in the currency office, they used to count the rupees. You know what they did; they did riot count the rupees. They counted the bags; they weighed the bags; each bag was supposed to contain 2,000 rupees — that had to be taken on trust — and then multiply the number of bags and you get a crore of rupees.

Like that, you count the molecules of the atmosphere. It is only a sort of estimate. But more than that we can actually see the scattering of light simply by looking through an instrument; you can find out whether a molecule is short or long, whether it is spherical or tetrahedral shape and so on. The study of the blue sky is an immense field of research, an unlimited field of research, which was opened up and is still being pursued.

The quest, you see, is the more the deeper you go. Then the question arises what about light? I cannot possibly enter into all that. Because, my idea, as I told you is just to give you a simple glimpse into how a familiar phenomenon is linked up with deeper problems of Physics and Chemistry. That is the lesson we learn today. From the familiar fact, it is not necessary to hunt round the textbooks to find problems of science. You keep your eyes open and you see that all round you the whole world bristles with problems to solve; but you must have the wit to solve it; and you must have the strength of mind to keep going at it until you get something. This is the lesson which I want to bring home to the younger generation in front of me. What is the use of all this? Here again, I want to stress the philosophy of my life. Never to ask what is the use of all this.

As I told you before, it is the striving that is worthwhile. Because we have certain inherent powers given to us to use — observation and thinking — we must use them. The more we use them, the sharper they become, the more powerful they become and ultimately something will come out of it so that humanity is benefited, science is benefited. Ultimately the aim of scientific knowledge is to benefit human life. And that comes automatically because the problems with which we are concerned in science are always those that lie nearest to hand. They are concerned with things about us. So long as we deal with the problem which arise out of our environment, you never can say that any particular piece of work can be useless. The most important, the most fundamental investigations, though at first might seem an abstraction of nature, are precisely those, which in due course, affect human life and human activities most profoundly. This is a very heartening thing because one should not think that scientific work in order to be valuable, should be useful. Scientific work is valuable because it will ultimately prove its value for the whole of human life and human activity. That is the history of modern science. Science has altered the complexion of things around us. And precisely those scientists who have laboured not with the aim of producing this or that, but who have worked with the sole desire to advance knowledge, ultimately prove to be the greatest benefactors of humanity.

## LETTERS

### Letters between S. Chandrasekhar and C. V. Raman

[*Here we are presenting some early correspondence between S. Chandrasekhar and C. V. Raman. These letters reveal the relationship that existed between uncle and nephew, two amongst the greatest scientists India has produced*].

Already by 1927 Chandrasekhar had decided to devote himself to research; '.. . like my uncle . .. at that time I knew the names of only two Indian scientists, Ramanujan and Raman. They were in a sense my role models'. When he was in the first year B.A. Hons., Chandrasekhar spent the summer of 1928 in Raman's laboratory in Calcutta. At the age of 17 he wrote his first scientific paper 'The Thermodynamics of the Compton Effect with reference to the Interior of Stars' and Raman published it in the *Indian Journal of Physics* (1928). The next year Chandrasekhar wrote his second paper entitled "The Compton Effect and the New Statistics', which appeared in the *Proceedings of the Royal Society* (1929). According to colleagues present at the time, Raman remarked that 'This young man shows all the signs of being a genius. He will surely leave an indelible mark on physics.' Chandrasekhar left for England in July 1930. On board the ship he wrote his famous paper 'The maximum mass of ideal white dwarfs' (published in the *Astrophysical Journal*, 1931). Since then till 1944 Chandrasekhar sent reprints of every one of his publications to Raman who always acknowledged them. Raman's letters usually had a congratulatory part, a chatty/newsy part and an enquiry about his nephew's well being and scientific progress. The letters were always typed, began with 'My dear Chandrasekhar' and ended 'Yours affectionately, C. V. Raman'. Most of Chandrasekhar's letters were hand-written, and often had a nostalgic part, asking for news from India and the state of science here.

### *Early Letters*

Extracts from a typical letter written soon after Raman left Calcutta and moved to Bangalore:

> Bangalore 19 July 1933
>
> My dear Chandrasekhar,
>
> I am delighted to receive the reprints of your series of papers on 'Distorted Polytropes' and hope that you will continue to have striking success in your future work as in the past. I have now been over three months at Bangalore and I am not fully acclimatised .... As I am only member of the physics staff progress in organising the new department has been very slow.
>
> Ultimately, I think the department should have at least three lecturers, one for theoretical physics, one for experimental physics and one for applied physics. But I am not making these appointments until men with requisite capacity and energy are available ...
>
> I hope you will find time to write to me a few lines occasionally about your progress.
>
> Yours affectionately,
>
> C. V. Raman.

In early-1934 Raman proposed that Chandrasekhar (just 23 years old) be a Founder Fellow of the Indian Academy of Sciences which Raman was establishing.

In 1935 Raman seems to have assured himself that there was one with '... requisite capacity and energy' and offered Chandrasekhar an Assistant Professorship (not lectureship) at the Indian Institute of Science.

Extracts from Chandrasekhar's reply:

> My first impulse was to send a cable accepting the offer; but on second thoughts I am becoming diffident as to whether I could do justice to the position .... I am afraid I may prove a disappointment for them (the experimental physicists) ....
>
> There is one other rather delicate matter. I have had reports that a certain part of the press ... is violently antagonistic to you. I realise of course that such attacks are launched by people ... who are jealous of the powerful school you are building around yourself. I am a little afraid that... (the press) ... might start a fresh scheme of scandals, if I were appointed to a position at your Institute
>
> Yours affectionately,
> S. Chandrasekhar.

Kameshwar Wali in his biography suggests that this letter refusing the job was written by Chandrasekhar with tongue in cheek to pull the wool over the eyes of an 'an elderly uncle...'. He may be right. But there could be another point of view. Over the years, Chandrasekhar rejected more than a dozen job offers from India, including the Chairmanship of the Atomic Energy Commission. One could well understand his not accepting offers like the AEC Chairmanship, Vice Chancellorships, Directorships, etc., because of the administrative chores associated with them. On the other hand, at least seven others, were amongst the best academic positions that the country could ever offer any active scientist-faculty positions at the Indian Institute of Science; the universities of Dacca, Allahabad, Andhra, TIFR, Jawaharlal Nehru University, etc. Consistently he found valid reasons to reject them, but always with ambivalence.

One part of him had a nostalgic yearning to come back, while the other was suspicious whether conditions in India would be conducive to his scientific development. His decisions must have been made more difficult by his colleagues wanting him to stay back. Wrote Otto Struve to C. V. Raman (24 May 1941) when the Allahabad offer was made (to occupy the chair previously occupied by M. N. Sana and K. S. Krishnan).

> When I asked Chandrasekhar to come to Yerkes I knew he was one of the most brilliant young astrophysicists of the world .. .. I should have regretted it greatly, if Chandrasekhar had decided to leave .. . (for Allahabad).

### *Nostalgic Letters*

> My dear uncle,
>
> I was delighted to learn this morning that you have been awarded a Franklin medal. Please accept my sincere congratulations on this most deserved recognition. I feel that the terms of the award are particularly appropriate and it is fitting that your leadership should be thus explicitly recognised ....
>
> As Krishnan and Bhabha are two further Fellows of the Royal Society, Indian physics has certainly come of age. I wish that circumstances had been that I too could have taken some part in this renaissance .... (underlining is mine)
>
> Yours affectionately,
> S. Chandrasekhar.

### *Fellowship of the Royal Society*

By 1941 the stack of reprints had increased to nearly 60, and Raman decided to propose Chandrasekhar to the Fellowship of the Royal Society (for the year 1943). On 24 June 1941, he sent a cablegram:

> DESIRE PROPOSE YOU FOR FELLOWSHIP. CABLE CONCURRENCE MENTIONING NAMES OF FIVE BRITISH FELLOWS WELL ACQUAINTED WITH YOUR WORK ....
>
> - RAMAN

The reply was immediate:

> Many thanks, Milne, Fowler, Eddington, Jeans and Whittaker.
>
> - Chandrasekhar.

Raman decided that E. A. Milne of Oxford who had collaborated with Chandrasekhar in 1932 should be the one to second the proposal.

28 July 1941

My dear Prof. Milne,

I have been watching with pleasure and admiration the splendid work which Dr. Chandrasekhar has been doing in the field of astronomy and astrophysics; and have felt that it would be appropriate to put him up for election to the Fellowship of the Royal Society. I have prepared the accompanying certificate on his behalf and am enclosing it herewith for your kind consideration.

I shall be most grateful if you could kindly consent to be his seconder and also arrange to obtain the signature on the forms of other Fellows in Great Britain who are familiar with Chandrasekhar and his work and forward the papers to the Society.

Professors Fowler, Eddington and Whittaker and Sir James Jeans amongst others know Chandrasekhar and his work well. I am sending them copies of the certificate requesting them to support....

Yours sincerely,
C. V. Raman.

Raman received letters agreeing to support Chandrasekhar from Sir James Jeans:

> I have signed it with much satisfaction.

R. H. Fowler, H. H. Plaskett:

> I am delighted that you have taken the initiative in bringing his name forward.

and A. S. Eddington:

> I appreciate Chandrasekhar is fine work in astrophysics and particularly in dynamical astronomy and have much pleasure in supporting his candidature.

and Milne:

> I am glad indeed you have nominated him this year, for as it happens a number of astronomers are being proposed just now. I am glad to help to sponsor Chandrasekhar as he and 1 have been such good friends ever since his first coming to Cambridge from India.

He also wrote to K. S. Krishnan, H. J. Bhabha and Birbal Sahni the Indian Fellows and they too signed the certificate.

On 21 March 1944 Raman's cable read:

> Warmest greetings from Bangalore physicists rejoicing in your election to the Fellowship of Royal Society.

Chandrasekhar's reply was:

> 25 March 1944
>
> My dear uncle,
>
> It was a special pleasure receiving your cablegram and the greetings from Bangalore. Under the circumstances it was natural that my thoughts should have gone back to the summer of 1928 when as an undergraduate 1 had the unique privilege of witnessing a band of physicists exploring the possibilities of a great discovery made by one of them and with that disinterested enthusiasm which is possible only under a great master in the presence of fields of knowledge freshly revealed. That was sixteen years ago and meantime our scientific interests have

diverged but the impression made on me then has remained with me ever since....

Yours affectionately,
Lalitha and S. Chandrasekhar

Announcing Chandrasekhar's election Raman wrote an article in *Current Science* (1944) which ended with:

> Chandrasekhar is one of that small rare group of men who combine a profound grasp of physical theory and principles, an unrivalled grasp of mathematical analysis and a deep and abiding interest in the phenomena presented to us by Nature in the fields of physics and astronomy. The names of Newton, Laplace and Einstein spring to the mind when we contemplate the history of astronomical science and the debt to men who have exhibited this combination of qualities. In the achievement of Chandrasekhar during the past fifteen years we have at least a promise of a career which should place him in the front rank of the world's great astronomers. The cordial wishes of all our readers will go out to encourage him in his future activities and to wish him and the talented young lady who shares his home at Yerkes observatory an uninterrupted welfare and happiness.

Chandrasekhar must have been very happy as his childhood dream of becoming an F.R.S. was fulfilled. One could comment that since his colleagues in England had not proposed him and had even given higher priority to others, Raman's spontaneous initiative proved timely and welcome.

### *Proposal for the Nobel Prize*

17 November 1948

My dear Chandrasekhar,

I have an idea of proposing you for the Nobel Prize in Physics. I wonder whether you would consider such a move premature....

Yours affectionately,
C. V. Raman.

To this Chandrasekhar replied:

29 November 1948

It is certainly flattering to know that you are considering proposing me for the Nobel Prize. Besides the fact that astronomers are not eligible for the Prize (they would not consider Russel or even Bethe for his discovery of the carbon cycle)... why, for example, have they not considered G. I. Taylor whose claims for the Prize seem to me obvious. I am not being falsely modest in any sense, but 1 sincerely feel that it would be inappropriate to have my name forwarded to the Nobel Committee....

Yours affectionately,
S. Chandrasekhar.

Raman persisted and in 1949 he wrote:

21 December 1949

My dear Chandrasekhar,

...I do not think however the argument that astronomers are ineligible for the Prize is correct. ... If I could have (such) a statement of your achievements it would be easier for me to say there is a prima facie case for you or not ....

Yours affectionately,
C. V. Raman.

Chandrasekhar refused again:

28 December 1949

I do not think that anything I have done qualifies for the Nobel Prize.... In the very remote possibility of my qualifying for the Nobel Prize would it not really be more appropriate if an astronomer... more conversant, with my work, than I have any right to expect of you, sends in my name....I do request you to regard my refusal as final,... I assure you of my very great appreciation of your interest.

Yours affectionately,
S. Chandrasekhar.

It so happened that I went to see Raman in early-January 1950 when the above letter of refusal had just arrived. After reading it he showed it to me along with the previous letter of 21 December 1949. Replying to many of my queries he started musing:

> I thought of proposing him to the Prize as he is definitely Nobel Prize material. The more important reason was because of the paper he wrote from Copenhagen when he was just 21 or 22. He concludes that in a star having a mass greater titan a particular value, the perfect gas equation of state does not break down. The consequence of this is that as the pressure increases due to the inexorable gravitational contraction the star cannot but go through a central singularity. Absurd is what normal common sense would say; so would I have said. But Chandrasekhar, in my view, is different. All his later papers completely vindicate his original stand. If this prediction turns out to be true he was clearly opening up a completely new chapter in Physics.

Twenty-five years later Chandrasekhar was awarded the Nobel Prize. Had Raman been alive it would have warmed the cockles of his heart. His cup of joy would have overflowed with the knowledge that Chandrasekhar got the Nobel Prize for the work he had guessed as being worthy of it.

It is not as if Chandrasekhar had not considered previously the possibility of the Prize for his work. '... thought of the Nobel Prize had my work in the early-30s received recognition without the unhappy controversy with Eddington'.

***The Raman Institute***

> 1 August 1943
>
> My dear uncle,
>
> This is just to say how very pleased I was to learn from some announcements I have lately received from the Indian Academy of Sciences, at long last you have now the opportunity to build an Institute entirely

according to your fashion .... I feel confident that the building of the Institute will be a crowning achievement in a life full of achievements ....

Yours affectionately,
S. Chandrasekhar

In almost every letter after this Chandrasekhar enquires about the progress of the Institute. Raman kept him informed at each stage — about the construction of the main building, the workshop, the hostel, the admission of students, etc.

***Some other Letters***

Raman, in a series of letters, poses many questions to Chandrasekhar about the origin of the magnetic field in sunspots, the limit of faintness of the stars visible with the naked eye, how the celebrated Olbers paradox was resolved by modern cosmological theories and so on. For all these questions Chandrasekhar pens replies and sends him relevant papers/ reprints, etc.

The following two letters could be of some interest:

22 October 1960

My dear uncle,

I was delighted to receive the other day a copy of your 'Lectures on Physical Optics' with your inscription. I had earlier seen this book with Pancliaratnam when he visited us last summer. I was most impressed with this book at that time, and I am very happy now to possess a copy.

By accident it happens that I am lecturing on advanced optics and I intend to make use of your book in these lectures ....

Yours affectionately,
S. Chandrasekhar

Chandrasekhar once remarked to me (after Raman's death):

> There is no doubt that in optics he was a master and belonged to the small band of greats like Rayleigh, Michelson and others.

A letter addressed to Chandrasekhar when he was in India:

9 December 1961

My dear Chandrasekhar,

A few days ago I received from Oxford University Press a presentation copy of your treatise on 'Hydrodynamics and Hydromagnetic Stability ...'. The magnificent way in which it has been printed, illustrated and got up is beyond all praise. The beautiful photographs and drawings interspersed throughout the volume would attract many readers who might otherwise have been put off by the rigours of the mathematical analysis. You have rescued from oblivion the work of many investigators in this field which might otherwise have remained buried in the learned periodicals. They have reason to be grateful to you for surveying their results and presenting them along with your own thoughts and contributions. It is remarkable how many different fields of study the book illuminates and is likely to illuminate during the years to come.

I am grateful to you for the presentation.

Yours affectionately,<br>
C. V. Raman.

Dr. S. Chandrasekhar (F.R.S)<br>
C/o Shri R. R. Sharma, ARIBA, AIAA<br>
Chartered Architect,<br>
1, Southern Avenue, Madras

(This letter will put the incident described by Wali, in a different light. It is possible that it was not forwarded to Chandrasekhar).

Raman in his later years had become cynical and had put on a very gruff exterior. Perhaps because of this, or for other reasons, many concluded wrongly that his relationship with Chandrasekhar was not good. Reading these letters one cannot but conclude that during this period (1930-67, Raman died in 1970) there was a very affectionate personal relationship between the two. After Chandrasekhar left for England in 1930 they met each other probably four or five times. Here again from all accounts the meetings were cordial, often hilarious, each poking fun at the other. There were of course serious discussions.

Chandrasekhar's letters, especially the one just after his election to the Royal Society, indicate his admiration for Raman for his initiative and leadership in science. Raman's regard and admiration for Chandrasekhar was unbounded. Making him a Founding Fellow of his Academy, offering him a faculty position at the Indian Institute of Science, proposing him for the Fellowship of the Royal Society and insisting that he put him up for the Nobel Prize were all indications that the uncle recognised the genius of his nephew from their meeting in 1928 to his dying day.

13

# Raman's Life at a Glance

***November 7, 1888:*** Chandrashekhara Venkata Raman was born at Tiruchirappalli in Southern India. His father was a lecturer in mathematics and physics and so from the first he was emerged in an academic atmosphere.

***1901:*** Joined Presidency College, Madras.

***1902:*** After his schooling days he entered Presidency College, Madras.

***1904:*** B. A. (from Presidency College) with Gold medals in Physics and English.

***1906:*** First Publication in Philosophical Magazine.

***1907:*** Completed M. A (First Class) Married with Lokasundari. Appointed as Assistant Accountant General, Finance department at Calcutta.

***1910:*** Transferred to Rangoon.

***1911:*** Transferred (and promoted) to Calcutta.

***July 1917:*** He joined the Calcutta University as Palit Professor in *July 1917*. That Ashutosh Mukherjee was touched by Raman's total devotion to science is obvious from his following remarks: "For the Chair of Physics created by Sir Taraknath Palit, we have been ...He joined the Calcutta University as Palit Professor. That Ashutosh Mukherjee was touched by Raman's total devotion to science is obvious from his following remarks: "For the Chair of Physics created by Sir Taraknath Palit, we have been fortunate enough to secure the services of Mr. Chandrashekhara Venkata Raman, who has greatly distinguished himself and acquired a European fame by his brilliant research in the domain of Physical Science.

***1918:*** Explained Complex Vibrations of strings of Musical Instruments.

***1919:*** Elected Honorary Secretary, Indian Association for Cultivation of Science (IACS).

***1921:*** Represented University of Calcutta at British University Congress at Oxford. Explained blue of sea.

***1922:*** Came to light, the research, based on a type of light scattering called Raman scattering, which was developed by Indian physicist Chandrashekhara Venkata Raman. When light is aimed at an object, packets of light, called photons, bounce back. While most of these of these photons come back with the same amount of energy, Raman noticed that some of them were different. In a technique called Raman spectroscopy, these unique photons bounce back after exciting the material with a laser.

***1924:*** Elected as Fellow of Royal Society, London.

***1925:*** Visited Russia to participate 200$^{th}$ anniversary of the Russian Academy of Sciences.

***1926:*** Started Indian Journal of Physics.

***1928:*** Sir Chandrashekhara Venkata Raman experimentally observed that, when light is scattered, photons are created at slightly different wavelengths (both higher and lower). A molecule absorbing a photon, and then re-emitting a photon while transferring some rotational or vibration energy (to or from) the photon, causes the effect. The additional wavelengths are characteristic of the material doing the scattering and thus result in a powerful spectroscopic tool.

***February 28, 1928:*** The Day is observed in memory of Sir Chandrashekhara Venkata Raman, who on this day, made known his epoch-making discovery "Raman Effect" to the world.

*1929:* President – Indian Science Congress.

*November 14, 1930:* Sir Chandrashekhara won the Nobel Prize for his work on the diffusion of light.

*1932:* Resigned as a professor – (from Calcutta University).

*1933:* Director of Tata Institute of Sciences (now known as Indian Institute of Science), Bangalore Honorary D.Sc. conferred on him by Bombay University, Madras University, Banaras University, Dacca University and Paris University,

*April 27, 1934:* The Indian Academy of Sciences was founded by the Nobel Laureate, Chandrashekhara Venkata Raman, with the objective of "promoting the progress and uphold the cause of science, both in pure and applied branches."

*1935:* He returned to India to visit Yukteswar and to help establish his Yogoda Satsanga work in India. During this visit, as told in his autobiography, he met with Mahatma Gandhi, the Bengali saint Anandamoyi Ma.

*1935-36:* Raman-Nath theory of diffraction of light by ultrasonic waves put forth.

*1939:* Resigned as the Director of IISc, but continued as Professor and Head of the Physics Department. Went to Paris to attend the International Congress on Physics.

*1940:* Raman-Nedungadi discovery of soft behaviour in quartz.

*1942:* Received Franklin Medal.

*1947:* Found his own institute known as Raman Research Institute at Bangalore.

*1948:* Retired from IISc Presided the annual session of Indian Science Congress. Director of RRI Appointed as National Professor.

*1951:* Published *The New Physics: Talks of Aspects of Science.*

*1952:* The two-seater petrol engine car (costing a mere Rs. 2,000/-) rolled out. But production was stopped subsequently, because of the Government's refusal to grant the necessary license. His inventiveness was not confined to machinery alone. He is said to have grown ten feet high Cotton plants, millet plants with high yields and several injections for plants that made possible what Chandrashekhara Venkata Raman (Sir C. V. Raman) called "Botanic marvels".

*1954:* The provision of Bharat Ratna was introduced. The first ever Indian to receive this award was the famous scientist, Chandrashekhara Venkata Raman. Since then, many dignitaries, each a whiz in varied aspects of their career have received this coveted award.

*1657:* He received Lenin Peace prize of USSR.

*September 1964:* Bhabha's widely quoted remark "no power is as expensive as no power" at the third UN conference on peaceful uses of atomic energy in Geneva registered with many from underdeveloped countries aspiring to tame nuclear energy. "Icons like Bhabha ...Bhabha's widely quoted remark "no power is as expensive as no power" at the third UN conference on peaceful uses of atomic energy in Geneva registered with many from underdeveloped countries aspiring to tame nuclear energy. "Icons like Bhabha appear only rarely," said Bikash Sinha, director of DAE's cyclotron project in Kolkata. Nobel Laureate Chandrashekhara Venkataraman described Bhabha as the modern equivalent of Leonardo da Vinci.

*November 21, 1970:* Sir Chandrashekhara Venkata Raman, a Nobel laureate in physics, died in Bangalore of a heart attack. He was 82 years old. President V. V. Giri said that in the death of Dr. Roman, India had lost a "grand old man of science" who had brought fame to the nation.

14

# Golden Words of Raman

### *On the Role of a Scientist*

The true role of scientists is the discovery of Truth, they have no concern either with the application or misapplication of the results of scientific discoveries. All the same, scientists owed an obligation to society, to improve it.

### *On the Misuse of Science*

Men of science are completely helpless in the matter of misuses of science. Only men like Buddha, Christ, and Mahatma Gandhi, and not scientists, could solve human problems by influencing human conduct.

### *On Atomic Power*

It is my conviction that out of every 100 dollars used for developing atomic energy, 99.99 dollars would be for war and only 0.01 dollars for peace. We Indians are a peace loving people. We want to be left for ourselves. I silently pray God to protect us from the Atom Bomb.

### *Success*

I would like to tell the young men and women before me not to lose hope and courage. Success can only come to you by courageous devotion to the task lying in front of you and *there is nothing worth in this world that can come without the sweat of our brow.* I can assert without fear of contradiction that the quality of the Indian mind is equal to the quality of any Teutonic, Nordic or Anglo-Saxon mind. What we lack is perhaps courage, what we lack is perhaps driving force which takes one anywhere. We have, I think, developed an inferiority complex. I think what is needed in India today is the destruction of that defeatist spirit. We need a spirit of victory, a spirit that will carry us to our rightful place under the sun, a spirit which will recognise that we, as inheritors of a proud civilization, are entitled to a rightful place on this planet. If that indomitable spirit were to arise, nothing can hold us from achieving our rightful destiny.

### *Comparing to Compton Effect*

Ah, but my effect will play a great role for chemistry and molecular structure!

### *On a Complaint that Raman was Giving Preference to the Students of Madras University*

Yes, that is the only university which does not teach the students anything, and when they come to me they do not have to unlearn nonsense as students from other universities have to!

### *Comment about the National Laboratories*

Shah Jehan built the Taj Mahal to bury one of his favourite women. The National Laboratories were built to bury scientific instruments.

### *About His Experiences in Bangalore (at IISc)*

Bangalore is a nice place and I thought there were people here who were interested in science. I did not come here to make money. I wanted to make Bangalore the centre of science in Asia. Then at the Indian Institute of Science they gave me hell. You may be scientist, but you are no administrator, they said. They cut the grants and they even said I had embezzled money.

What I suffered was indescribable. You must have political support to succeed, you see, and I had none. Then I quit and set up my own Institute. I am my own master and I am happy about it. This Institute of mine is a fitting reply to all the torture heaped on me. I work here quietly, silently. The work of science is done quietly and silently. Look at our National Laboratories. They have become vested interests for some people."

### *On the Silver Jubilee of the Discovery of the Raman Effect*

The more I look back on my career, the more I feel that it has been a long history of frustration, disappointment, struggle and every kind of tribulation. But there have been a few gleams of success. It was poverty and the poor laboratories that gave me the determination to do the very best I could.

It is worth noting here for the youth of today, Raman when he discovered in 1928 the Effect bearing his name, his formal education was only — an M.A. in physics!

### *Way of Life*

I think your education is imperfect, if you do not realise my young friends, that life is not merely a question of getting food, clothes and shelter. Man does not live by bread alone. This has been realised from ancient times. I think that the finest things in life are not these, but music, colour, flowers, beauty, aesthetic sense, the satisfaction derived from these. It is these finer things in life that makes life worth living.

### *Criteria for Success*

Ambition, Courage and Endeavour have been my watchwords.

### *Advice to Research Scientists*

Develop self-confidence, self-reliance and a little desire to work. Young friends do this and research will come afterwards.

### *On Importing Equipment for Research*

There will be no science in India if we continue to rely on imported equipment for research work. I call it paying for our ignorance — nay, paying for our incompetence. Science can and shall advance in very simple ways. We often pay Rs. 50,000 for something we can make for Rs. 5,000. The difference we pay for our ignorance.

### *Memorial for Gandhiji*

The best way for perpetuating the memory of Mahatmaji is to inculcate into the minds of the coming generation of the best teachings of Gandhiji. Each boy and girl from the primary standard to post-graduate course must be made to read the best sayings of Gandhiji.

### *On the Education of Women*

No one who is a patriot, no one who looks to the future of India can fail to be impressed by the importance of women receiving the best and the highest kind of education. No nation of which one half was sunk in superstition and ignorance could ever hope to rise.

### *Advice to Youth*

You, our young men come to the Universities and leave them to face the world...a world which may seem to be an unsympathetic harsh world. I would like to tell the young men and women before me not to lose hope and courage. Success can only come to you by courageous devotion to the task lying in front of you and there is nothing worth in this world that can come without the sweat of our brow. We have abundant human material in India. Speaking as a teacher of 24 years' experience, I can assert, without fear of contradiction that the quality of the Indian mind is equal to the quality of any Teutonic, Nordic, or Anglo-Saxon mind. What we lack is perhaps courage, what we lack is perhaps driving force which takes one anywhere. We have, I think developed an inferiority complex. I think what is needed in India today is the destruction of that defeatist spirit We need a spirit of victory, a spirit that will carry us on to our rightful place under the sun, a spirit which will recognise that, we as inheritors of a proud civilization, are entitled to a rightful place on this planet. If that indomitable spirit were to arise, nothing can hold us from achieving our rightful destiny.

### *On Religious Life*

There is no Heaven, no Swarga, no Hell, no Rebirth, no Incarnation. This belief in the existence of the next world is the greatest force against true religious life. People are likely to lead a more rational and religious life, if they believed that what really mattered was the life of today. That is also the message of science to humanity.

# Bibliography


Albrecht, M. G. and Creighton, J. A.: *Anomalously Intense Raman Spectra of Pyridine at a Silver Electrode,* Journal of the American Chemical Society, 1977.

Baker, G. A. and Moore, D. S.: *Progress in Plasmonic Engineering of Surface-enhanced Raman-scattering Substrates Toward Ultra-trace Analysis,* Analytical and Bioanalytical Chemistry, 2005.

Bernhard, C. G.: *Nobel Prize Winners,* The H. W. Wilson Company, New York, 1987.

Bhagavantam, S.: *Chandrasekhara Venkata Raman. 1888-1970,* Biographical Memoirs of Fellows of the Royal Society, London, 1971.

Bhagawantam, S.: *Biogr. Mem. Fellows R.,* Soc., 1971.

Birke, R. L. Lombardi, J. R. and Gersten, J. I.: *Observation of a Continuum in Enhanced Raman Scattering from a Metal-solution Interface,* Physical Review Letters, 1979.

Burstein, E. Chen, Y. J. Chen, C. Y. Lundquist, S. and Tosatti, E.: *Giant Raman Scattering by Adsorbed Molecules on Metal Surfaces,* Solid State Communications, 1979.

Camafeita, L. E. S´anchez-Cort´es, S. and Garc´?a-Ramos, J. V.: *SERS of Guanine and its Alkyl Derivatives on Gold Sols,* Journal of Raman Spectroscopy, 1996.

Demming, A. L. Festy, F. and Richards, D.: *Plasmon Resonances on Metal Tips: Understanding Tip-enhanced Raman Scattering,* The Journal of Chemical Physics, 2005.

Downes, A. Salter, D. and Elfick, A.: *Finite Element Analysis of Tip-enhanced Raman Scattering,* Proceedings SPIE, 2006.

Fabelinski I, L.: *Priority and the Raman Effect,* Nature, 1990.

Festy, F. Demming, A. and Richards, D.: *Resonant Excitation of Tip Plasmons for Tip-enhanced Raman SNOM,* Ultramicroscopy, 2004.

Fleischmann, M. Hendra, P. J. and McQuillan, A. J.: *Raman Spectra from Electrode Surfaces,* Journal of the Chemical Society - Chemical Communications, 1973.

Furtak, T. E. and Macomber, S. H.: *Voltage-induced Shifting of Charge-transfer Excitations and their Role in Surface-enhanced Raman Scattering,* Chemical Physics Letters, 1983.

Futamata, M. Borthen, P. Thomassen, J. Schumacher, D. and Otto, A.: *Application of An ATR Method in Raman Spectroscopy,* Applied Spectroscopy, 1994.

Goulet, P. J. G. Pieczonka, N. P. W. and Aroca, R. F.: *Overtones and Combinations in Single-molecule Surface-enhanced Resonance Raman Scattering Spectra,* Analytical Chemistry, 2003.

Hartschuh, A. Anderson, N. and Novotny, L.: *Near-field Raman Spectroscopy using a Sharp Metal Tip,* Journal of Microscopy, 2003.

Hartschuh, A. Pedrosa, H. N. Novotny, L. and Krauss, T. D.: *Simultaneous Fluorescence and Raman Scattering from Single Carbon Nanotubes,* Science, 2003.

Haslett, T. L. Tay, L. and Moskovits, M.: *Can Surface-enhanced Raman Scattering Serve as a Channel for Strong Optical Pumping?,* Journal of Chemical Physics, 2000.

Hayazawa, N. Saito, Y. and Kawata, S.: *Detection and Characterization of Longitudinal Field for Tip-enhanced Raman Spectroscopy,* Applied Physics Letters, 2004.

Hirakawa, A. Y. Okada, H. Sasagawa, S. and Tsuboi, M.: *Infrared and Raman-spectra of Adenine and its N-15 and C-13 Substitution Products,* Spectrochimica Acta A, 1985.

Hulthen, E.: *Kompletterande Utredning Roeande Raman-effekten,* Report of the Expert for the Nobel Committee, Berlin, 1990.

Itoh, T. Biju, V. Ishikawa, M. Kikkawa, Y. Hashimoto, K. Ikehata, A. and Ozaki, Y.: *Surface-enhanced Resonance Raman Scattering and Background Light Emission Coupled with Plasmons of Single Ag Nanoaggregates,* Journal of Chemical Physics, 2006.

Jayaraman, A.: *C. V. Raman - A Memoir,* Affiliated East-West Press Pvt Ltd., New Delhi, 1989.

Jeanmaire, D. L. and Van Duyne, R. P.: *Surface Raman Spectroelectrochemistry: 1 Heterocyclic, Aromatic and Aliphatic Amines Adsorbed on the Anodized Silver Electrode,* Journal of Electroanalytical Chemistry, 1977.

Jeziorowski, H. and Kn¨ozinger, H.: *Raman and Ultraviolet Spectroscopic Characterization of Molybdena on Alumina Catalysts,* Journal of Physical Chemistry, 1979.

Jiang, J. Bosnick, K. Maillard, M. and Brus, L.: *Single-molecule Raman Spec-troscopy at the Junctions of Large Ag Nanocrystals,* Journal of Physical Chemistry B, 2003.

Keswani, G. H.: *Raman and his Effect,* National Book Trust of India, New Delhi, 1980.

Kim, S. K. Joo, T. H. Suh, S. W. and Kim, M. S.: *Surface-enhanced Raman Scattering (SERS) of Nucleic-acid Components in Silver Sol - Adenine Series,* Journal of Raman Spectroscopy, 1986.

Kneipp, K. Moskovits, M. and Kneipp, H.: *Topics in Applied Physics, Volume 103: Surface-Enhanced Raman Scattering,* Physics and Applications, Springer-Verlag, 2006.

Kneipp, K. Wang, Y. Kneipp, H. Perelman, L. T. Itzkan, I. Dasari, R. and Feld, M. S.: *Single-molecule Detection Using Surface-enhanced Raman Scattering (SERS),* Physical Review Letters, 1997.

Koglin, E. Sequaris, J. M. and Valenta, P.: *Surface Raman Spectra of Nucleic acid Components Adsorbed at a Silver Electrode,* Journal of Molecular Structure, 1980.

Kohlrausch, K. W. F.: *Der Smekal- Raman-Effekt, Struktur der Materie in Einzeldarstellungen-12,* Verlag von Julius Springer, Berlin, 1931.

Krishnamurti, P. Sir C. V. Raman: *A Short Biographical Sketch,* The Bangalore Press, Bangalore, 1938.

Kueppers, G., Weingart, P. and Ulitzka, N.: *Die Nobelpreise in Physik und Chemie, 1901-1929,* Materialien Zum Nominierungsprozess, B. K. Verlag GmbH, Bielefeld, 1982.

Lueck, H. B. Daniel, D. C. and McHale, J. L.: *Resonance Raman Study of Solvent Effects on a Series of Triarylmethane Dyes,* Journal of Raman Spectroscopy, 1993.

Maher, R. C. Cohen, L. F. and Etchegoin, P.: *Single Molecule Photo-bleaching Observed by Surface-enhanced Resonant Raman Scattering (SERRS),* Chemical Physics Letters, 2002.

Majoube, M. and Henry, M.: *Fourier-transform Raman and Infrared and Surface-enhanced Raman Spectra for Rhodamine 6G,* Spectrochimica Acta A, 1991.

McQuillan, A. J. Hendra, P. J. and Fleischmann, M.: *Raman Spectroscopic Investigation of Silver Electrodes,* Journal of Electroanalytical Chemistry, 1975.

Miller, Foil A., Kauffman, George: *C. V. Raman and the Discovery of the Raman Effect,* Journal of Chemical Education, 1989.

Miller, Foil A., Kauffman, George: *C. V. Raman and the Discovery of the Raman Effect,* Journal of Chemical Education, 1989.

Moskovits, M. Dilella, D. P. and Maynard, K. J.: *Surface Raman-spectroscopy of a Number of Cyclic Aromatic Molecules Adsorbed on Silver - Selection Rules and Molecular Reorientation,* Langmuir, 1988.

Moskovits, M.: *Surface Roughness and Enhanced Intensity of Raman Scattering by Molecules Adsorbed on Metals,* Journal of Chemical Physics, 1978.

Nampoori, V. P. N.: *Illustrated Biography of C. V. International School of Photonics,* Cochin University of Science and Technology, India, 1988.

Neacsu, C. C. Dreyer, J. Behr, N. and Raschke, M. B.: *Scanning-probe Raman Spectroscopy with Single-molecule Sensitivity,* Physical Review B, 2006.

Nie, S. M. and Emory, S. R.: *Probing Single Molecules and Single Nanoparticles by Surface-enhanced Raman Scattering,* 1997.

Olson, L. G. Uibel, R. H. and Harris, J. M.: *C18-modified Metal-colloid Substrates for Surface-enhanced Raman Detection of Trace-level Polycyclic Aromatic Hydrocarbons in Aqueous Solution,* Applied Spectroscopy, 2004.

Otto, A.: *What is Observed in Single Molecule SERS and Why?* Journal of Raman Spectroscopy, 2002.

Pettinger, B. Picardi, G. Schuster, R. and Ertl, G.: *Surface-enhanced and STM-tip-enhanced Raman Spectroscopy at Metal Surfaces,* Single Molecules, 2002.

Pettinger, B. Ren, B. Picardi, G. Schuster, R. and Ertl, G.: *Nanoscale Probing of Adsorbed Species by Tip-enhanced Raman Spectroscopy,* Physical Review Letters, 2004.

Picardi, G.: *Raman Spectroscopy and Light Emission at Metal Surfaces Enhanced by the Optical Near-field of a Scanning Tunneling Tip,* Freie Universit¨at Berlin, PhD thesis, 2003.

Pieczonka, N. P. W. and Aroca, R. W.: *Inherent Complexities of Trace Detection by Surface-enhanced Raman Scattering,* ChemPhysChem, 2005.

Pisharoty, P. R.: *C. V. Raman,* Publications Division, New Delhi, 1982.

Ramaseshan S.: *Scientific Papers of C. V. Raman,* Indian Academy of Sciences, Bangalore, 1988.

Schneider, S. Brehm, G. and Freunscht, P.: *Comparison of Surface-enhanced Raman and Hyper-Raman Spectra of the Triphenylmethane Dyes Crystal Violet and Malachite Green,* Physica Status Solidi B, 1995.

Sen, S. N.: *Prof. C. V. Raman - Scientific Work at Calcutta,* Indian Association for the Cultivation of Science, Kolkata, 1988.

Tsang, J. C. Demuth, J. E. Sanda, P. N. and Kirtley, J. R.: *Enhanced Raman scattering from Carbon Layers on Silver,* Chemical Physics Letters, 1980.

Venkataraman, G.: *Journey Into Light-Life and Science of C. V. Raman*, Penguin Books India (P) Ltd., New Delhi, 1994.

Venkataraman, G.: *Raman and his Effect*, Universities Press (India) Ltd., Hyderabad, 1995.

Vosgr¨one, T. and Meixner, A. J.: *Surface- and Resonance-enhanced Micro-Raman Spectroscopy of Xanthene Dyes: From the Ensemble to Single Molecules*, ChemPhysChem, 2005.

Wali, K. Chandra, C.: *A Biography of S. Chandrasekhar*, The University of Chicago Press, Chicago, 1991.

Whitman, A.: *Nobel Prize Winners*, The H. W. Wilson Company, New York, 1987.

Xiao, Y. Chen, Y. and Gao, X.: *Comparative Study of the Surface-enhanced Near Infrared Raman Spectra of Adenine and NAD+ on a Gold Electrode*, Spectrochim-ica Acta Part A, 1999.

Zhao, L. L. Jensen, L. and Schatz, G. C.: *Pyridine-Ag-20 Cluster: A Model System for Studying Surface-enhanced Raman Scattering*, Journal of the American Chemical Society, 2006.

# Index

E



F



G



H



I



J



K



L



M



N

## T



## U



## V



## W



## X



❑❑❑